Limerick

100 STORIES OF THE CENTURY

By Denis O'Shaughnessy

Author's previous books:
"A Spot So Fair" (1998);
"The Pig Buyer and the Pope" (1999).

ACKNOWLEDGMENTS

Sponsors: Shannon Development, St. Mary's IDP, Cowhey's Mall Bar; Silke's, William Street; TSB, Argosea, Sean O'Halloran & Sons, Painting Contractors; O'Riada's, Catherine St.; Limerick Ryan Hotel, Saunders Aluminium, Frontline Estate Agents, Polyprint, Golden Vale plc, AIB, O'Driscoll's, Corbally Bar; Garden World, Ellen St.; Limerick Corporation, St. Mary's Credit Union.

Photographs: With originals unavailable, several of the photographs published in the book had to be copied from newspaper files, which diminished quality. Hopefully their historical content will compensate for this deficiency. Thanks to Jim Kemmy Museum, Michael Martin, George Spillane, Dessie Judge, Limerick Leader, Cork Examiner, UL Library, Irish Times for photographs supplied.

Special thanks to Jim McDermott, Larry Walsh, Des Ryan, Earl Connolly, Tony Browne, John Deeley, Eoin Stenson, photograhphic unit IT Div. UL; the staffs of Limerick Library and UL, for their help.

Cover Picture: King John's Castle, 1900.

Back cover: Siege of Limerick 1922: armed Free Staters in mufti with a requisitioned train.

Printed by Leader Print

The book

This book is a collection of one hundred stories representative of all Limerick life of the century just gone, with gleanings of great tragedies and triumphs, pathos and humour, examples of the great religious ethos through most of the century and consequent intolerance. You will read of the hard and happy times, the doubts, the sacrifices and initiatives of our forebears as they struggled to find their feet after gaining independence following centuries of subjection.

These stories are deliberately laid out in a form that is not chronological: the book is not a history of Limerick in the 20th century, but rather a selection of stories gleaned in the main from the files of local and national newspapers.

Several of the stories that were barely touched on in the millennium edition of the Limerick Leader have been considerably enlarged upon, with accompanying photographs where possible; many other stories have lain dormant and their resurrection here will raise many an eyebrow of even those who thought they knew all there was to be known about 20th century Limerick.

Way back at the dawn of 1900 very little fuss was made in Limerick at the birth of a new century: it was generally held that this did not start until 1901, and a Papal Decree declared that Midnight Mass on New Year's Eve would be celebrated in all the churches to usher in the 20th century. For those, and there are many, who contend that the new millennium has yet to dawn, this is further vindication of their argument and they will be pleased at the timing of the publication of this book as we face the year 2001.

The author
October, 2000.

Contents

Page

Mystery of the Monster of Limerick Docks 6
James Dalton: spy or patriot? 8
A case of unrequited love and other court dramas....................13
The Pimpernel of Prospect 15
A night of terror....................................16
Hunger strike at Knockalisheen 19
Men of Annaholty: their measure taken 22
Some memorable Corporation meetings 24
And a lively Co. Council meeting............................26
Death of a Duke....................................28
Poets laud Munster's win over all-Blacks 30
Shoppers tread on haunted ground 31
The great dog hoaxes of West Limerick....................33
Humour of the century 35
A night to remember....................................37
Drunken ducks in Bruree 39
Whatever happened to Christopher Lynch?..................40
Last man to be hanged 43
Death on the Shannon....................................45
The caustic wit of Bishop O'Dwyer 46
Death in Mount St. Vincent 48
When Musical Marie took Limerick by storm 52
Shades of War in Thomond Park............................55
Troubled times: Riots at O'Connell Monument................56
Death of Sean South....................................57
The last Siege of Limerick 58
The pig scam of Newcastle West............................61
Murder on the Shannon Scheme 63
Cold War in Ballinacurra................................67
When the Shannon froze over............................68
Wit of the famous Judge Adams 70
When the Lyric rose up against 'Biddy' 73
A Limerickman in Hitler's Germany........................76
Snobby high-brows in Eden Terrace 78
Cries of the drowning in Castleconnell......................79
The old lady and County Library fire 81
Sorrows of a tenor....................................81
Execution of a spy 83
Stevie and the new pyjamas 85
Mysteries of Shannon Airport air crashes 86
County folklore: laying the chairs........................90
In praise of a reformatory 91
Attempted suicide: a criminal offence 92
John McCormack dies....................................93
Boherbuoy Band attacked by Healyites....................94
Shoot-out at Doolin....................................96
Gold in Ballybunion....................................97
And also in Bulgaden....................................97
The ravages of the flu of 1951 98

Massacre in Dromkeen 100
Joy in Newcastle West... 103
Bishop O'Dwyer: 'a very queer man' 105
Leader condemns Rising... 106
Limerick people in world tragedies 107
The strange case of Maurice Lenihan's portrait........................... 110
The most hated man in Limerick 112
Letters to the Editor 117
Leader lashes Noel Browne and *Times* 121
The empty chair... 122
Dromcollogher: city of the dead 124
Limerick's 1931 wedding of the year 129
Curraghchase: the burning of a mansion 130
When dancing was an occasion of sin 133
Record salmon at Castleconnell... 135
A remarkable West Limerick woman.. 136
Carry-on at the Markets Field.. 138
Mother Theresa refuses honour 139
Royal wedding in Limerick 141
Diana you were wonderful 141
Tragedy in St Mary's Park 143
The statues that moved a nation 144
Golf in Ballybunion: 50p a round.. 145
The man who closed Ferenka 146
Greyhound in the bed 147
Limerick MP's not sound suffragists.. 148
Stories of the Emergency 149
de Valera speaks out against Shannon Scheme............................. 158
Fear of the Red menace hits the city.. 161
Back Garryowen says Mary Ann Walsh 163
Rumours of the war... 163
When Mackey was king 164
Limerickwoman witnesses shooting on the Titanic 168
The children that nobody wanted.. 171
Stevie Coughlan, Dev and the Jews 173
An innocent victim of The Troubles 177
The Jewish Question 179
The Yank and the Eucharistic Congress....................................... 182
Forgotten outrage: the riots of 1935.. 184
Death of Donogh 186
Haughey speaks on morality 187
Dessie is kicked out of Fianna Fáil 188
A rugby mad city.. 190
The great liquor boycott... 191
April Fool's Day Jokes.. 191
Coonagh fishing comedy and Abbey outrage 192
Great fire disasters... 193
John B. Keane: miscellaneous items 195
Visit of John F. Kennedy 197
Kidnap makes world headlines... 198
Holocaust portents in tragic suicide... 199

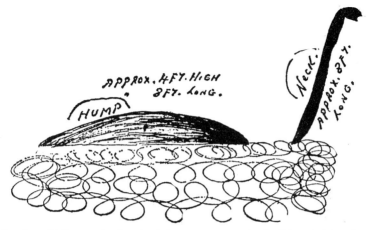

Stephen O'Gorman's sketch of the sea monster in the Limerick Docks in 1922.

Mystery of the Monster of Limerick Docks

The appearance of what was described simply as a monster in the Docks in Limerick in 1922 caused no amount of excitement in an era not unused to sensations, with the Civil War coming to a close. Hundreds of people were reported to have thronged the quays to see the phenomenon and Free State soldiers actually fired shots at the creature. Two witnesses to one of the greatest mysteries of the Shannon have recorded their impressions of the incident.

Mr. A. E. Aldridge of Gloucestershire, master of a schooner in the Docks at the time, has left a written account of the sighting. He and his crew were getting the ship ready to sail on high tide in the afternoon when the mate called him from the cabin: "Captain! Come up here at once!"

What happened next proved the greatest of sensations and has remained a matter of conjecture and mystery down the years.

"When I reached the deck I saw the quays on both sides of the river crowded with people and they were watching the most amazing sea creature they or I had ever seen or read about.

"This object was close alongside my vessel, in fact it was only a few feet away. My first impression on seeing it was of its resemblance in size and shape to a small submarine. It was large and black and shining, and it had a very long neck and at least twelve feet long, held proudly erect and shaped like a swan's. It waved its small head from side to side and its bright shining eyes seemed to express alarm.

"Behind its long neck for a distance of ten or twelve feet was a massive black cone-shaped hump, which rose a few feet out of the water, but no part of the creature's body could be seen between the hump and the neck, this part being submerged."

Mr. Aldridge then stated that at that stage the monster was heading upstream at a very slow speed and seagulls in the vicinity flew off in fright. He then described how the creature eventually turned and headed downstream.

But this extraordinary story was not yet concluded, as the schooner captain has recorded.

"After we had passed Foynes it was nearly dark when I and the crew heard a blowing sound, like a porpoise makes when it surfaces for air, and we saw the long neck of the sea creature shoot out of the water; then it disappeared. It returned within a few seconds surfacing to blow and take in air again. This it did again and again and we eventually left it behind. This was the last we saw of it."

In a letter to the Leader in 1974 following the publication of Mr. Aldridge's account of the sighting of the monster, Stephen O'Gorman, with an address in Birmingham, wrote to corroborate the schooner captain's account of the incident and his description of the creature that caused such a sensation in the Docks was extraordinarily similar to that of Mr. Aldridge's.

Stephen was a teenager at the time and was playing handball in Shannon Street with several of his pals when suddenly they noticed that people were gathering in large numbers at the quayside. "We immediately joined them and to our amazement saw this strange creature in the middle of the river. It was travelling very slowly towards Sarsfield Bridge."

Stephen went on to give the same description of the physical appearance of the creature as that of Mr. Aldridge, describing as he did the hump and how the long neck continually moved from side to side and at no time did it submerge. Stephen, who made a sketch of the monster, reproduced above, continued his story:

"The creature travelled as far as Limerick Boat Club and then turned back and I ran across to the Cleeve's side of the river to follow it. A group of Free State soldiers with rifles came dashing by (I believe they came out of the Strand Barracks) and they kept pace with the creature. When it passed the end of the Docks, where the old St Michael's Rowing Club used to be, they opened fire from Cleeve's Bank and every so often they repeated the shooting until the creature passed Barrington's Pier and finally disappeared into the distance.

"They did not hit it, merely content to hit the water just behind it. I believe they were just trying to encourage it on its way."

In the years that ensued, Stephen emigrated to England and when on many occasions he mentioned the sensational occurrence to different people, he was invariably greeted to a big smile, even by Limerick people.

Stephen, on reading his story being corroborated by the English sea captain, wound up by saying: "Now it is my turn to smile."

James Dalton: spy or patriot?

Limerick City, in the late afternoon of Saturday, May 15th, 1920, was normal enough, if one could call it such. It was a period of great turbulence – the War of Independence being at its height. On that Saturday one of the city's outstanding sportsmen of some years previous, James Dalton, also a prominent Sinn Fein activist, went with his father-in-law Patrick Kelly for a drink down to his local, Humphrey's public house in Clare Street. The pub was situated a few hundred yards from Dalton's house at No. 5, where he lived with his wife Annie and eleven children.

James Dalton

Shortly after 6 pm, both men left the public house and Dalton after parting with his father-on-law, started to walk casually towards his house. His daughter, 15-year-old Kitty, who was playing nearby, came towards her father and prepared to greet him.

What happened next caused one of the greatest sensations and consequent mysteries of the whole War of Independence, made national headlines, was the subject of a Dáil debate, and later brought in such national figures as Dan Breen into the controversy.

On that fateful afternoon, what was described by eye-witnesses as a group of three to four men suddenly appeared out of a laneway and came up to Dalton, who then made to go back towards Humphrey's. He did not make it: he was felled by a fusillade of revolver shots and when struggling on the ground further shots were fired into his back. The group, according to young Kitty Dalton, the only witness of the incident to be called at the inquest, then escaped down Meany's Bow. She ran towards her father who was lying on the ground and asked him was he alright. He only said "goodbye."

Word spread quickly through the city of the tragedy and knots of people gathered near the scene of the murder. Armed R.I.C. men eventually dispersed the crowds.

The shooting had national reverberations. "Well-known Limerickman shot dead. Two point-blank volleys from band of men" were the headlines on the Sunday Independent the following day and "Sensational Shooting Affair" was the heading in the Leader. It was also reported that a young girl, Eily Lowe, was wounded in the shooting, not seriously.

Dr. W. P Dundon, house surgeon, at the adjourned inquest on 27th May, said when Dalton was brought shortly after the shooting to Barrington's Hospital, life was extinct. He performed the post mortem with Dr. Graham and six bullet wounds were found on the body. When questioned by Mr. J. J. Dundon, solr. for next of kin, witness was of the opinion that two of these were fired into the back.

Dalton was a member of the Commercials football team, winners of the All-Ireland football title for Limerick in 1898; he was also an outstanding boxer, being Irish lightweight champion from 1904 to 1907; he was an accomplished athlete and also trained the Limerick hurling team in seasons 1918 and 1919, who had come close to winning the all-Ireland title. Like another great city sportsman of the time, Pa Healy, noted rugby international, oarsman and heavyweight boxing champion, both men had the distinction of boxing in the famous Sporting Club in London, an honour that was bestowed only to those who had reached the top echelons of their sport.

Dalton had been highly involved in the Sinn Fein movement, being one of those who marched to Killonan only to find the 1916 Rising was aborted countrywide. He was one of the first speakers to open the De Valera election campaign in East Clare and also took a prominent part in the Longford-Roscommon and East Limerick Elections. In 1896 he was president of the Irish Trade Congress, being a compositor with Guys Printers in George's Street at the time. At the time of the shooting he was employed as a clerk in the Limerick Gas Works.

This was the second attempt on Dalton's life according to the Leader report. Some weeks previously a shot was fired at him from a laneway in Clare Street and the top of one finger was blown off. Subsequently the words "A bullet is waiting for Dalton the spy" were painted on walls throughout the city.

At the inquest the full story leading to the shooting was revealed by the victim's brother, Joseph Dalton, 1 Mallow Street, described as an outstanding officer in the Movement. He outlined his brother's involvement in the national movement. "My brother was an ardent nationalist, prepared to lay down his life for his country, and though he had not been active for some years part, he still held the same political views, being of the opinion that there was now no need for him to work so hard.

"In December last he was seen entering the house of a member of the Limerick police at 1 a.m. and to leave in the morning; that incident gave rise to a scandalous rumour through the city. Arising out of that rumour, no charge was made against his brother by any political organisation.

"On St. Stephen's Day the deceased lodged with the representative of Dáil Eireann a demand for a full inquiry into his actions and the official finding (though not published until a few days after the shooting) exonerating his brother, was well known in the city a week before he was shot dead. Prominent members of the local Sinn Fein Executive gave evidence in his favour. In view of this I am of the opinion that no political organisation was responsible for my brother's death."

The official Dáil verdict on Dalton's appeal read:

"The main point was not in dispute, that the plaintiff (Mr. Dalton) had entered a certain premises at 1 a.m. and remained there 'till morning, the fact which brought suspicion on him. Having heard the evidence I was of opinion that the plaintiff had been guilty of a grave indiscretion and error of judgment in acting as he had done, and that his conduct very naturally gave rise to such suspicion. As against this, I was clearly of opinion that there had been no guilt or dishonest motive on his part, and that the suspicions in this respect were unfounded."

Dalton in Killonan in 1916 when the Easter Rising was aborted.

Some considerable questioning of Joseph Dalton by District Inspector Marrinan followed at the inquest and he queried the power of the Dail court over the deceased, to which the witness replied: "As a citizen of the Irish Republic; it was the court that governs the country."

The Inspector repeatedly asked had the court, which the witness admitted that he and his brother had attended, the right to sentence a man to death. Witness declined to answer the question. Inspector Marrinan then asked "were you aware that a good many evilly disposed people had given your brother a lot of trouble - didn't they shoot him?" Mr. Dalton: "that was public property, I was aware that he was shot."

Both Mr. J. J. Dundon, solicitor for next of kin, and Inspector Marrinan vehemently condemned the shooting. Mr. Dundon, addressing the jury, stated that he did not think there was anything he could say that could add to the horror and pity that they might feel for the brutal crime which was committed. Mr. Dalton had been exonerated against the serious slander made against him. As a result of what had happened within the past few years all over Europe the value and sanctity of human life might be said to have depreciated in the eyes of the public.

Inspector Marrinan said a fellow citizen had been done to death in broad daylight in a Christian and civilised country. Deceased was a respectful and fearless man according to his views, and he was done to death as he was going home to his family. They were unfortunately familiar with the means by which caused his death. It was a case of getting shot in the back with the cowardly cruel assassins slinking away, and the sanctity of human life trodden on in the dust with the victim's blood.

The Inspector then made a strong and lengthy attack on the Dáil court, asking the jury did they know what they were doing by accepting the verdict of a tribunal with power to decree life or death. By doing so they were giving legality to assassination by accepting the evidence of a secret tribunal.

The Inspector then caused a sensation by refusing to return to the Coroner (Mr. James F. Barry, J.P.), the document containing the verdict of the Dáil court, maintaining the inquest should not have accepted a record from a secret court. After a long debate the Inspector held out and refused to hand over the document. The Coroner, said: "I will oblige any man, and I have tried to do so, but I don't think it is a ungentlemany thing to take anything off the Coroner's desk and refuse to return it (applause).

The incident then ended and as the inquest drew to a close, Inspector Marrinan mentioned that he had in his possession a sum of five one pound notes riddled with bullets that he found in deceased's clothes. The Coroner ordered the money to be handed over to the widow and children.

The jury returned the following verdict: "We find that the deceased died from shock and haemorrhage caused by bullet wounds inflicted by some person or persons unknown, and the jury wish to express their sympathy with the widow, family and orphans of the deceased."

In 1924, in a lecture at the Athenaeum, "Reminiscences of War", Rev. Fr. Philip, O.F.M., recalled the tragic death of Jim Dalton. "Shortly after the shooting I called at the hospital and there was handed a bullet marked paper which had been removed from his pocket. It was the original verdict of the Dail, signed by the Cabinet, which cleared his name and proved him an honourable man," said Fr. Philip.

The controversy surrounding the shooting continued for many years afterwards, even up to 1966, when an IRA activist, imprisoned in Brixton at the time of the shooting, and who signed himself simply "Paidin" wrote: "Dalton had one great fault, he had a high opinion of his own cleverness and thought he could match his intellect against the greatest in the land. This caused his downfall and his death. One night he was seen by a night watchman coming out of the house of a 'G' man named Mahony. Instead of reporting this to the proper quarters, the watchman spread the story and naturally it went far and wide, and for some months Dalton was the object of suspicion and hatred by the majority of citizens. He was cleared of all charges of treachery, but was blamed for indiscretion. A few days later he was shot to death by a group of men. As far as I am aware, he got no chance to defend himself before any tribunal set up by these men. They constituted themselves judge, jury and executioners without the formality of a trial. There is no doubt about it, Dalton was murdered."

The same year, the famous I.R.A. man, Dan Breen, though in failing health, wrote from St. Joseph's Nursing Home in Bray to Michael Hilliard, Minister for Defence, stating that he was very interested in clearing the name of Jim Dalton, "shot in Limerick in the Tan War. Dalton was innocent, and was shot in order to cover up for others. It is a shame his name was never cleared and the right people named," Breen claimed.

In his reply, the Minister reiterated the findings of the Dail enquiry before the shooting which found that Dalton was innocent of the charges proffered against him. The letter continued: "After his death, An Dail unanimously voted Mrs. Annie Dalton, his widow, a national grant of £500 as a vindication. She was also granted an allowance under the Army Pensions Act, 1923, in respect of her husband's death, for herself and her qualified children.

"A posthumous award of the Service 1917-1921 Medal with Bar has now been made to the late James Dalton. Will you please advise my Department of the name and address of the next-of-kin of the deceased in order that the medal with bar may be issued?"

That is briefly the outline of the shooting of James Dalton, one of the most sensational and controversial incidents in the whole War of Independence campaign in Limerick. No-one was ever charged with his murder, even though at the inquest, his daughter Kitty said she could identify one of the assassins, a tall young man who had no moustache. For safety reasons, the young girl was sent to live with relatives in Dublin for a year after giving her evidence.

Dalton's wife Annie died in 1933 and it is said she brought with her to the grave the names of those who had cruelly taken the life of her husband thirteen years previously. Her sons went on to found the City Printing Co. in Rutland Street which flourished for many years afterwards.

A case of unrequited love and other court dramas

There was a major court case in Hospital in the 1920's following what was claimed was eighteen years of unrequited love. The plaintiff, like the defendant, was middle aged, and sued her unwilling lover for £300 for breach of promise. She claimed a date had been set for the wedding and she had bought new clothes and made arrangements for the big day.

In the cross-examination it came to light that the defendant at one stage had second thoughts about the big day as he felt he was "too delicate."

"That was only a fad", the plaintiff claimed.

The defence also claimed that the plaintiff said she would drown herself if the defendant did not marry her, which was not denied. "I was so tired of waiting I would do something."

And it was also suggested that she abused the defendant publicly in the streets, calling him "an old crocodile" and a '' dirty, low, mean cad.''

At this accusation the plaintiff started laughing which caused the Justice to say "are you amused?"

She replied: "What I said was that he was a dissipated old thing." She also added that the defendant could be "sulky" at times.

The Judge dismissed the case without hearing evidence for the defence, maintaining there was no corroboration which was necessary to sustain an action for breach of promise. The Judge spoke of the parties' relations for 18 years and proceeded to say that the action was brought for the purpose of blackmail. He then referred to the "shocking state of affairs" which had prevailed in the village of Hospital and concluded by saying "this shocking and disgusting case should never have been brought to this Court."

In Charleville around the same time two shopkeepers contested a case that was a forerunner of what is now termed "neighbours from hell." One, a lady shopkeeper, and the other, a male harnessmaker, wound up in court to air their differences. All the trouble stemmed from the yard common to both shops at the back with the shopkeeper claiming there was constant intrusion on her half. On one occasion she admitted, when the plaintiff intruded into her half she threw a jug of water on top of him "but he then stormed into the kitchen waving a hammer and said he would kick the heart out of her."

The most startling piece of evidence given by the harnessmaker was that his neighbour sang "Bantry Bay" to annoy his wife. There was no elaboration as to why this should be the cause of such annoyance. Both were bound to the peace.

What was described as an amusing case was held before Justice J. M. Flood in 1939 when a Pallasgrean man sued a widow, who had promised to marry him, for the sum of £8 14s. 6d. in lieu of various gifts he had bought her over a period of twenty years.

The defendant denied promise of marriage. "The plaintiff was constantly hanging around my place and eventually I had to make complaints to the Guards. I am not in a position to marry as I had a life interest in the holding under the terms of my late husband's will."

The plaintiff, who described himself as an eligible bachelor, said he had known the widow for 20 years and that she had promised to marry him. Included in the gifts he had given her over the years were a pair of gloves, a pair of shoes, a hat, a pig, a turkey, an item for drawing teeth and a corset.

"Certainly a most miscellaneous list,"commented the Justice to a roar of laughter.

It was established that the pig was the most important of the presents given over the years and several questions were asked by defending counsel. "Did you say that when she asked you select a pig down at O'Dea's that you said you would give her two? Did you say to her that you would give her two bonhams to keep the place warm?"

Plaintiff: "I did not."

It was established that the first time the plaintiff asked for any of the presents back was when on an unannounced visit the door was slammed in his face.

Asked if he got any gifts in return, plaintiff said all he ever got from the defendant was "fourpence worth of a handkerchief."

"It was a mean offer," solaced Mr. d'Arcy, "and she told you to go and blow your nose?" (laughter).

The widow said she never had any intentions of marrying the plaintiff and the justice commented that if this was the case it was strange that she accepted the miscallenous gifts from the plaintiff over the years.

There were plenty of more laughs at the expense of the poor plaintiff before the Jutsice dismissed his claim, stating that it was obvious that he was taking a chance and in fact hoping to marry into the farm.

An elderly Croom farmer when charged in 1945 for having an unlicensed bull, was fined £10 by Justice Kenny in the Circuit Court.

"You must be joking," said the outraged farmer, who was described as being elderly.

"Indeed I'm not," said the judge. "£10 or three months in jail for default."

On a plea of reduced circumstances the Judge reduced the fine to £5.

The defendant then excused himself from the court and came back shortly with the required number of notes in his hand.

Marching up to the bench, and amidst loud laughter, he asked the Judge how much he would settle for if he got cash down.

The indignant Justice spluttered: "Get out of here while the going is good or I will reimpose the original £10 fine."

The Pimpernel
of Prospect

The Monday, August 9th issue of the Leader of 1943 contained many items of war news from the theatre of war all over Europe and Asia. Allied advances in North Africa were reported and a new Russian offensive launched which threatened the main line of German retreat from Kharkov; these were some of the headlines of the war report.

Alongside all this news of the greatest conflict in history appeared a local story, which set against the great tragedies enfolding throughout the world, provided light relief for readers, even if some were terrified by the actions of what was termed Limerick's Elusive Pimpernel.

> *They seek him here,*
> *They seek him there,*
> *The residents seek him everywhere.*
> *Is he in Killeely or Pennywell.*
> *Limerick's midnight Pimpernel.*

This was the introduction to the story which stated that for the past week Limerick feasted itself on a new "terror" story – the story of a midnight visitant who flashes a light, shines it for a second on his face, disappears with the speed of lightning, hangs by his finger-tips from roof-tops and frightens women into fits of hysteria.

The report went on:

Staking his claim to the area around the new housing scheme at the Bombing Field in Prospect, the Elusive Pimpernel makes his sudden appearance armed only (as far as current reports go) with a flashlight.

There is no report that he has attempted to enter a house or commit violence, and the descriptions of the marauder by those who allege they have seen him are so vague as to be practically useless to police investigators.

Meanwhile, with the story gaining strength with each passing night, the residents in the locality have apparently banded themselves together to catch this daring night-pad.

So far their endeavours have been in vain. Some people have become so alarmed by the story that they are afraid to sleep at night, and watch has been kept in back gardens in anticipation of the marauder's arrival.

His last manifestation is supposed to have occurred on Friday night in Schoolhouse Lane, in the neighbourhood of Leamy's School, when there was a general hue and cry, but again the "gentleman of the light" vanished without obligingly leaving any traces.

Since then there has not been any report that he has been seen.

Perhaps his battery has become exhausted.

A night of terror

There were many nights of terror during the War of Independence in Limerick and one that had the most tragic outcome took place on Monday, February 2nd, 1920, when indiscriminate shooting by the military claimed the lives of two completely innocent victims.

Lena Johnson, aged 21, and described as being beautiful looking, was hurrying to her home in Thomondgate after finishing her night's work as an attendant in the Coliseum Cinema in O'Connell Street. There had been great agitation in the city when earlier on crowds of youths were reported to have taunted a patrol of military as they approached the corner of Roche's Street. Shots were fired, albeit blank ones, according to the police.

There may have been some semblance of authenticity in the claim initially, but as events unfolded for the next hour or so, the ammunition used thereafter was anything but blank.

More military were called out and Limerick took on an appearance of a city under siege

Lena Johnson, aged 21, shot dead on Sarsfield Bridge, February 2nd, 1920.

with armoured cars and even tanks now charging down the main thoroughfares. Intimidation of the citizenry was now the key word.

Indiscriminate firing from the patrols became the norm and several shop windows were pierced by bullets. William Street and Sarsfield Street were the next to be strafed and those leaving the Theatre Royal and other picture houses walked into the thick of the shooting and had to take cover as best as they could. Many had narrow escapes from being shot dead.

Not so lucky was young Lena Johnson. Hurrying home as fast as she could to escape the terror that now stalked the streets of the city, she had just gained Sarsfield Bridge when a shot that proved fatal entered her abdomen at the left side and the bullet exited in her back. Lying stricken on the ground, her moans attracted the attention of members of the Shannon Rowing Club, and a half dozen of them rushed out and brought the stricken woman into the clubhouse.

Witnesses said that when shot, she shouted out "J—, Mother, I am shot," and Denis Punch, Cross Road, Thomondgate, who came on the scene, said the deceased said to him to take her in his arms and asked to have her mother and a priest sent for. Mrs. Noonan, another witness, said looking from her bedroom window in Sarsfield Street, she saw the police fire indiscriminately and Miss Johnson fell to the ground.

In the clubhouse, the dying woman was attended to by Dr. Kelly and removed to Barrington's Hospital by the Fire Brigade ambulance. She died there a short time afterwards. Immediately after Miss Johnson was shot, word was sent to the Franciscan Priory close by, and Rev. Fr. Philip, O.F.M., was at once on the scene and anointed the poor girl, who was suffering great pain.

Lena was not the only victim of that night of terror. Earlier on, Augustinian Lane, off Roche's Street, was described as the storm centre of the trouble with the police alleging that a revolver shot was fired at the patrol from the lane. The blank shots that were purported to have been fired by the police soon turned to real ones. Roche's Street soon became the centre of the action and the house of Mr. Thompson the undertaker was riddled with rifle bullets as were several others in the vicinity.

It was during this fusillade that the second fatal shooting of the night occurred. Richard O'Dwyer, whose public house was described as standing at the opposite side of Catherine Street, was standing at the counter when several shots were fired into the premises, one shattering a mirror and the other one hitting him in the head. Soon afterwards his wife and others rushed into the public house after hearing the shots only to discover that the publican had died instantaneously.

One of the lucky ones was Laurence Murphy from Barrington's Mall who was shot in Patrick Street but escaped with a leg injury which was treated in Barrington's Hospital.

There were poignant scenes at the funeral of Lena Johnson from St. Munchin's Church, with the procession estimated at a mile long with many mourning carriages. The footpaths were lined with an immense crowd and the grief-stricken family: parents Frank and Bridget Johnson, Charles and Patrick, brothers; Mrs. Meade, Mrs. Slattery (sisters), were the object of huge outpourings of sympathy. There were many floral tributes including some from the staff of the Coliseum, where Miss Johnson was employed.

At the inquest on both victims, the military authorities were roundly condemned. The Mayor, Michael O'Callaghan, made a statement and while condemning the fact that the city fathers had no control over the military patrols, appealed for calm. "We should conduct ourselves in a way that would not besmirch the Cause or tarnish in any way the memory of our gallant martyred dead" (applause).

Mr. P. Kelly, B.L., also spoke and said it was quite clear what happened. Sergeant Conroy got wounded and when the police inside in William Street Barracks saw their comrade bleeding they were maddened and exasperated and they came out on the street, fired at random, and took the life of the poor girl returning from work. "I cannot understand why there was not a holocaust on this night in question," he added.

In the case of Miss Johnson, the verdict returned by the jury was "death was caused by shock, the effects of a bullet wound inflicted by a rifle fired by the police without orders from their superiors, an act which we strongly condemn, as there was no provocation, and it is what the jury consider murder in the case of Helena Johnson."

Much the same verdict was returned in the case of Laurence Murphy, who was buried in his native Tipperary.

Leading his fellow citizens at the funeral of Miss Johnson was Michael O'Callaghan, Mayor of Limerick. Little did the Mayor, or any of the mourners that day, think that a short year later, in another night of terror, that he too would be murdered by Crown Forces.

The funeral of murdered Mayor Michael O'Callaghan passing Bank Place. Note the attending clergymen wearing white sashes, a funeral custom of the time.

Hunger strike at Knockalisheen

On the October 27th, 1956, reports came through that over 2,500 people had been killed in the Hungarian uprising against the Soviet Union overlords.

A month later Knockalisheen Army Camp, situated a few miles outside the city in the Meelick direction, and which had been used by the army during the Emergency years, was opened to 35 families, comprising 161 people, from the war-stricken country.

"Hungarians Are Happy In Their New Surroundings" was the Leader heading after the families settled in. "The courtesy and kindness that have been extended to them are so much appreciated that they have fallen in love with Ireland," went on the report. "Gone for these Hungarians was the day of terror under Russian rule. Instead, there was the peaceful atmosphere of 'The Hill of the Little Fort' where these visitors have found a peace and contentment that they had not known for years."

A mighty cheer went up in the camp a few weeks after settling in when it was announced that the refugees would have 200 lbs. of venison for dinner. The meal was compliments of Mr. G. Deeny, Station Manager, of Seaboard and Western Air Lines at Shannon, who shot a deer while hunting at Whitegate.

Four of the Hungarian women were picked to help the Army cooks in the preparation of meals and the army men present were compiling a list of words in Hungarian to help the situation. Four interpreters were helping out including Mrs. Dorrit O'Shaughnessy of Glin and Mrs. Eva Kovarry, Rath Luirc.

Several functions were organised throughout the city and county to raise funds for the relief of the refugees and sewing machines, radios, clothing, etc., were donated. The Red Cross were very active helping out and it was announced that they had received an anonymous donation of a £1 note in the post. The Imco sponsored programme on Radio Eireann devoted their whole air-time to playing Hungarian music in an attempt to make the refugees feel at home.

It was announced by "Spectator", the Leader soccer cor., that one of the refugees, who preferred to call himself simply "Janos"' had signed on for the local city team. It was claimed that he had played for Hungary against Czechoslovakia just before the uprising and, this, coupled with the signing of Frankie Johnson from Waterford, signalled "that brighter days were now around the corner for Limerick."

The Red Cross were active over the Christmas period in the camp and many gifts were donated, specially for the children. The Red Cross had donated a radio, which was much appreciated by the refugees.

Sadly, it was all downhill after this. In a very depressed era, with little or no job opportunities here, the men in the camp got restless and by April an ultimatum was given by the camp committee to the authorities that they would go on hunger strike if employment were not provided, and failing this that they would be given visas to go to other countries.

The hunger strike started on April 29, 1957, and the camp was described as bearing a close resemblance to Goldsmith's "Deserted Village" with none of the families venturing out from their huts. Despite a tempting menu, which included roast beef, veg., and rice pudding, no one turned up to collect the meal. Camp commandant Edward Murphy, of the Red Cross, said that there was no onus on his organisation to provide jobs, but that they had got employment for many and also provided visas for others.

A reporter visiting the camp was struck by the fact that not one of the refugees was to be seen anywhere. "They are all keeping indoors, even the children, an indication that the organisers of the strike must be enforcing a discipline reminiscent of Gestapo methods. The silence prevailing was both mystifying and baffling. An enquiry as to how the children were kept in subjection was left unanswered but it was suggested that fear must be playing a predominant part in the whole set-up. Not a sound is to be heard, not even the cry of a baby!"

By Wednesday, May 1st, reports said that "desperation point" had been reached and that two men had collapsed from hunger and that fifty of the women had also joined the hunger strike.

A conference involving all the people running the camp and the refugees representatives met the following Sunday and was attended by high drama. Captain McCann, camp medical officer, was hurriedly requisitioned on three or four occasions to go to the nearby schoolhouse, where the condition of the strikers was worsening. Two had to be removed to the camp hospital.

As the sick refugees were removed on the stretchers, the many women who had congregated outside the conference hut, anxiously awaiting the outcome of the deliberations, wept bitterly. One woman fainted and was taken to the camp hospital. There was a sharp and short span of excitement when three of the camp leaders rushed from the conference on hearing the screams of protest from their women folk against the taking of photographs of a refugee being conveyed on a stretcher to hospital.

The conference had the desired result and "Hunger Strike Called Off" were the headlines on the following day. "After a conference lasting two and half hours, the Hungarian refugees called off their hunger strike. It had lasted for 85 hours" ran the introduction.

Dr. O'Neill, Bishop of Limerick, played a major role in helping to resolve the dispute and Mrs. Tom Barry, chairman of the Red Cross, when pressed for a statement, said: "It was agreed that the Government had done, and was doing, everything possible for the refugees."

There were smiling faces to be seen everywhere in the camp following the settlement but two of the hunger strikers, including one who had a serious gastric operation in Hungary, were reported to be seriously ill in Barrington's Hospital.

Following the closing of the camp at Knockalisheen, camp commandant Edward Murphy resigned his position in the Red Cross due to what he claimed was the lack of co-operation from the Society's headquarters in Dublin during the duration of the refugee camp in Knockalisheen.

Food being doled out to the women and children during the strike of Hungarian refugees in Knockalisheen.

Men of Annaholty: their measure taken

For generations, the men of Annaholty were privileged drinkers, cocking a snoop at their fellow imbibers in nearby Castleconnell. Living three miles outside the village gave them drinking privileges afforded to travellers and when locals had to leave the various hostelries at normal closing hours on Sundays, the men from Annaholty bid them good night and settled down to drink at their leisure.

Bona-fide travellers they were called and this happy state of affairs lasted for many years until the fateful afternoon of Sunday, October 7th, 1951. Guard Flanagan, stationed locally, decided to pay a visit to Winifred Fitzgerald's pub in the village to make sure that the law was being complied with and that no wayward drinking was taking place. It was 4.45 pm, a quarter of an hour outside normal drinking hours, and to his amazement the front door of the pub was open. He immediately decided to raid the pub, which was then the term used for Gardai entering pubs suspected of serving outside the allotted hours.

In the court case that followed Guard Flanagan said he found five men drinking in the bar and a sixth escaped through the back-door but he (Guard Flanagan) followed him and brought him back. "I only came for a box of matches" claimed the one who had made the aborted dash for freedom.

Guard Flanagan then began to take names. The men from Annaholty, in number four, smiled benignly. "Bona-fide men Guard, pass on," they said.

Guard Flanagan, obviously a highly conscientious upholder of the law, and possibly piqued at finding nearly all of the apprehendees bona-fide, decided to test the Annaholty men's claims for immunity.

Soon afterwards, armed with his measuring tape, he set off on his bicycle and measured the distance from the men's homes to Fitzgerald's and triumph was his when all four were found to be inside the three mile limit. It didn't matter that one of them was only a mere 300 yards short of the three miles, being measured at 2 miles 1,213 yards from the pub, and the rest not much further off the mark either. Not bona-fide. All were charged with breaking the law.

Justice Gleeson was somewhat sympathetic. "They nearly made it. They were only a few hundred yards short of being bona-fide," he said.

Replying to a question by Mr. T. E. O'Donnell, solr., Guard Flanagan said the sensible way for anybody from Annaholty to cycle or drive to Castleconnell would be by Daly's Cross, which would be slightly longer than via the Bog Road; it was the distance over the Bog Road he measured.

Justice: The sensible thing would be to wait at home when the premises are shut legally to them.

John Kinevane, barman, said all the men told him they were travellers. He thought he was entitled to serve them. The licensee was ill at the time.

Three of the Annaholty Four claimed they honestly believed they were bona fide travellers in Mrs. Fitzgerald's Bar. One of them said he had believed this for the past twenty years.

Justice Gleeson: Well you know differently now.

The Justice dismissed the case against the publican and four of the men who were either in Court or represented. He fined one man 15s and the other 10s.

So ended the good times for the Annaholty men and from then on, like their fellow Castleconnell imbibers, had to meekly leave the village hostelries when the barmen gave the time-worn call, "Time, gentlemen, please!"

Families of famous horse dealers were united in 1951 when a triple wedding took place in Limerick. The happy couples were pictured on an open site in the city containing their horse drawn caravans.

Some memorable Corporation meetings

The column "Random Gossip" in the Leader of 1948 was bemoaning the fact that Corporation meetings were now tame affairs in comparison to those of former times when "scenes" were of frequent occurrences and the air was made more or less thick with recriminations.

"You are like a little barking dog" said a burly Councillor on one occasion many years ago to a diminutive "City Father" who was frequently interjecting remarks made during a speech by the former.

"What can you expect from a pig but a grunt" came the quick retort.

The columnist went on to say that the Corporation "gallery" of today

Steve Coughlan.

too is very different from that of former years – and does not seem to possess anything like as much ready wit. "I rise to a point of order," said a certain councillor getting to his feet in the olden days. "Faith you'd rather rise to a pint of porther" immediately snapped out one of the "gods."

If the scribe was around in 1972 he would have a different story to tell. All hell broke loose at a Corporation meeting which was described by reporter Tony Purcell as the most explosive in 20 years. "There was so much ranting and raving that 'Mohammed Ali' would have looked a poor second," he wrote.

The trouble started when Ald. Mick Lipper stood up and congratulated Clr. Paddy Kiely, Fianna Fail, on his election to the Mayoralty and said he was sure he would maintain the high standards set by his predecessors. But instead of leaving it at that Ald. Lipper added: "Because of the skulduggery, conspiracy, bribery and corruption which has taken place in the elections of Mayors in the past I was the first person to moot that our election of Mayor should be carried out in a proper and dignified manner. I know Mayors who were elected by asking the price for the high office and some of them are still members of this council."

Ald. Lipper then attacked Ald. Pat Kennedy for his actions in previous mayoral elections, winding up by saying; "I hate chancers, you want to take the glory and get all the publicity. You're more publicised than Christine Keeler."

Ald. Kennedy ably defended himself but Steve Coughlan chimed in: "Behold the man, *ecce homo,* the Messiah is here. When I spent 40 minutes with Mr. Liam Cosgrave last week he told me that Kennedy was a head case."

Clr. Gus O'Driscoll and Ald. Kennedy both joined in simultaneously and stated that Mr. Cosgrave "told us that he could make no sense out of what you (Mr. Coughlan) was saying to him".

Ald. Kennedy now entered the fray with all guns blazing: "Mr.

Mick Lipper

Cosgrave doesn't understand political buffoons. You are the greatest political buffoon the country has seen."

In the long and distinguished history of Mayors of the City, no one ever had a greater baptism of fire than Cllr. Kiely in his first council meeting in office. Sensibly he adjourned the meeting to let matters cool down, the report went on.

Even during what could be described as half-time, the antagonists were still having at it. "The Fianna Fail councillors looked on with amazement at these scenes, and laughter was heard from the small gallery. The scenes were unforgettable," the report went on.

The recess seemed to have worked wonders with Cllr. O'Driscoll setting a conciliatory tone. "We should forget what has gone before and get on with the important business. He pledged his party's support to Clr. Kiely and apologised for what had taken place in his first night in the chair."

Ald. Lipper was also conciliatory when he stood up but then in a dramatic incident when he was about to refer to Ald. Kennedy again, Clr. O'Driscoll caught him by the lapels of his coat and made him sit down.

"Thus ended the stormiest opening to a Limerick City Council meeting in years. No doubt, when the new Mayor recalls the highlights of his year of office next June, he will remember the greatest baptism of fire he endured while presiding over his first council meeting," the report concluded.

.... and a lively Co. Council meeting

In the early 1950's so much heat was generated at a County Council meeting that chaos reigned with blows eventually being struck. "Sit down, and don't be dancing around there like a mad bull. How dare you come in here with a lot of drink in you and insult our officials."

Such were the pleasantries delivered by the chairman J. W. Canty, when he confronted Mr. P. Fitzsimons, who was airing a long-standing obsession about the merits of stone wall fencing for council cottages against that of the wire type. He aggravated Mr. D. Ryan, B.E. to such an extent that the engineer walked out but was persuaded to return by Messrs. John Mackey and D. McAuliffe.

The chairman accused Mr. Fitzsimons of taking the floor for an hour and when he refused to sit down the sport started.

Mr. Fitzsimons: You say I'm drunk. Go out and get a doctor.

Chairman: It's a psychiatrist you want, dancing and lepping there like a mad bull.

Mr. Fitzsimons: You bloody sitting bull up there. I am on my feet here.

Member: Barely (laughter).

There was several appeals made to Mr. Fitzsimons to sit down with the chairman saying they were sick and tired of hearing about that. "We have had this type of thing from you for years."

Undeterred, Mr. Fitzsimons continued despite objections and being told that the decision had been taken in the matter being discussed. "There was a cottage erected near my land and my cattle and sheep could go in over the road fence."

Chairman: For God's sake sit down. We have finished with that. You'll get a stroke or something if you keep dancing madly around the place like that.

The chairman then threatened to adjourn the meeting but Mr. Fitzsimons said: You will not adjourn it. I'll stay on my feet until you agree with me.

Mr. Canty, ringing the bell, and leaving his seat: The meeting is adjourned. Move back there, Mr. Fitzsimons.

Mr. Fitzsimons: I won't move back for you, Canty.

Chairman: You ignorant b————. Be God you will.

With that the chairman slung off his coat and rushed at Mr. Fitzsimons who came to meet him. A couple of blows were struck but the other members rushed in and separated the two.

Mr. Fitzsimons: Do you think I'm afraid of you, Canty?

Chairman: You bloody idiot you. You won't make a cod of me you ignorant b————.

Mr. D. McCauliffe: Don't bother with him John. Don't dirty your hands. He's not worth it, the bloody b————. (To Mr. Fitzsimons): You bloody disturber. You're always wrong.

Mr. Fitzsimons: When was I wrong?

Mr. McAuliffe: Always, since you came in here. You never did a right thing in your life.

Mr. Canty went back to the chair after being told he had the support of the house, but it was then pointed out that he had already adjourned the meeting, which he did immediately.

Mr. Quish: Let us go in the name of God.

Mr. Fitzsimons, game to the very end, shouted: I defy any engineer in the county——

Like one, the councillors interrupted with a chorus of "shut up" and the meeting broke up.

Sarsfield Bridge, 1968. What are they looking at? See page 94.

Death of a Duke

Limerick city was the centre of the motor racing world in 1935 and 1936 when the top drivers from England and Europe took part here in the Grand Prix. Many titled people from abroad competed and these included Prince Birabongse of Siam, who entered under the name "Bira." The Prince, described as coloured, aroused much personal interest amongst the general body of spectators. "Everyone wanted to get a look at His Highness, who appears to have created a very favourable impression." He was described as being a very talented figure, being one of the most famous racing drivers in the world and a gifted artist in bronze.

Prince Birabongse of Siam (left) with the Duke of Grafton prior to the start of the race in which the Duke was to lose his life when his car went out of control at the junction of Roxboro Road in the Grand Prix of Limerick in August, 1936.

The Grand Prix proved a huge undertaking but was voted an outstanding success. It proved a spectacular event for the thousands who came from all over the country as the racing cars swept through the centre of the of the city on a circuitous course that ran through the suburbs as far as Punch's Cross in Ballinacurra, back into Edward Street, Carey's Road, Roxboro and back down William Street and into O'Connell Street.

Sadly, tragedy marred the race in the August weekend of 1936 when 22-year-old John Fitzroy, the 9th Duke of Grafton, was killed when his car went out of control after coming out of the bend at Roxboro and entering Sexton Street. A witness to the accident was local solicitor, T. E. O'Donnell, who was a marshal. At the inquest he said he saw the car coming round the bend from Carey's Road and it then left the ground. The car then skidded for about 25 yards and the back portion hit the pier at the entrance to the Christian Brothers Schools and then burst into flames.

Albert Bennett, 11 James Street, another witness, said the car burst into flames after the crash and he ran over with his fire extinguisher. "The Duke had no clothes on him, they were completely burned off. He was lying in flames and even though he appeared to be badly burned, he said 'I am all right. I am not too bad.' ". Even though the Duke managed to walk, with help, to the ambulance, he died in Barrington's Hospital from his burns shortly afterwards.

Hugh Caruthers Massey, Hampshire, a personal friend of the deceased and with whom he said he had studied in Cambridge, identified the remains. The mother of the dead Duke, Lady Gavin Hume Gore, arrived in Limerick the day after the accident and was the recipient of many condolences on her great tribulation. The remains were removed to Dun Laoghaire to catch the mail boat to Holyhead.

Winner of the race was A. Hutchinson from Belfast and a Miss Ellison and Cholmondoley Taper were sixth. Prince Bira set up a lap record.

Whether the tragic death of the Duke had any bearing on the affair or not, but that was the final Grand Prix held in Limerick.

Racing in Limerick in the Grand Prix of 1936.

Poets laud Munster's win over the All-Blacks

"ALL BLACKS CRASH" were the giant headlines in the Leader when after seventy-three years trying, an Irish team (Munster) at last beat the All Blacks in the never-forgotten match in Thomond Park in October 31st, 1978, on the score of 12-nil.

Film star Richard Harris, filming in South Africa, fired off a telegram of congratulation addressed to the Leader in which he said his ten months stint "on the dry" may have come to a jubilant end because of the famous victory. "I wish I had been there," he added.

The match was hardly over when poets rushed into print, like Athlunkard Street's Arthur Lysaght: "Ah, glory, it was great, in October '78,/when the All Blacks fell to Munster in the field;/they were striving hard to win/with their fifteen well-tried men/but the stalwart men of Munster made them yield."

John B. Keane wrote: "Were you in Thomond Park/for that classic rugby lark/did you cheer when Christy Cantillon touched it down?/were you there when Tony Ward/dropped them high and sweet and hard?/when the men of Munster donned the world crown."

John B. continued: "A day may well dawn when a Ministry of Sport could rank highest in all cabinet posts. In that not too unlikely event, men, women and children who were present at the Munster triumph would be well advised to hold on to their tickets and programmes in case they would ever be applying for pensions or medals as the fair guarantee for being present that afternoon."

G. P. Carey of Essex added his effort, the last verse of which was: "Saxon, Briton and Scot/though they gave all they got/could not stem the black tide grim and gory/but, Mumhan abu, what no other could do/the Gael has the glory."

Charlie Mulqueen said the Munstermen played with such commitment and character that it would make them household names for as long as rugby is played in the province. "Seamus Dennison's great early tackle on Stu Wilson set the trend. Failure then could have opened the floodgates."

Russ Thomas, the All-Blacks manager, said "the pressure you put on us with that early try won the day, I could not single out any one player for special mention, they were all magnificent."

Official attendance at the match was 13,000 but over the intervening years so many have claimed to have been there on the historic occasion that it is said that attendance figures on that day have risen to the 100,000 mark.

Munster were the only Irish team ever to have beaten the All-Blacks.

Shoppers tread
on haunted ground

For the many shoppers who traverse Dunnes Stores in Sarsfield Street, there appears to be nothing out of the ordinary about the premises, purchased by the company in the early 1970's.

Back then, however, when the premises was sold by Stokes and McKiernan, some of the former employees of this wholesale firm had several harrowing stories to tell about hauntings. The premises was formerly Spillane's Tobacco Factory.

One former employee told of how one evening when he was working up in the loft to his amazement this figure approached him. Before he could catch his breath the figure had disappeared in front of his eyes. Another had much the same experience, but the figure

Spillane's tobacco factory, later Stokes & McKiernan, and now Dunnes Stores

appeared and then vanished several times. The man was described as between 48 and 50 years, 5' 6', dressed in tweed and he had grey hair.

"I went stone cold. I got a terrible fright even though it was a very bright and cheerful day," claimed the one who saw the apparition. Other workmates were called but there was no sign of the ghostly visitor.

The incidents culminated in the sighting of the figure on the roof of the building and the Gardai were called in to investigate and four of them ascended onto the roof. Onlookers watched from the street below but were amazed when the men in blue walked by the mysterious figure as if it wasn't there.

"Why don't they do something," they cried in unison.

When the Gardai came down they were accosted by eager questioners. "There was no-one there. We could see no-one," was their terse reply.

Anyone seen a middle-aged man, dressed in tweed and with grey hair in Dunne's lately?

Catholic Emancipation Centenary celebrations parade passing through O'Connell Street in 1929.

Limerick - 100 stories of the century

The great dog hoaxes of West Limerick

A correspondent in the 1930's recalled the great dog hoaxes of West Limerick, which happened in Newcastle West during the time of the Boer War and later in Abbeyfeale.

During the war many mules and donkeys were sold to the British Army at fairs in the district and when posters were put up to the effect that on a certain date buyers would attend that town to purchases all classes of dogs in as large numbers as were available, and at the highest prices, many thought that it was but a continuation of the good times for those with such animals to sell.

The result was a "fair" of extraordinary large dimensions and of the most diverse composition, for dogs of almost every kind and in immense numbers were brought in from all quarters! As the appointed day dawned for the sale, hundreds of dogs, voicing their protests against such unreasonable travelling, assisted the traders of the old town of the "Templars" to rise from their beds a great deal earlier than was comfortable.

It is on record, however, that shop assistants found many a window guard serving a new purpose that morning, holding a new sort of livestock to which cattle fairs had previously been strangers. Numerous dogs of low and no degree, were whiling away the early hours of the morning barking for a purchaser, but there appeared to be nothing doing. Later things became more active in the queues and some whirling contests developed. These were generally of the one-round species, which made a ring of some of the shop counters and sometimes wound up inside them, where the shop assistants appeared to referee with a pike instead of a sponge.

When, as no buyers turned up, and it became obvious later in the day that the whole thing was a hoax, the most amusing situations arose. Most of the would-be sellers retired to licensed premises to console themselves, while little boys busied themselves tying saucepans and other such utensils to the dogs' tails, so that towards evening almost every publichouse in the town was in a state of pandemonium from the leashed canines struggling and snarling and fighting each other. Many of the poor dogs got a watery grave on their way home that evening, but their fate was mild by comparison with that to which the practical joker would be subjected were he found by those whom he had duped.

Some of those fooled however, managed to retain some of their sense of humour.

"Did Mike sell the dog?" asked one woman of a duped neighbour. "Indeed he did," was the reply, "but a damn bad salesman he is too. He got only £3 while he could have got £5 easily if only he had held out a few minutes more.

The woman was too irate to say more than blurt out: "I wouldn't doubt the old fool!' The correspondent colourfully described the scene as the duped dog owners, who were described as being part responsible for the greatest concentration of undesirable curs and mongrels in the history of West Limerick, prepared for a dignified retreat. "Hannibal, Alexander and Napoleon conducted a few retreats, but with more or less success in their days, but it would be interesting to know how any of the trio would have extracted his dignity under similar circumstances to those that faced the innocent canine vendors."

One would have thought that news of the hoax would have reached Abbeyfeale and that dog owners there in later years would have been on their guard. But no. The Abbeyfeale correspondent wrote that in April, 1931 the bellman of Abbeyfeale announced that a Mr. B———, some well-known Cross-channel buyer of greyhounds would attend at Abbeyfeale Market to buy all sorts and breeds of greyhounds. For miles around greyhound owners arrived in the town but waited in vain for the supposed buyer from cross-channel.

Humbugging smiles and comments raked the retreat of the victims of the heartless joke as they struggled homewards. At Abbeyfeale, one such victim innocently admitted that he did not mind so much "coming in", it was the "going out" that killed him.

In the retreat from the town, "like seasoned generals some of the would-be sellers withdrew under cover of the night. Others departed as the shadows were lengthening, leaving some old friends behind. One or two of the latter still tugged at the ropes that held them to the window guards of the pub, from which their owners were last seen to depart."

Upper Maiden Street, Newcastle West, early 20th century

Humour of the century

Tragedies, by their very nature, are the lifeline of newspapers and a perusal of the century's files bear this out. However, humour, whether in court reports of a more leisurely age or in gleanings of the city or county council or other public bodies, often shone through.

Con Cregan, the eminent editor of the Leader for most of the first part of the century, following his retirement in 1960 recorded many humorous anecdotes. He wrote once of the old Limerick Board of Guardians, which consisted of an unwieldy body of about a hundred members, representing both Counties Limerick and Clare. By their substance, it was not surprising that there were many diverse characters on board. Seemingly there was a discussion at a meeting of the Board one day on an incident in which a patient who was supposed to have breathed his last had been actually removed by mistake from the workhouse hospital to the morgue before life was fully extinct.

On hearing this an outraged member got on his feet and seriously and formally proposed that "in future no corpse be removed from the house until he is dead."

Such incidents were then known as ''bulls'' and Con recalled the famous Boyle Roche, who one time uttered immortally "no one could be in two places at the one time unless he was a bird."

In the 1930's, James McAuliffe recalled the great wit, Bill Lenane, who once operated as a travelling jobbing man in the Charleville area. He had the title of the wittiest man in the Limerick/Cork Border area and whether the company was lowly or exalted he invariably came out on top by his witty sallies and ripostes.

By nature of his job, Bill sampled many of the ''delights'' of lodging houses in his day and had many caustic stories to tell of them. He happened to stay one night in a house to rest his weary bones, and when he lay down in his bed he was immediately attacked from front and rear by a leaping army of fleas.

On rising next morning he registered a strong protest with the landlady about the ordeal he had undergone but she wouldn't believe him.

"Well,", said Bill, "if you want proof of it Mrs. look at my neck after them, 'tis like a music book".

Still defending the integrity of the establishment, the landlady claimed that "she caught the last flea in that bed of yours yesterday and killed him."

"Faith then if you did," said Bill, "all his pals attended his wake during the night!"

Another day Bill was working for a farmer in Co. Limerick and being dinner time and Friday, the woman of the house put up a salty herring on his plate swimming in a sea of transparent liquid masquerading as brown sauce. Bill stared at the feast long and hard and when his host enquired why he wasn't tucking into the meal, Bill replied," "O I'm waiting mam, 'til the tide goes out!"

A Mission was taking place in Charleville and Bill went to confess his sins to a priest who unknown to him was rather severe. "You're standing on the brink of hell" his Redemptorist confessor admonished the penitent.

"Isn't it a quare place then, Father," replied Bill, "you perched your little confession box."

Richard Adams, Q.C., a local judge in the early part of the century, was a noted wit, his fame being such that a reporter travelled from London to hear him in action. One could hardly imagine the formidable Dr. Edward Thomas O'Dwyer, Bishop of Limerick, as being a wit but he too had his moments: both their stories are recorded elsewhere in the book.

O'Connell Street in the 1950s.

The West End in Kilkee, made impassable during the storms of 1951.

A night to remember

A ferocious storm struck these islands at the height of the Christmas festivities of 1951. The gales coincided with a spring tide and many parts of Limerick were seriously flooded due to the Shannon and the Abbey rivers overflowing. Eighty miles an hour winds were reported and in Newcastle West, the family of Mr. Patrick O'Carroll-Nash had a narrow escape from death when a large elm tree came crashing down on the back of the residence. Luckily, the family were in the front of the house at the time and escaped injury.

The West Clare coast took a terrible beating and the sea wall in the West End in Kilkee was thrown down and the road made impassable. There were some extraordinary stories emanating from Lahinch, where fish were thrown on to the esplanade and driven up onto the Golf Links road.

Mr. Setright, the driver of the Limerick bus, was able to bring home a nice ling to his wife. "Most of us got some kind of a fish. Conger eels were on the tables the next day and some people even had turbot." Local man Paul Barrett was on a roof putting slates back when he found a pollock, blown out of the sea, caught between the only two slates that were left. "I had it for my dinner," he told a Leader reporter, "it tasted lovely."

Colonel Patrick Brennan had an extraordinary story to tell of his near neighbour in the village, a returned Yank named John Reidy, who lived in a house called the Bath-house, only two yards from the pier. John used go across to the Colonel's house each evening but so severe was the storm on the St Stephen's Night that he tied the end of a long rope to his door-knob, caught the other end, and over he came for his visit. "When John went to bed he tied himself to it for fear he might be sucked out through the window by one of the big waves," added the Colonel.

Michael Skerrit, who also lived alongside the pier, had a miraculous escape from drowning when a huge wave broke in his front door. He was attempting to put up a barricade when a worse wave followed sweeping right through the house, knocking him down, breaking his back door, and on its way back, nearly sucking him with into the Atlantic. His narrow front door-way saved his life as it blocked his passage into the sea.

Workmen on the esplanade the following day said they "enjoyed" the biggest storm they had seen since 1923. One of them described the worst feature of the night. "A huge tidal wave swept down Marine Parade and carried everything with it as far as the golf house. After it went back, eight hundred yards of roadway was literally alive with fish of all description strewn around."

The downside of the storm was that two O'Donnell families from Lahinch, who had started a small fishing industry out of Liscannor, lost both their trawlers in the storm. Col. Brennan also said that young lads who used caddy during the summer supplemented their earnings in the winter by collecting "fithon", or sea rods, the extractions of which are used for the making of such things as nylons. "All the rods they had harvested are washed out to sea," he said.

One of the great sea dramas of the century took place during the storm. In an age when a captain was expected to stay with his doomed ship, the world watched as Captain Kurt Carslen, stayed with the "Flying Enterprise", listing at 80 degrees and lashed by 15 foot waves in mid Atlantic. Films of the Danish captain, his mate Kenneth Dancy, and their damaged ship were taken from circling aeroplanes and flashed on newsreels showing in cinemas all over the world. The ship was eventually towed to Falmouth and on his way to New York, where a ticker tape reception awaited, him, Captain Carlsen's plane touched down at Shannon.

There to greet him was Steve Coughlan, Mayor of Limerick, who presented him with an actual lifebouy from the Port of Limerick and a bottle of Irish whiskey. The Mayor said: "I am sorry I was not in a position to extend you some Irish hospitality during your recent terrifying ordeal, but I can assure you that the people of this country followed with keen interest your heroic endeavours to save your ship." The thousands waiting in New York to greet the captain were disappointed as engine trouble, when the plane was 250 miles out into the Atlantic, forced it to return to Shannon from where it left the next day.

Drunken ducks in Bruree

At the turn of the century, Bruree was en fete. John Gubbins of Bruree House had won the Derby with his horse "Galteemore" and excitement was high in anticipation of the return of the horse, its owner and trainer. In honour of the great victory Mr. Gubbins arranged a celebration for all those in and around the village who cared to participate in it. A lavish supply of intoxicants was provided and in the process of sending it around a large barrel of stout fell and smashed on the ground. The liquid flowed freely down the channel and this gave the ducks the opportunity for their unwonted spree!

A newspaper account written about the incident said: "The ducks imbibed copiously and after a while, according to the local gossip of the time, they waddled around in a defiant and truculent attitude similar to that of the mouse that puts out its chest after fortifying itself at a leaking whiskey tap and exclaimed: 'where are the bloody cats now? I'd ate a million of um.' "

John Gubbins was a great sportsman and had the very rare honour of winning the Derby twice in the space of four years: in 1898 with "Galteemore" and in 1902 with "Ardpatrick." Many interesting stories were current for a long time in the Bruree district in connection with these victories. It was told, for instance, that one day "Galteemore", as a young foal, got caught in a gate and was in danger of getting choked. The wife of one of the workmen on the estate released the future Derby winner and when John returned from Epsom after the race he sought out this woman and filled her apron with pound notes.

Performing in the Olympia Theatre in Dublin in 1952 were Laurel and Hardy and pictured with the famous duo were, from left: Callie Connolly, Earl Connolly, Jim Marshall, Jim O'Carroll, Mrs. Murphy and Mrs. Stan Laurel.

Christopher Lynch being coached by Count John McCormack at the world famous tenor's home in Booterstown, Co. Dublin. It was 1945, and McCormack was to die the same year.

Whatever happened to Christopher Lynch?

Newspaper reports all through the 1940's hailed Rathkeale man Christopher Lynch as the natural successor to the world famous tenor, John McCormack. In 1943 when he sang in Dublin the Irish Independent critic Harold R. White was reported as saying: "the most promising Irish tenor in years, and definitely a young man with a future, must have been the judgment of the great majority of the audience who heard the young Limerick tenor."

Count John McCormack, with his own career coming to an end, took over the Limerickman as his protege and devoted considerable time to passing on the benefit of his rich experience. "The singer most likely to succeed me, and a promise of which I have not heard better in a quarter of a century," stated McCormack. Lynch was at the bedside of the famous singer when he died in 1945. It was reported in the same year that the Rathkeale man turned down the then considerable sum of £250 per week for a contract to sing in the United States. He had made his mind up to go to Italy for final coaching before appearing on any international stage. He gave one final concert before he left, in the Savoy in Limerick, which was booked out and he received a reception which was described as "ecstatic."

On his return from Rome, where he studied under the world renowned maestro Signor Morelli, the young Rathkeale man, before his departure to the USA, gave a farewell concert in the Savoy to which many failed to gain admission. Supported by violinist Jack Cheattle, leader of the Radio Eireann Orchestra, and Miss Jennie Reddan, piano, the concert was described as one of the most outstanding musical events in the life of the city. "Those who came in the role of captious critics, were to the forefront in clamouring for more, recalling the great tenor again and again. His voice was more golden than gold."

Hundreds were left outside the doors of the Deel Hall, Rathkeale when the tenor gave a two-night concert in his home town. The correspondent waxed lyrical in describing the occasion. "People came from a radius of 30 miles by bicycle, farm carts, traps and donkey carts in severe weather. He received an ovation that rocked the very building and had to give numerous encores. It was very touching when at the finish of his programme he sang 'Mother Macree' with evident emotion – just across the footlights was his own mother." At a reception afterwards the tenor was the recipient of a championship G.A.A. medal: he had played in the goalkeeper position with the home club.

Rave notices greeted the Rathkeale man's appearances across the States. Writing in the New York World Telegram Edmund Leavy said: "there is magic to his music to warm the heart and mist the eye," and eminent music critic Martin W. Bush said the tenor sang with uncommonly clear enunciation and elicits heart-tugs where many another would fail.

He was giving an average of 150 concerts a year across the States and clocking up to 50,000 miles, appearing in all the principal cities. It was added: "When this is coupled with his radio and television work (on the later-day miracle-medium of American entertainment he has proved a phenomenal success), it can readily be realised that the life of a singer in the big time can be a gruelling one."

In 1949 it was reported that Lynch sang the Midnight Mass in St. Patrick's Cathedral in New York and the following year a Leader report said that admirers of the young tenor would be delighted to hear that they were to get an opportunity to hear Christopher sing at a special concert in Limerick. The Rathkeale man was coming home on holidays after his three year stint in America. "So June 30th next will find him arriving at Cobh with his charming wife, Dympna, and his three lovely children, Brian, Marese and baby Christopher Gerard. Music lovers may be assured of a treat in hearing him on the few occasions afforded this summer. Reports from the States confirm that his voice has attained a maturity and tone which are a delight to the ear, confirming beyond doubt the verdict by the late John McCormack when he said he has a beautiful voice, a charming personality and undoubtedly the best prospect I have heard in twenty-five years."

Lynch made his television debut in the United States the same year "where he is proving a great attraction." It was a popular series of musical programmes sponsored by Firestone and on the programme he sang such numbers as "Younger than Springtime" and "Believe Me If All Those Endearing Young Charms."

The following year, in July, 1950, the Rathkeale born tenor made another triumphant return home and gave a concert in the Savoy. Like all such events in the past decade at this venue, the recital was packed out and he had to respond to many requests for encores. And the Leader was once more in seventh heaven about the voice, stating that his singing stamped him out as one of the world's greatest tenors. "His glorious voice, embellished with a fine stage presence, was to be heard to advantage in a repertoire of five groups that ranged from the highly classical to popular refrains."

That was to be Lynch's last concert in the Savoy, and when his voice, according to contemporary reports, seemed to be at its finest and maturest, there were no further newspaper reports of his career which inexplicably seemed to have come to a sudden end.

O'Callaghan's Strand, early 1950s.

Last man to be hanged

On the night of Wednesday, 18th November, 1953, Mary E. Cooper a staff nurse at Barrington's Hospital, paid a visit to her friend in Castletroy, Miss A. Curtin, a former matron at the hospital. Described as being around 60 years of age, Miss Cooper got the bus out from the city and after having tea and spending a few hours with her friend, prepared to return to the city. She was seen to the gate by the housemaid, Miss Margaret Egan, who expressed regret that she was unable to drive the Ford Anglia, owned by Miss Curtin.

It was an age, however, when it was not unusual for women to be abroad on their own after dark, Miss Cooper felt no fear, saying that the night was so lovely she was even sorry she did not walk out to Castletroy instead of taking the bus.

Miss Egan was the second last person to see Miss Cooper alive.

At around 11 p.m., Mr. and Mrs. John McCormack, who were motoring to their home in the neighbourhood, came upon the body of Miss Cooper. They immediately alerted the Gardai and a priest. The report said Miss Cooper's body was found facing the Castletroy direction about fifty yards from the old castle ruin, which stands opposite the golf links. She was lying on the grass margin, with a large tuft of grass jammed into her mouth. The body, identified by a doctor who knew Miss Cooper, was taken to Barrington's Hospital, in the Corporation Ambulance. The result of the autopsy by Dr. Hickey, state pathologist, described the various injuries to the body and said death was caused due to shock and asphyxia, resulting from suffocation, and certain organs were removed for further examination.

The deceased was a native of Killimer, Co. Clare, and the funeral was attended by "hundreds of citizens."

Early next morning, a 24-year-old carter named Michael Manning (alias Mangan), from Clare Street, was taken into custody and charged with Miss Cooper's murder. The murder was described as a "sensation" in the Leader report, which gave huge headlines, and several hundred gathered outside the courthouse attempting to get a glimpse of the accused when he was brought in and charged. Gardai had difficulty in keeping a clear passage for the accused.

The trial in the Criminal Court in Dublin was followed with huge interest in the city and crowds gathered outside the offices of the Leader each day of the court hearings to purchase either the Leader or the Chronicle to keep abreast of the news.

There was a poignant moment in the trial when Guard F. Slattery described a visit by the accused's father to his son in Mountjoy. "Why did you do it?" asked the father. "I was drunk," said his son, "I saw a woman walking in front of me on the road and when I moved up I jumped at her. There was a struggle, then a car came along and I jumped through a hedge and ran away."

Mr. Manning then said to his son: "I was never up for anything in my life except for having no light. Now you have disgraced me."

The thrust of the defence's case was that the accused perpetrated the crime when intoxicated, and that it was not premeditated. There was also a plea of insanity and Sir John Desmonde, for the defence, addressing the jury, said the charge should be reduced to one of manslaughter.

For the prosecution, Mr. B. Walsh, S.C, said that one thing was certain and that was that Miss Cooper was killed and the accused killed her. He departed from his usual routine of bringing the horse and cart to his brother's place for the purpose of leaving himself free to commit the crime. He had stuffed grass into the deceased's mouth to stop her from screaming. There was no evidence that accused was suffering from mental disease.

Summing up, the Judge told the jury that drink was no defence in this case, the accused being fully aware when he stuffed the victim's mouth with grass to stop the deceased from screaming. If they accepted the evidence given by the State, then the accused was guilty of murder.

Manning, in admitting the killing, stated that at the time of the attack he was drunk. "I saw this lady walking in front of me towards Limerick, on the left-hand side of the road. I walked behind her for a few minutes then I suddenly lost control of myself and jumped on her because she was alone. She screamed and I knocked her on the grass margin and stuffed her mouth with grass to stop her from roaring. She got quiet after five minutes but she began to struggle again, and asked me to stop. She just said "Stop, stop." The next thing a motor car with lights stopped beside me and I got up and jumped over the ditch."

On February 17th, 1954, after three hours deliberation, the jury returned a verdict of guilty and the judge, donning the black cap, sentenced the accused to be hanged on the following 10th March.

The execution was delayed for some time, following an appeal, which was turned down on April 3rd, and the accused was hanged in Mountjoy on Tuesday, 20th April, 1953. It was to be the last execution in the Republic.

Jury Considering Verdict In Limerick Murder Charge

THE trial of Michael Manning, the Limerick carter charged with the murder of Nurse Catherine E. Cooper, concluded in the Central Criminal Court this evening. At the time of going to Press the jury are considering their verdict.

The Judge concluded his charge to the jury at 2.45. At 4.50 the jury re-appeared to seek clarification on a legal point.

Result of trial in later edition.

QUESTION OF FISHING RIGHTS ON THE SHANNON

(To the Editor, "Limerick Leader")
A DHUINE UASAIL, Last year when Sean O'Carroll was in...

TO-NIGHT'S GREAT SYMPHONY CONCERT

MR. Erskine Childers, Minister for Posts and Telegraphs, is coming to Limerick this evening to attend the Symphony Concert...

Death on the Shannon

On Easter Sunday, 1906, six men from Coonagh, a small fishing village a few miles downstream from Limerick city, crossed over the Shannon to Tervoe in a gondola, a flat-bottomed fishing craft. On the return journey, with the wind favourable, a large sail was put up and all went well until about half-way across the river. A sudden squall blew up, which caused the boat to upset, with all the occupants being thrown into the extremely cold water. There was but one survivor, Michael Punch, who managed to hold on to the upturned boat. He threw some of the

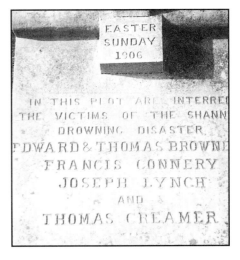

oars to his floundering companions, but had the traumatic experience of seeing them drown one by one with nothing left but their caps floating on the water. There were scenes of great grief when the victims (Edward Browne, Joseph Lynch, Thomas Creamer, Thomas Browne, Francis Connery), most of them in their early twenties, were buried in Mount St Laurence. The report of the drowning said that the flat-bottomed craft was not suitable for a sail.

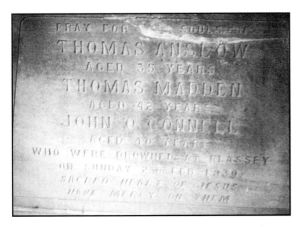

On Sunday, February 2nd, 1930, three anglers, John O'Connell, Pennywell; Thomas Anslow, Pennywell , and Thomas Madden, Canal Bank, were returning in their angling cot from a pleasant day's salmon fishing in Plassey. They made a halt on their return journey and gave a lift in the boat to a young man named John Airey. Darkness had fallen as they approached Plassey Bridge and driven on by strong currents following heavy rains, the boat hit one of the supports of the bridge. It was smashed and all the occupants thrown into the raging torrent. All were drowned except Airey, who managed to hold on to a portion of the boat before he was rescued.

The caustic wit of Bishop O'Dwyer

Edward Thomas O'Dwyer, Bishop of Limerick, was one of the most formidable figures ever to oversee the Diocese of Limerick, being both a villain and hero to many during his bishopric in the momentous years from 1887 to 1918. Highly dictatorial and fearless in his comments, he did however on occasions display a keen sense of humour, mostly caustic, and here are a few examples taken from local newspaper files:

When Mons. Hallinan, D.D., who was to succeed Dr. O'Dwyer in 1918 as bishop, was P.P. in St. Mary's, the bishop visited and the weather being fine, they went for a walk in the garden. Now at that time there was a glue yard in nearby St Francis Abbey, the proprietor of which was a great benefactor of St. Mary's. As the wind was blowing in a certain direction the odours from the factory were wafted towards them. Suddenly the Bishop said:

"How can you stand that terrible smell?"

"What smell, my Lord?" asked the Monsignor, who probably like a lot of people had a poor sense of smell, or else had become acclimatised to that particular odour.

"The smell from the glue yard of course."

"I don't find any smell my Lord."

"No,' retorted Dr. O'Dwyer, 'because Mr. _____'s banknotes are stuffed up your nose."

Dr. O'Dwyer was not remiss to telling a joke against himself. On one occasion he remonstrated with an American priest who was smoking a cigar on the train to Dublin.

"To what diocese do you belong" the bishop asked the priest.

"Chicago, Illinois, USA."

"And do you consider it consistent with the dignity of the Catholic priesthood to smoke in public?"

"Well, I don't see any harm in doing so, but by the way, who are you?

"I am the Bishop of Limerick," returned Dr. O'Dwyer with great dignity.

"Well, you have a darned good job and you ought to mind it," retorted the American as the train moved off.

The bishop was president of St. Michael's Temperance Society when some of its members conceived the then daring plan (it was early century) of throwing open their Sunday night dance to the public to help swell funds. They had of course to get the permission of his eminence and they were delighted when he agreed that it was a great idea. Seeing the delegation to the door of his palace in Corbally, he soon brought them down to earth when adding the proviso that no women would be allowed attend the dance!

According to historian A. J. O'Halloran, the bishop was noted for his "put downers" as exemplified by the following story. During the infamous Parnell split, O'Dwyer, like his contemporaries throughout the country, aligned himself against the "Uncrowned King" but neither he nor his clergy took an overt part in the strife that raged between the two factions. With the idea probably of winning his powerful advocacy on behalf of his party, a prominent member of the Anti-Parnellite group waited on him, and proceeded to bewail in unctuous tones the grave scandal caused by the lapse of Charles Stewart Parnell. Bishop O'Dwyer listened to him a while and then demanded brusquely:

"When where you last at Mass?"

Now since the honourable member was sadly remiss in fulfilling this most essential spiritual duty, as the Bishop very well knew, he immediately wilted, forgot his mission, and speedily took his leave!

A grand bazaar and fete was organised in Dromin in September 1905 in connection with the renovations of the church. Organiser was the P.P., Fr. Canty, and an immense gathering of clergy and laity saw the Bishop open the proceedings in the schoolhouse.

His Lordship was in scintillating form and spoke of recent slurs cast against the Irish by the English.

He told the story of a jarvey up in Connemara who when his English passenger enquired as to the ruins of a farmer's house was told by the driver " 'twas the chapels that did it your honour."

When asked to explain, the jarvey told him '' 'twas one of the grandest houses and one of the grandest families around and on St. Stephen's Day you would see six sons on horseback after the hunt. There were dinners going on there every day of the week. The owner drank nothing before dinner but after dinner he took his sixteen tumblers of punch without a murmur (laughter).

"A pity," said the Englishman, "but what caused the ruin of that great family?"

"Building a chapel, your honour," said the driver. "They were doing very well until a parish priest came here, who built a chapel below there, and that chapel ruined more people around here than any other thing since the time of the famine" (laughter).

The Bishop concluded the story: "That Englishman, some tailor from Leeds or greengrocer from Manchester, went back and told his circle of friends how the clergy were destroying the people of Ireland, and that were it not for the English Government and the landlords and the Protestant religion there would not be one of them left in the country at all (great laughter).

"That is the sort of nonsense we are asked to answer and explain. For my part I treat it with such contempt that I would not be bothered going to any trouble to answer it at all" (hear hear).

Death in Mount St. Vincent

Around 5 o'clock in the afternoon of 3rd November, 1908, two orphans in Mount St. Vincent, O'Connell Avenue, run by the Mercy Sisters, complained of sickness and headache and were sent to bed. Soon there were others showing signs of a like malady and by 10 o'clock up to twenty of the children had fallen ill. As the night wore on, up to sixty had become affected. Mother M. Joseph, in charge of the orphanage, with another sister and the resident nurse, stayed up all night with the sick children.

A doctor had been sent for earlier on and after examining the patients considered the illness was caused by some type of poisoning. All the victims were showing the same symptoms, suffering from vomiting and severe headache. The doctor maintained as there were no alarming symptoms, he would take his leave, giving instructions as to the treatment which he said would counteract the attack.

What followed proved one of the great tragedies in the history of the city. Before dawn had broken, seven young children had succumbed to what the jury described at the inquest as Cholera Nostra due to meat poisoning, "and we are further of opinion that at the time of cooking the unsoundness of the meat could not be detected."

Two more deaths were to follow, making it in all a total of nine fatalities.

The first death occurred at 7 a.m. the

The grave of the children of Mount St. Vincent's in Mount St. Laurence Cemetery, in which six of the 1908 poisoning victims (Sarah King, Nora Meaney, Francis Storey, Lilly O'Dea, Mary Ryan, Bridget O'Donoghue) are buried. Elizabeth Gleeson, May Kelly and Jessie Smart are buried in family graves. The average age of the victims was 15.

next morning, November 4th, and as news of the terrible disaster filtered through, all the medical men in the city were soon in attendance. Despite doing all they could, the fatalities soon started to rise. Descriptions were given of the horrific suffering of the children by the nursing sisters: "The poor children were writhing in agony of excruciating pain: the intensity of suffering rendered them unconscious of what was going on around them."

It was reported that a saintly Franciscan, Fr. Dillon, was taken to several of the bad cases, and he prayed at the bedside of each. Then he knelt in the middle of the dormitory and prayed aloud. He was considered by everyone to be a saint and the Sisters believed it was owing to his prayers that several whom they thought could not possibly survived, were spared.

During the two days in which the children died, large crowds gathered at the entrance to the Mount, "including relatives and sympathisers of the afflicted children and some pathetic scenes were witnessed. The wailing of the women was sometimes heartrending, while it was also touching to witness the eagerness with which the latest tidings of the condition of the other poor sufferers was awaited. A number of policemen were also on duty at the entrance, and while their demeanour was sympathetic they had very little trouble with the subdued and awe-stricken bystanders."

The tragedy caused great shock and many messages of sympathy addressed to the superior, Mother M. Joseph, poured into the convent from all parts of the country. The chairman of Knockea Branch of the Ratepayers Association, Mr. H. O'Connell, said: "We can picture that no parent could feel the loss of their children more than the fostering nuns from whom these nine young souls have been so sadly separated." He then proposed that their assembled meeting tender on behalf of their parish the most heartfelt condolence to the good and sorrow-stricken nuns and relations of the children."

Eminent medical men, like Professor McWeeney, bacteriologist, sent to investigate the case, were loud in their praises of the efficient method in which everything connected with the sick children was carried. out. A Protestant military doctor who attended said that the hospital was as perfect as any of their military hospitals.

The Right Hon. Lord Emly, chairman of St. John's Hospital Governors, conveyed the board's heartfelt sympathy to the nuns and relatives. "In common with our fellow citizens, we fully recognise the untiring devotion and attention bestowed by the good nuns on the children under their care, which has earned for the orphanage the high reputation that it so deservedly enjoys."

A telegram was received from Rome conveying to the community and children the blessing of the Holy Father.

There were poignant scenes at the funeral with the nine victims being laid out in pale blue habits. Five of the victims were buried on Friday 6th, and "the spectacle presented by the five hearses containing the remains of the victims, followed by a long train of mourning coaches, was pathetic in the extreme, and was watched by thousands of silent witnesses with bared heads who were in many instances moved to tears as the cortege passed by on its way to the Mount St. Vincent plot in Mount St. Laurence Cemetery."

The report went on to state that "the outcome of the inquest, which had been adjourned, was awaited with much interest as speculations to the cause is rife and all sorts of theories are being propounded to account for the awful visitation."

The inquest heard Rev. Mother Joseph state that there were four classes of children in the institution, first, second, third, fourth, or the babyhood class. Out of the fifty-five of the first class that had the beef dinner on the 3rd, fifty-three of them fell ill that night and Sarah King was first to die followed by Mary Quirke. She was satisfied that there was no rat-poison about the place at the time of the occurrence; Mr. McCormack of Roche's Street was the contractor for meat; the price was 8d. for choice bits and 5d. for the rest; 8d. was the price all round for mutton. Mr. McCormack was contractor for a number of years; the meat was never sent back for being bad.

Sr. Martha and Sr. Fintan gave evidence of the manner in which the meal was prepared and how different meats that were cooked during the week were added to make up the stew. Both emphasised the cleanliness of the cooking utensils and the absence of any type of rodents in the kitchen. Replying to a question from the Coroner, Sr. Martha said that a lap of mutton delivered on the 24th October was cooked the following Thursday.

Mr. McCormack, butcher, Roche's Street, said he had been supplying meat to Mount St. Vincent for twenty years. He had bought the beef from Jeremiah Roche, High Street, and in his opinion the beef was sound. Mr. Roche said he had slaughtered the beast, bought in a fair in Abbeyfeale, in a small slaughter-house in Benson's Lane, off Mungret Street. Following cross-examination, Mr. Roche protested against the way he was being questioned, and defied his questioner or anybody else to find a breach in his character.

Professor McWeeney, bacteriologist, sent down by the Local Government Board to investigate the case, said that the cause of death, cholera nostras, was the same in all instances. The germ could withstand a high degree of heat without being killed. Infected animals in many cases could not be detected and he instanced a case in Holland where an inspector not alone passed meat but kept some for his own use and died of the effects of eating it. He was of the opinion that the article of food in this case was some beef which arrived in the institution on October 24th and had been kept for five days since it was roasted; this beef formed part of the stew which constituted the dinner of the older girls on Tuesday, the 3rd inst., and some of which was eaten cold by six girls of the second class. How the beef came to be infected he did not know; the beast may have taken ill before being slaughtered, another possibility was that the beef might have been infected by sick mice whilst in the larder.

At the conclusion of his evidence, in answer to a question, Dr. McWeeney said that the provision of an abattoir would be of enormous advantage in securing the freedom of meat from infectious disease.

The Leader editorial on November 20th said: "Since the dreadful consequences of this awful occurrence became known, not alone the citizens and residents in the county, but the entire country has awaited with the utmost concern the results of the analysis and investigations made by that distinguished scientist, Professor McWeeney.

"The verdict returned by the jury at the inquest exonerated all concerned, and the intelligent reader who has carefully followed the proceedings at the inquest will endorse the conclusion arrived at, viz., that the deaths of these poor children were due to one of those unfortunate and unforeseen calamities to which all things are at any moment liable."

The Bishop of Limerick, Most Rev. O'Dwyer, thanking the Corporation for passing a vote of sympathy with the Sisters of Mercy on the calamity, said "it had been a great comfort to him to have been the medium of conveying to the Rev. Mother and the Sisters of Mercy the resolution with reference to the awful affliction which it has pleased our good God to permit to come upon them; and it is no less a happiness to me to be allowed to express to you the heartfelt thanks of the poor nuns for the generous and loyal manner in which you, Mr. Mayor, and the Borough Council, and indeed the whole body of our fellow-citizens, have rallied to them in this hour of difficulty and trial. If any human considerations can mitigate their sorrow, it is the knowledge that this great calamity has only quickened on all sides the feelings of esteem and affection in which their community is held by everyone who has any experience of its manifold and beneficial activities in this city."

Mount St Vincent, O'Connell Avenue at the time of the tragedy.

When Musical Marie took Limerick by storm

The 1920's to the 1950's was Limerick's greatest era of the cinema. In October, 1953, seven cinemas, all of them in close proximity to the city centre, advertised current attractions in the Leader. These included "Titanic" in the Savoy starring Clifton Webb and Barbara Stanwyck; "Salome" at the Lyric with Rita Hayworth and Stewart Granger, and the "Merry Widow" at the Grand Central with Fernando Lamas and Lana Turner.

The same page carried an advt. announcing the arrival of an English pianist named simply "Musical Marie" who at the Transport Union Hall (formerly Catholic Institute Hall) in Sarsfield Street would be attempting to break the world record of playing the piano non-stop for 132 hours set up by an unnamed German. Admission (until further notice) would be a shilling with children half price, and could be viewed up to 12 midnight with the Press and the police observing the record attempt after that.

In an innocent age, and with every little in the way of diversions, Marie's musical marathon attempt took the city by storm and queues formed regularly to see this stupendous musical marathon. As the week went on, and excitement gripped the city with large crowds queuing up to see the musical wonder, the admission price was increased, with Marie playing the odd request.

Local newspapers carried regular news reports of the pianist's progress with headlines such as "Musical Marie is Confident of Success" and reports going on to state that after 53 hours non-stop playing, the pianist's legs and wrists were swollen and that she complained of stomach-ache. To sustain her in her trial, Marie after two days had consumed seven jars of honey and thirty eggs, which she took with two bottles of brandy. "Two nurses are standing by and Marie is quietly confident of breaking the record. Many have turned up to wish her luck and to leave gifts, one of these a white terrier as a lucky mascot."

As the week wore on there were constant reports of her progress and more importantly, the crowds were still flocking in ever increasing numbers to the Transport Hall. Reported to be a devout Catholic, Marie said she was a firm believer in the power of prayer. "Please God," she said, "I shall beat the world record when I conclude at midnight on Saturday night."

As the week progressed and weaker grew the 40-year-old pianist, the Friday night Leader said that it was safe to assume that never in Limerick's history had so much interest been taken in anything than this battle against fatigue, sleep and nerves taking place on the small stage there. Earl Connolly wrote: "She has baffled the thousands who have gone to see her with her will-power and determination to win this record for Limerick. Her marathon is the talk of Limerick and every home is taking a keen interest in her every hour at the piano. Adults and children alike are following the bulletins with as much interest as if she was a relative, and there is no doubting the affection that Limerick has for this devout Catholic who firmly believes that the prayers of all her well-wishers will carry her through the tortuous hours until midnight on the Saturday."

She made it. As midnight approached on Saturday night a crowd estimated at 6,000 thronged the vicinity of Transport Union Hall and a mighty cheer went up when it was announced that Musical Marie had broken the world record. For fifteen hours previously, many more thousands had filed past her as she neared the end of the marathon. The last tune she played was "Now is the Hour" and when she finished up with the National Anthem the huge crowd lining Sarsfield Street stood to attention.

Marie was then lifted from her stool by St. John's Ambulance men and brought by ambulance to Cruise's Hotel where she recovered enough to make several appearances at the window to deafening cheers from the thousands gathered below.

In their attempts to get a glance at the musical wonder, the crowd were reported to be unruly at times and several cars were damaged when spectators climbed onto them. The City Fathers were not amused by the carry on and on the following Monday night Musical Marie was the subject of much debate at the council meeting.

Ald G. E. Russell said he did not know what the feelings of the Council were but he for one took very strong exception to the spectacle. "It was most degrading particularly when it was held adjacent to one of the city's principal thoroughfares."

"Indignation was widespread . . . a positive disgrace. . . it wouldn't have been allowed happen in Cork" were some of the comments from Councillors J. P. Liddy, Ald. Russell and Ald. J. Reidy.

The Mayor: I understand they took close on £1,000.

Ald Reidy: I heard it was £1,400.

A sad sequel to the musical record attempt took place the following January when the Limerick Steamship, and Mr. Philip Murray, Douglas, Cork, claimed compensation from the Limerick Borough Council arising from damage to their vehicles outside Cruise's Hotel on the Saturday night.

The Judge, Mr. Barra O Briain, who seemed to be hopelessly out of touch with the local scene, asked what kind of instrument Musical Marie was playing.

Mr. Kenny, for the plaintiffs, said "a piano."

Judge O'Briain: "I thought it was a gramophone when I heard all the talk about a record."

Sergeant D. Buckley said he estimated the crowd outside Cruise's to be between 3,000 and 4,000. At one period there were up to eight or nine people standing on the roofs of cars trying to get a glimpse of the pianist. The doors of the hotel had to be locked and traffic had to be diverted at the William Street crossing.

There were several witnesses to the disorderly nature of the crowd and Paul Leavy, porter in Cruise's, said they were very rough and some of them forced their way into the hotel. It was also stated that the crowd were originally quite orderly but went berserk when the lady was brought in the ambulance.

The Judge described the case as a very interesting one and said that the Malicious Injury Act was one of the few good legacies left behind by the former British regime,

He held that malicious damage was caused to Mr. Murray's car and awarded the sum of £58 10s., but in the case brought by the Limerick Steamship for damage to their Ford Custom car (the driver, James Boggin, was collecting passengers in Cruise's), he held that the claim must fail as the crowd were orderly at the time the damage occurred, that was before the arrival of the celebrated lady.

Shades of War in Thomond Park

While the Leader of March 2nd, 1942, was full of news of progress of the war, Jimmy O'Donovan, alias "N.M.", rugby correspondent at the time, had his own story to tell of another war . . . a match played the previous day that in ferocity would have matched any of the hand to hand combats of the battles being fought in Europe!

It happened in a replay between Old Crescent Boys (now Old Crescent) and Young Munster in the Munster Junior Cup at Thomond Park. So ferocious were the bodily exchanges that when referee Paddy O'Sullivan called the final whistle no less than nine players who had been banished from the game were looking on from the sideline: nine were left on the Young Munster team and twelve on the Crescent side. Not surprisingly, Crescent won by 16 pts to 3. It was an era when the names of those sent off in the course of play were not published.

The correspondent blamed a section of the crowd for inciting the players; he did not mention the team they were supporting but did leave slip that their chief hobbies consisted of a tirade of constant abuse at the referee for any decision he gave against Young Munster, and inviting the members of that side to commit acts not in accordance with the rules of the game.

"That in itself was bad enough but when the game was over the referee was surrounded and attacked from all sides by the players and non-playing members of the defeated club and several players who intervened paid the piper for their trouble. A description of the play is utterly impossible only to say that throughout the eighty minutes the idea of the beaten team was to crease their opponents no matter how, hence the marching orders."

Laffan, and a player described only as "Fox", and Paddy Reid, accounted for the three Crescent tries, with the latter adding a drop goal and penalty. Young Munster's only score was a penalty try.

"N.M." summed up: "In every case of the dismissals, some of which included players defending themselves, not one in a thousand could find fault with the referee's decisions. Now the question arises, what is to be done to put a stop to such unsportsmanlike actions? Those in charge of the game must assert their authority in such a manner that will leave no loophole for a recurrence."

Unfortunately this did not happen and led to the resignation two weeks later of the President of the Branch, D. J. O'Malley, who was Mayor at the time. The result of the special meeting of the Munster Branch saw suspensions of twelve months upwards meted out to several of the Young Munster players.

"Not enough" said Mr. O'Malley, who left the meeting after the decision was announced. "The offending club should have been suspended," he said in a statement afterwards. "I could not legislate for rugby football in Munster where organised blackguardism took place and where the committee failed, in my opinion, to mete out sufficient punishment to the offending club by suspending them."

Troubled times: Riots at O'Connell Monument

With the legacy of the Civil War still very much in evidence, and with so many who had fought on opposite sides now involved in different political parties, the situation throughout the country through the first part of the 1930's was volatile and there were regular reports of these political disturbances.

On Saturday, September 23, 1933, there were violent scenes following a United Ireland Party (Blueshirts) meeting at the O'Connell Monument, scene of the great political gatherings at the time. As a result of the clashes thirty-three people were treated in Barrington's Hospital, five being detained. One member of the Garda, Sergt. Morgan, was stabbed with a knife in the abdomen and thigh. A number of Guards had to throw themselves on the road when, chasing stone-throwers down Mallow Street, shots were fired from the direction of the Lyric.

Earlier on, a big crowd had gathered outside Cruise's Hotel where the principal speakers, General O'Duffy, Mr. W. T. Cosgrove, and Mr. James Dillon, T.D., were having tea. A cordon of Civic Guards, drawn up in front of the hotel, prevented the crowd lining the footpath at the opposite side from approaching the hotel, outside which "Blueshirts" who had come from all over the country in buses, had gathered. The people at the rear of the cordon indulged in a good deal of booing and there were repeated cries of "Up de Valera."

The trouble started when the parade proceeded up O'Connell Street led by the Collins Pipe Band. En route, the processionists were attacked from different points and some fierce baton charges took place. There were several other baton charges during the meeting at O'Connell Monument and the opening remarks of the chairman, Ald. James Reidy, T.D., could not be heard, but he was able to continue his speech without interruption. When General O'Duffy was speaking a struggle was observed between a Guard and a man resulting in the Guard being stabbed. His assailant, an Irish-American, was arrested. There were further disturbances when the meeting broke up, with more stone-throwing and baton charges.

General O'Duffy, dismissed as Commissioner of the Garda in 1933, had formed a party called the National Guard, which sprung from the Army Comrades Association, made up of former members of the Free State Army in the Civil War. The official uniform was the blue shirt, the style of the fascists of the time. O'Duffy now joined up with Cumann na nGaedhal and other opposition parties in the Dail and thus the United Ireland Party, later Fine Gael, was born with the General as leader. Dissatisfaction with O'Duffy and his methods soon surfaced and the older members of the Cumann na nGaedhal demanded his resignation. William Cosgrave replaced him as leader in 1935 and the era of the Blue Shirts came to an end, but the label is sometimes recalled when referring to members of the Fine Gael Party.

Death of Sean South

Headlines in the Leader following New Year's Day, 1958, brought the stunning news that a Limerick man had been shot dead in the Six Counties. "Two young men were killed in last night's raid on Brookeborough Barracks, Co. Fermanagh. One was identified as Fergal O'Hanlon (25) of Park Street, Monaghan. The other, it was stated, come from Limerick and was the leader of the party taking part in the raid." A later report said: "as we go to press, a message from Dublin says it is understood that the Limerickman who lost his life is Mr. Sean South from Henry Street."

Thousands of mourners, from the city and county, and all over the country, attended South's funeral. In a huge outpouring of sympathy, the cortege, on its removal from Dublin, was met at the city boundary at Pennywell by a huge concourse of mourners and the remains were removed to St. Michael's Church.

From all over the country, all walks of life, public representatives, including TDs, councillors, chairmen and mayors, attended the obsequies and a vast concourse marched in the funeral to the Republican Plot in Mount St. Laurence Cemetery on 5th January.

In an appreciation, the deceased was described as unselfishly sincere and an ardent lover of Ireland as ever breathed. Deeply religious, he was widely read and cultured and was in every action of his life actuated by the highest ideals and motives. He was very shy and gentle as a child, but behind that shyness and gentleness one could always sense some hidden strength and determination. He had an all-consuming love of the Irish language and there was no-one in Limerick more determined about its revival. His great hero was Padraig Pearse, whose ideals he tried to emulate.

Barricades in O'Connell Street during the siege of Limerick, July 1922.

The last siege of Limerick

The last siege of Limerick took place during the Civil War that raged through the country in 1922. For eleven days, during the month of July, Irregulars (Republican) and Free State troops fought running battles through the streets of Limerick. As fighting continued, there were many civilian casualties as the result of gunfire, and St. John's and Barrington's Hospital were over-run at times with many of the injured.

All the civilian casualties had sustained their injuries as they tried desperately to run the gauntlet of snipers' bullets to get to shops (those that managed to stay open) for provisions. O'Connell Street was the scene of some of the worst sniping and was reckoned to be the most dangerous place in the city. Terror stalked the streets and only armoured cars could safely negotiate the principal thoroughfares. The extent of the fighting could be garnered from the fact that a nun, walking in the seclusion of the grounds of the Training College in Mary Immaculate in the South Circular Road, was injured by a stray bullet.

The Limerick Chronicle, for the first time in its then 225 years history, failed to publish for several days during the battle. When the siege was lifted, on July 22, the Chronicle published dramatic headlines. which in the style of the time, carried several sub-headings: "The Limerick Siege. Bullet-Swept Streets. Heavy Casualty List. Three Military Barracks Burned."

The Civil War had broken out the previous month with the bombardment of the Four Courts in Dublin. Irregulars invaded Limerick in the early days of July, and under General Liam Lynch they occupied the Strand, Ordnance (Mulgrave Street), Castle and New (now Sarsfield) Barracks, while the Free State troops, under Donncha O Hannigan, occupied William Street Barracks and several of the big drapery houses in O'Connell Street.

There was an uneasy truce for some days as both leaders, a short time before comrades in the Fight for Freedom, desisted in engaging their troops, but eventually, on strict orders of GHQ, the Free Staters were ordered to attack the Ordnance Barracks, occupied by Republicans.

On Friday, July 7, the first shots were fired in the last siege of Limerick. It would last until the 21st of that month.

For a fortnight, all businesses in the city came to a standstill, and foodstuffs became extremely scarce. Starvation became a real threat especially for the poorer families, and bread delivery men risked their lives daily to try and alleviate the situation.

Terror stalked the streets and those that ventured out did so at their peril, with some being killed and many wounded in the process. The centre of the city was the scene of most of the sniping and many families in the area fled to diverse locations outside the city such as Mungret College where they were looked after by the Jesuit community.

There were several overtures during the siege to effect a ceasefire but whatever chances of that happening went by the board when a Free State soldier named O'Brien, a native of the city, was shot dead in Nelson Street, his companion, Private O'Connell, having been disarmed a few minutes previously. From that moment, all efforts at a truce vanished and both sides took up com-

Free State troops departing William Street Barracks, July 1922, with the armoured car "Danny Boy" in foregrokund.

manding positions or points of vantage. With barricades springing up all over the place, it became a beleaguered city with mills, business houses, private houses, even belfries of churches all being requisitioned by the troops.

One of the turning points in the battle came when on Thursday, July 20th, the Free State troops trained heavy artillery on the Strand Barracks, the occupying Irregulars eventually surrendering when the front portion of the building was hit. This incident precipitated a withdrawal of the Republicans from the city and around midnight a string of cars were seen, or heard, to be leaving the city, heading south. It signalled the end of the battle and the lifting of the siege.

The Irregulars were not finished yet, however, and shortly after midnight several violent explosions rent the city air. A mine had been detonated inside the gates of the New Barracks and such was the intensity of the blast that roofs of several houses in the Wolfe Tone street area were damaged. Most of the barracks was burned to the ground in the conflagration that followed the explosion. The Ordnance Barracks in Mulgrave Street was burned to the ground and the Castle Barracks fired and the modern part burned out. But the old part of the castle, which had withstood the Williamite siege of 1690, remains intact, the Chronicle reported.

After the withdrawal of the Irregulars, a communiqué was issued from William Street Barracks (occupied by Free State troops), stating : "We have agreed in this area to a truce, to enable a conference to be held which might bring about peace."

At this stage the greater part of the Republican forces had retreated south, to make what was in effect their last stand in the Bruree/Kilmallock/Bruff area. But the trauma of the Civil War was to trundle on for the best part of another year, with the truce finally being signed on May 24, 1923.

Free State troops relaxing in William Street, July 1922 before their departure for the county in pursuit of the Irregulars.

The pig scam of Newcastle West

The monthly pig market in Newcastle West in September, 1952, got off to an unusually good start for farmers. A buyer from the North of Ireland from early on, to the dismay of other buyers present, started to pay prices far in advance of those given by the regular Limerick pig buyers.

Local farmers queued up as the stranger paid up to 40/- and in some cases 50/- a head above the normal price. In no time over 100 pigs were sold to the Northern buyer and the sellers couldn't believe their good fortune when their benefactor even refused to accept luck money traditionally proffered to the purchaser. Delivering the pigs to the station, the sellers felt very satisfied on a good morning's work.

They then gratefully received their cheques. But then the sport started. The local branch of the National Bank refused to cash the cheques amidst huge consternation.

What was described as the Six County buyer luckily was still in town and when he was accosted by the angry farmers he placated them saying there was some mistake and that everything would be alright within an hour or two. He then proceeded to put a phone call through from the Post Office watched by the anxious buyers. However, another hour or two passed and nothing happened to improve matters for the now thoroughly alarmed farmers.

The situation eventually came to a head when it was announced that the sellers would be restored their pigs from the station, where they had been booked in wagons in readiness for transport.

There was further consternation when the various owners sought to identify their own pigs. It took a long time to segregate the animals, a job in which Sergeant J. Daly gave a helping hand. Having got their pigs, the farmers returned home to tell of the strange happenings of the morning. In addition to their pigs, they had something else to show: the cheques that had been given them by one "T. Davidson." That was the signature they bore. The mysterious unknown buyer from across the Border had told the farmers concerned that they might keep the cheques, which varied in amount from £20 to £300, according to the number of pigs "sold."

What happened caused great annoyance and indignation as the farmers returned home with their unsold pigs. To make matters worse for the pig sellers, there was no immediate prospect of another market.

The correspondent was told that the unusual development had taken an adverse effect on the sale of bonhams, which usually took place at the concluding stages of the market, when producers had disposed of their pigs.

It was not recorded whether the farmers ever tried to cash the cheques again. Or the comments of the Limerick pig buyers, which must have been choice.

It was in a way history repeating itself when during the Boer War a mysterious hoaxer announced that dogs of all shapes and sizes would be bought in the town. But that is another story which can be read elsewhere in this book.

Newcastle West Parents Association social in 1967 with Bishop Murphy in the background.

Murder on the Shannon Scheme

On the Friday night of December 21st, 1928, a German foreman mechanic named Jacob Kunz, aged 45, was making his way back to his lodgings after finishing his day's work on the Shannon Scheme at Ardnacrusha. The Scheme, the greatest engineering project the country had ever seen, was nearing completion and would be operational six months later.

Described as an extremely inoffensive man, Kunz had the habit of keeping his savings on his person, the notes being sewn into the inside of his jacket. This was known to some workmen who worked under him on the Scheme and was eventually to lead to his death by murder.

As he approached the Long Pavement Station, around 7 pm, an

Superintendent Mooney in charge of the Parteen murder investigation.

assailant lay in wait and attacked him from behind with a iron bar and robbed him of his savings, which amounted to £80, a substantial sum then when it was considered that weekly rate for thousands of labourers on the Scheme amounted to 32 shillings (£1 12s.) at its conception. The victim also had hidden on his person £409 10s., which his assailant failed to locate.

First to come on the scene was Michael Lynch, a worker on the Scheme, from Quarry Road, who found Kunz sitting on the rail extension near Gloster's Gate. Kunz, covered in blood, was unable to speak and when asked what was the matter replied: "sick, sick." With the aid of another man, Lynch took the German to a first aid station but the badly wounded man broke away and returned to the scene of the attack. Another witness, John Fitzgerald, went after Kunz and found him at the spot where he was attacked. He appeared to be making a search and said to witness: "my monies, my monies."

Johan Kunz, brother of Jacob, was sent for and was brought to the first aid station. There he found Jacob with a gaping wound at the back of his head, and he was vomiting blood. He was with him when he died in St. John's Hospital early next morning. His brother was paid £6 per week and they had an arrangement between them where Jacob kept both their money. Witness was handed £415 of his brother's money the evening of the attack.

The same evening, five men were questioned by police in connection with the attack and a week later John Joseph Cox, of Rosemary Place, Limerick, a former British soldier who fought in the First World War, was charged with the murder of Kunz. Presiding was District Justice J. M. Flood and so great was the crowd attempting to attend the trial that the doors had to be closed a half hour before proceedings began.

Cox, who was working under Kunz at the time of the murder, was eventually returned for trial to the

Sergeant Michael Staunton, Ardnacrusha, who gave evidence in the murder trial.

Central Criminal Court in Dublin before Mr. Justice Johnson. Over 40 witnesses were due to be called to give evidence and five of the jurors asked to be excused from duty due to their conscientious objection to capital punishment.

The defendant who pleaded not guilty, appeared in the dock wearing a Sacred Heart Badge in the lapel of his coat.

The prosecution claimed that the man who murdered Kunz was in the dock. "It was a crime against the nation and nature and was a dastardly crime to have been committed against an inoffensive foreigner. The prisoner, having made various contradictory statements, charged a young man named Cassidy with the crime. Cassidy was a blameless young man living with his mother. It was a desperate attempt on the part of the accused to extricate himself from the crime."

Counsel added that they were not relying on proof of the footprints leading up to the old ruin where the money was found that they were the footprints of Cox. They did prove that a solitary man walked along the bank from the scene of the crime and hid the money in the old ruin. The man who wrote the letter to Mrs. Cox stating where the money was concealed and which the police intercepted was the man who murdered Josef Kunz. He would ask the jury to come to that conclusion when they had heard the evidence.

The prosecution produced the pants and boots that were worn by Cox on the night of the murder. Detective Officer Mulroy said that on the soles of the boots were marks like indentions caused by wire fencing. Casts were made of the indentions and these corresponded in shape and size to the boots that were produced. The end of the pants was covered with clay.

Further evidence was given that at various points along the bank corresponding footprints were found on the railway bridge crossing the river, and on to the Salmon Weir Bank. These were traced to an old ruin near Park Bridge, and here the stolen money was recovered.

The accused entered the witness box and in firm voice said he was born in Limerick in 1887. From 1914 to 1917 he had continuous war service and had some very thrilling experiences. He was discharged as medically unfit and after joining the Free State Army, also had to take his discharge. He then got employment in the Shannon Scheme and was at one time a foreman but lost it because he refused to "bring the blood out through the men."

Cox then swore he was nowhere near the scene of the murder on the evening of the 21st, stating that he had visited Ardnacrusha that morning to have an injured hand attended to. He claimed he travelled in and out by Flannery's bus, who ran a service to the power station, but the prosecution discounted this as neither the driver or conductor questioned remembered him being on board. Another bus conductor swore that he saw defendant on the bus going to Ardnacrusha at 4 p.m on the day in question.

The defendant said that a young man named Cassidy who also worked on the scheme, had cursed Kunz and said that he (Kunz) would not be long there. On another occasion Cassidy told him he would have money for Xmas wherever he would get it. He met Cassidy on the 21st December at Coffey's Corner, and Cassidy said that he had got the money and what would he do with it. Cox told him to hide the money until Christmas was over. Cassidy then gave him a bundle of notes to put away. "I took it, walked down Athlunkard Street and put it under a stone near an old house at Park Bridge. When he was at Ardnacrusha barracks he sent out a note to his wife telling where the money was."

The trial lasted four days and at its conclusion Justice Johnston directed that the jury should not consider a manslaughter charge as the defence had given no evidence of such. After two hours and five minutes deliberating, the foreman of the jury returned to the court and in a subdued voice the foreman stated "guilty," with a strong recommendation to mercy. The jury were of the opinion that death may not have ensued if the skull of the victim had been stronger.

The final scenes were dramatically recounted:

"These were dreadful moments, the solemnity of which could be better imagined than described. A deadly pallor came over the accused's face, his lips quivered and a vacant stare came into his eyes. He said 'not guilty' with a vacant stare in his eyes when asked if had anything to say why the sentence of death should not be passed upon him.

"The Judge then assumed the black cap and in a whisper passed the death sentence, saying that the prisoner was to be taken to the prison from whence he came and there hanged by the neck until he was dead on 11th April, and may God have mercy on his soul."

Mr. Kavanagh, for the defence, rose to make application for leave to appeal, which Judge Johnston refused.

The execution was deferred when a successful application was made for leave to appeal on the grounds of a misdirection of the jury on the question of manslaughter and the admission of a certain statement alleged to have been made by Cox to Supt. Mooney in evidence. This appeal was heard in the Criminal Appeal Court before Chief Justice Sullivan and Mr. Justice Hannan and the verdict was refusal for leave to appeal. The execution, originally fixed for 11th April, was now fixed for Thursday, 25th inst.

An extensive appeal got under way for the reprieve of the death sentence on Cox, with many thousands signing the petition. In a poignant letter to the Leader, Mrs. Mary Cox thanked all the various bodies, including all the Corporation members, the Women's International League and the director and secretary of Messrs. Siemens (contractors for the Shannon Scheme) for their efforts. "I also thank all those who have left no stone unturned to have my husband reprieved on behalf of his innocent four children, so as he should repent for whatever wrongs he has done."

All the appeals were in vain, with the Government considering a last-minute request on a stay of execution but turning it down.

Cox was hanged in Mountjoy Jail on April 25th, 1929.

The Leader recorded his last moments: "He met his death with fortitude. He spent his last remaining hours in prayer. He retired at 12 o'clock on Wednesday night and woke at 4 yesterday morning and having dressed, remained in prayer until Mass was celebrated at 8 o'clock. When facing the scaffold at 8 o'clock he called back to the warders: 'Goodbye, all. I shall pray for you up above.' Death was instantaneous, His family and relatives visited him the previous night."

Scene of the murder in the Longpavement (left), and on the right, old ruin near Park Bridge in which the bundle of notes mentioned in the case was discovered

Cold War in Ballinacurra

An air attack in the vicinity of Southville Gardens in 1965 saw a mass evacuation of residents of the area to Knockalisheen Camp in Co. Clare.

It was, however, a simulated attack, being the height of the Cold War, and the Limerick Civil Defence were going through their paces in the event of this country being embroiled in war.

It was reported that casualties were light but shortly afterwards it was reported to Central Control in the Town Hall that a radio-active cloud was approaching the Ballinacurra area. Immediately Central Control in Town Hall, with Co. Assistant Warden Frank Garvey and his assistant, Miss Mae Clancy, in charge, alerted Strand Barracks where a fleet of fire trucks, ambulances and other rescue equipment sprang into action.

Within an hour one hundred people were evacuated to Knockalisheen where on their arrival they were registered and were given a feed of soup, bacon and sausages and vegetables. The time was 3.30 pm.

In charge of the operation was city manager, Mr. T. P. McDermott, assisted by M. O'Sullivan, Civil Defence; 100 civil defence workers, Red Cross (under John F. Hurley), Knights of Malta (John Quinn), and St. John's Ambulance (Patrick Moloney), the Gardai under Inspector T. W. Barrett, all played their part in what was described as a "very impressive performance" by J. G. Buskmaster, Deputy Director of Civil Defence Headquarters.

1940 | **ALFRED J. SEXTON'S SALES.**

CITY OF LIMERICK.

THE LYRIC THEATRE.

A remunerative and gilt edge security, forming a most attractive investment,

FOR SALE BY PRIVATE TREATY

(AS A GOING CONCERN),

Comprising imposing corner detached structure, soundly built, widely known and conveniently situated. They are approached by double door entrance from Glentworth Street, with box office in large hall, with entrance to parterre, stalls and balcony. Entrance to gallery is through a double gate entrance from Pery Square, which entrance is also used in connection with the fire escape from the balcony, gallery and ballroom, exits from the parterre and stalls.

The Cinema is substantial, commodious, fully equipped with stage and the necessary curtains and screens; annexe from cinema projector (fireproof). The parterre, with entrance from hall, is fitted with tip-up seats, and has accommodation for 107 people, with centre and side isle. The stalls, with separate entrance from the hall, with tip-up seats, has accommodation for 234 people. The balcony, approached from box office by wide and easy stairway, has accommodation for 150 people, and fitted

In 1940, while the Battle of Britain was taking place, Sexton's sold the Lyric Theatre, Glentworth Street, to a conglomeration of Limerick business people, one of their many top sales of the century.

When the Shannon froze over

What was described in the Leader as the "coldest night ever" was Sunday night, January 14, 1963, when temperatures of 24 degrees below freezing were reported.

"Parts of the River Shannon were frozen over and today Limerick is a city of burst water pipes and frozen oil heaters. Several factories and schools closed down due to oil freezing in the boilers," said the report.

This was just the beginning of what was said to be the coldest snap of the century which lasted from the end of December right into March.

Reports of the big freeze-up in the city and county were regularly reported. For the first time in living memory the Shannon could be crossed dry-footed from the shore at Corbally to St Thomas' Island and the Abbey River at Athlunkard Boat Club was an ice flow stretching almost half-way across, and undulating in its formation where it was built up at different levels of the tide. Several seagulls were trapped in the ice near Barrington's Hospital and when some small boys went to free them they found the birds frozen to death. The thickness of the ice in the canal was measured at five inches.

In Killaloe, the Shannon had an Arctic appearance with many ice flows stretching across the lake and the river front frozen solid.

Several blizzards occurred during the freezing spell and reports from all parts of Co. Limerick graphically described the Arctic conditions.

Scores of mountainside houses were completely isolated along the bleak mountains, extending from Tournafulla and Mountcollins to Barna, Templeglantine, Rooskagh, Ballyoughane, Carrickerry and Athea.

The Brosnan family, living on Limerick's highest mountain at Clash, Abbeyfeale, were marooned by snow drifts, some reaching to 20 feet, for seven weeks. Neighbours John, Joseph and Patrick O'Connor dug a tunnel of 100 feet in length to bring food to the stricken family, 87-year-old Matt, his brother 77-year-old Timothy and his wife, Joan.

James Hunt of Killean, Glin, was unable to open the front door of his house with the snow drifts when he returned to his home and he was reported to be in a coma after spending the night outside the house.

"Many families marooned and loss of livestock feared due to the conditions" were the reports from Ballylanders. The Bruff cor., while reporting that workers could not get to work in Shannon, said over 200 people availed of the skating on Lough Gur where the ice was a foot thick.

Dan Mulcahy, reporting from the west of the County, said that while conditions were bad in the towns, for families on the remote hillsides it was disastrous with many of them completely marooned.

It was reported that wild life were starving all over the place and had become almost tame due to the severity of the conditions. Birds, weak with lack of food, have been captured by children by the simple expediency of throwing coats over them. The birds are then taken home and fed until they are well again. Many stories are current about the "cheeky" robin who has shown itself to be almost fearless in its search for food.

Older residents of Herbertstown are agreed that the snow, ice and frost were the worst that have been seen since 1873.

In early February it was reported that coal stocks were seriously depleted in the city and some firms had imposed rationing. Hundreds of homes were without water due to frozen pipes and many damaged due to burst pipes. Several tried melting the snow but found it was not suitable for making tea. One enterprising man went around Ballinacurra Weston and sold gallons of water for 1/- a go. Most cheerful of all were the children who were having an extended holiday but frayed tempers were very much in evidence with households suffering from damaged furniture and ceilings from burst pipes, and the mostly fruitless search for plumbers, some of whom were reported to be working both night and day.

Old Crescent and Bohemians, unable to play since December due to the frozen pitches, went to the strand in Lahinch on February 3rd for a game and many locals turned out to see their first game in this code. The "pitch" proved excellent, of full length, and enabled both sides to throw the ball around in great style. The match was taken seriously and as a result exchanges at times were fierce, and indeed, on more than one occasion, tempers became frayed. Old Crescent won by two tries (Seamus Gubbins and Jack Fitzgerald) to one (Gerry Hayes).

Skating on Loughmore, Raheen, during the great freeze-up of 1963.

Wit of the famous Judge Adams

Richard Adams was County Court Judge in Limerick from 1884 to 1908 and was universally noted for his wit. His fame crossed the Channel and according to Bart Kennedy, a well known English writer, "his fame had penetrated into the heart of dull London."

Bart came over specially to hear the judge in action and wasn't disappointed. He spent the day in the court in Limerick and this was his verdict: "A wit and philosopher who dealt in genial wisdom of comedy," the writer said, and waxed lyrical on how the judge, by his wisdom, kindness and wit, dealt with the cases that came before him in Limerick that day.

Con Cregan, long time editor of the Leader, as a young reporter attended court when the judge was in action, and has recorded some hilarious incidents about him. The judge was strolling towards the railway station one day following a sitting in Rathkeale. With him was Fr Jerry Murphy, then a local C.C. Passing the church tower the judge looked at the time and remarked that he should hurry as he would be late for his train.

"Ah," said Fr. Murphy, "you're in plenty of time, that old clock is wrong."

The judge, in mock indignation replied: "I'm amazed at you Fr. Murphy. Do you mean to tell me the Church can err?"

According to Con Cregan, Judge Adams was at his best when local "characters" were in court. On one occasion a man was sued for the balance of his daughter's fortune. This defendant in the course of his evidence, said he didn't like the match at all and had advised his daughter against the marriage.

"What advice did you give her?" asked the Judge,

"I wouldn't like to tell you what I said," replied the witness.

"Oh, but you must," said His Honour with a twinkle in his eye, "this is a Court of Law and we must hear everything,"

"Well, said the witness, "I told her that if she burned a certain part of her anatomy (in fact he used a plainer description than that) she should lie on her blisters."

The Judge almost exploded with laughter at this piece of evidence.

A case that provided the judge with a perfect platform to show off his wit took place in Newcastle West in 1904 when a farm labourer cum fiddler named Daly sued a farmer named Mullins for breaking the fiddle over his head.

Judge Adams presided and was in his element, even if all the laughs were provided against the poor plaintiff, who obviously wasn't the brightest.

Plaintiff accounted how he, playing the fiddle, and another young lad, playing the tambourine, were passing the defendant's house when the defendant rushed out, grabbed the fiddle and broke it over his (plaintiff's) head.

Mr. Kelly, for the defendant: Is this broken fiddle a Stradivarius? (laughter). The plaintiff looked blankly at him.

Judge Adams: You are slightly going astray, Mr. Kelly. It should be Antonio Stradvario of Cremont (laughter). To witness: You claim to be a musician. If this fiddle was made by Stradvario it is worth you £500. What do you say to that?

Witness said he did not know (laughter).

Mr. Kelly, who was vying with His Worship for the laughs, said "this fiddle is not a dangerous instrument to strike a man with; it was deadly only when the plaintiff played it" (laughter).

His Honour, now having a field day, added that defendant played the fiddle on plaintiff's head and though intended to be musical, it was a most discordant blow, every string being out of tune (great laughter).

At this stage the court was convulsed with the defendant giving evidence that his cows were upset by the music. When queried as to the tune being played, the boy on the tambourine said he was playing the "Wearing of the Green" but the plaintiff said it was "God Save Ireland."

His Honour: According to this ye were playing two different tunes, no wonder the cows hissed at such a performance. Either that or they were Northern, Orange cows, rising in revolt at the rendering of "Wearing of the Green" (laughter).

Mr. Liston, for the plaintiff asked defendant: "if the King's Army Band were playing passing your door would you demand they cease playing?"

Witness said he would make the fiddles stop.

Mr. Liston: Oh, it was the fiddles the cows objected to and not other class of music? (laughter).

Judge Adams, summing up, said they had the organ grinder in London but those objecting did not go out and smash it. The fiddle was not by Stradivarius, or it would have cost the defendant £500 to replace it, but fortunately it was purchased from Mr. Patrick O'Shaughnessy of Newcastle West, "a personal friend of mine and an eminent musician," for 27s. 6d.

"It was absurd to say that these poor innocent cows in their native Munster would object to this music (laughter). He believed defendant was angry at the musical promenade, came out, and did strike plaintiff, breaking the fiddle. He would give a decree for £1 10s. and 7s. 6d. costs.

Described in another article as ''a fellow with infinite jest'', the Judge used come up against a very rural policeman whose style of giving evidence was so diffuse and unconnected as to irritate his honour on every occasion it was inflicted on him. One day the policeman, described as not being a very brilliant specimen, gave evidence in a case in which a horse, usually quiet, saw a red petticoat fluttering on a line, and not knowing what it was, bolted.

Judge Adams interjected: "Res ignota pro magnifico."

''Begorra yer Honour,'' retorted the policeman, "you took the words out of my mouth." The judge collapsed.

Judge Adams was a highly competent journalist before going to the Bar and at one stage was chief leader writer of the "Freeman's Journal." He was reported to have a great rapport with the members of his former profession.

He died in April, 1908, after fourteen years on the bench, and was mourned by all classes and creeds. Many anecdotes were related in his obituary like the one about a particular sitting of the judge when a complete stranger rushed to his bench before he could be stopped by the police. "Can I see Dick Adams," he demanded of the judge, which elicited the reply: "Yes you can. I am Dick Adams." Stranger: "I am proud of the privilege and honour of addressing Ireland's greatest wit." Judge: "Thank you my friend, I thank you" at which the stranger made a low bow and retired from the court.

When as Q.C., Adams was interviewed with others of his ilk by the Chief Secretary, John Morley, Adams had the nerve during the interview to tell a joke about a character named Jones. The secretary was convulsed with laughter and at the conclusion of the interview said: "Jones, I'll never forget you."

Time passed and so did T. A. Purcell, County Court Judge. Adams telegraphed the intelligence to Mr. Morley in London, and in the message he asked him to "Remember Jones." The reply came back "Jones is Remembered" and thus was Mr. Richard Adams, Q.C., made County Judge of Limerick.

The obituary concluded: "A humane and well loved man, he was possessed of a rich vein of humour all of his own which often led the court through vestibules of laughter to the temple where justice was seated."

There was good news in the post in 1952 for sisters Mrs. Tim Hurley of Hyde Road, and Mrs. Jack Upton of Cecil Street when they learned that they were to share $100,000 (£35,000) fortune left by their sister, Mrs. Mary Gallagher, Los Angeles, whose husband was a prominent businessman. Mrs. Hurley, is shown reading the solicitor's letter watched by Delma and Nancy Hurley and Jim Upton.

When the Lyric rose up against "Biddy"

Back in December, 1927, an English touring company called the Union Jack Photo Plays came to the Lyric Theatre in Glentworth Street for a week's run with a play called "Biddy". Described as an "Irish Stew," the play was written by an Englishman, Laurence Cowen, and the group looked forward to an enjoyable stay with good houses.

Little did they know what lay in store for them. First indications of trouble ahead started on the opening night, Monday, December 5th, when a group of young men picketed the play, distributing leaflets quoting adverse criticism from some Derry newspapers.

Rumours swept the city that on the second night there would be more vehement protests and crowds gathered outside the theatre to witness the fun.

But it was all happening inside and as the play progressed the cast were subjected to a continuous verbal fusillade consisting of booing and hissing. "Leave Limerick immediately," "pack up" and "go back to Houndsditch" were some of the cat-calls the actors had to endure. The play was stopped several times with the stage manager appealing to the audience to give the actors a chance. "This is an all-Irish cast, with just one exception," he stated.

One of the actors, named Charles Keogh, later came on and appealed for order stating that he was as good an Irishman as anyone in the audience. "So was Judas an Apostle" a member of the audience shouted back. "Beat it as quickly as you can. This show must be closed down, you're only a renegade," another shouted.

Keogh had enough and moving closer to the footlights, invited anyone who would care to come up and he would show them whether he was a renegade or not. His invitation was not accepted. At this stage people in the pit took up the refrain of the hymn "Faith of our Fathers" while Keogh, obviously demented at this point, jibed at them from the wings. Tension was now so high that the Guards present were put on full alert and the Inspector sent for reinforcements.

Most outspoken of what was described as "the vigilants" was Mr. Denis O'Dwyer, reported to be of the Harbour Commissioners, who addressed the crowd from the stalls: "The piece that night was worse than immoral; it was an insult to the Catholic faith and the Catholic clergy. He would appeal to all those people who took exception to the piece to follow him and leave the building," which was greeted by cheers and several left but some stayed on to make sure no attempt was made to go on with the play.

At this stage a member of the orchestra, who speaking in broken English, said he was glad he was not an Irishman. "You are a disgrace to the world," he added, which elicited cries from the audience: "to go back to Germany or the Shannon Scheme."

It was all too much for a female member of the orchestra, who frightened at the attitude towards her colleague, swooned and the other members immediately disappeared from view with her limp form and did not return.

The end was now drawing near and the last sally was made by a woman, who was understood to be connected with the management of the theatre. She took up a position in the balcony and, addressing the twenty or so young men left in the theatre, said with a marked English accent, that it was enough to make her tired. "They (meaning the management) had tried to do good for the people of Limerick and that was the thanks they got." She was interrupted at this stage by a man, who said they would not allow shows of that kind. "I will show you some of your dirty, immoral Limerick some day," she concluded in a high-pitched excitable voice, but her promise was only greeted with taunts, a young man nearby telling her to take them back to England with her.

At this stage the crowd on the street outside had grown to huge dimensions, a state of congestion existing from Tait's Clock to the door of the "gods" and from the clock tower to the junction of Glentworth Street and Catherine Street, on the other side (good humoured).

Inside, the last verbal fusillade had been fired and the house was empty within the subsequent few minutes, and the surging throng outside was informed by Mr. O'Dwyer, who had been in consultation with the management, that "Biddy" was finished and Limerick would know her no more, a statement that evoked a loud outburst of cheers.

So, what should have been a week's performance ended after two nights. The play moved on to the Gaiety Theatre in Dublin, and before its performance the author, Mr. Cowen, remarked on the scenes in Limerick, saying "it was the argument of the shillelagh; it was the method employed by the primitive man," adding for good measure that "it was the procedure known as hanging a man first and trying him afterwards."

He was taken to task in the columns of the Leader by Mr. O'Dwyer, the leader of the "vigilants" with an address at North Strand, Limerick. "Our protest was made in a most dignified and orderly manner. A strong feeling of resentment was produced in the great majority of those who witnessed the production that it culminated in compelling the cessation of the performance on the Tuesday night, when the most objectionable part was reached. It is significant to note that this objectionable part was deleted from the edition of the play as produced at the Gaiety Theatre."

According to the Leader reporter, the most objectionable part of the play, and when the main trouble started, was a scene where "the priest, who spoke the English of an uneducated person, was about to get 'the whole hierarchy of Ireland' a marriage dispensation for the 'squire' provided the latter paid for it by giving a piece of ground."

The sequel to the scenes in the Lyric came a year later when in the London King's Bench Division the Union Jack Photo Plays Ltd. sued the leasees of the Lyric, Messrs. G. Lawrence and S. H. Parsons, for damages, claiming that as a sequel to the scenes which followed the production of the play "Biddy," there was a breach of contract on the part of the Lyric management inasmuch as the play was discontinued after the first night. The defendants denied there was any breach of contract, as the then manager of "Biddy" withdrew the production of his own free will. A number of Limerick people were subpoenaed to give evidence.

The Judge held that after the second night's disturbance plaintiffs and defendants mutually agreed to rescind the contract (for a week's production) as they realised it was hopeless to go on with the play. Consequently he dismissed the claim, with costs. In the claim against the Gaiety Theatre, for £300 for alleged breach of contract in connection with the same play, judgment was given in plaintiffs' favour as the judge held that there was no legal excuse for the breach of contact in that case.

So ended the extraordinary story of "Biddy's" aborted visit to the Lyric with the Leader reporter summing up: "that the people of Limerick were not disposed to digest plays with Irish settings which have their birth in the brain of an outsider who was unacquainted with the native mentality as demonstrated in a most unequivocal manner in the Lyric Theatre last night."

A Limerickman in Hitler's Germany

A native of East Limerick (unnamed) spent some time in Germany in 1936, the year of the Berlin Olympics, and wrote in the Leader in August of that year of his experiences and views of that country as he saw it. Some of his comments were outspoken, racial, and some prophetic.

The hero of those games for many, except of course Hitler and the advocates of Aryan supremacy, was Jesse Owens, the super American black athlete who landed an unprecedented four gold medals.

The correspondent, who recalled the great Limerick athletes like Flanagan, Ryan and the Leahy's, said he himself got more pleasure from a well fought "quarter" at Kilmallock Sports than all the orgies of broken records he witnessed at the Olympics.

Commenting on the feats of Jessie Owens he wrote:

"To make a star of Owens must have cost as much as it did to turn out a Derby winner. The star Olympic sprinter must be somewhat of a freak.

"America, realising that she could never secure a monopoly of the sprints with her white athletes has turned to her negroes and converted them from cooks and waiters into national heroes.

"I like the negro. I lived in his native haunts for some years. And unspoilt by white vices he is a loveable child of nature, but I can't see why he is only a nigger with a prefix in 1935 and the saviour of his nation in 1936.

"And incidentally, it is the freaks of the black races that are sought out by the arm

Hitler dances a jig on hearing the news of the capture of Paris.

of American athletic touts. These negroes are different from any other of their type I have ever seen; they are all leg and spring, like racehorses or greyhounds and they can lope along at an extraordinary pace."

Commenting on the political situation in Germany the cor. said:

"Adolph Hitler is to be lauded for bringing this nation of eighty million from black despair and servility to the proud position it now holds in the world. He is now regarded as a god in his own country. He wanted these Olympics to be an advertisement for the new Germany, and no man made better use of this opportunity.

"I am a lover of nature, however, and the natural, so I dislike this new branch of democracy with its cold materialism, its systematic suppression of individuality, its soulless human progress, its State control and all its works and pomps.

"I wouldn't advise any Limerickman to go in search of liberty in the German Republic; he would find it in theory and probably enjoy it in jail.

"I saw German officialdom in full blast at the borders and only for I had my Leader pass, I would have been subjected to star chamber methods. I am not surprised at the wholesale arrests of helpless monks and nuns, it is hard to get into Germany but harder still to get out with your belongings.

"On my first Sunday in Berlin, I heard a children's Mass. The young people were as grave as septuagenarians and though I suppose I should have admired them, I felt a sort of compassion for them. The Jewish lads who dodged the Apostles and fought their way to Him were not so well behaved.

"How will the Catholic Church fare in this new campaign of repression of all individual liberty? I sincerely hope I am wrong in my hasty impressions, but it seems to me that anything more opposite in ideals than Hitlerism and Catholicity cannot be found since the days of the great contest between Imperial Rome and early Christianity.

"I could go on pointing out points of conflict, but that is sufficient and I am sorely afraid that my summary of the situation is not mere wild prophecy. Hitlerism has already shown its hand in the suppression of Catholic Youth Societies, with wholesale arrests of priests, monks and nuns; in interference in Church affairs, but above all in the revolting doctrine that the German child is born not to the Church, nor even to God, but to the German State, just as the Irish calf is born to the Irish farmstead.

"When the present age of fear is over, when Hitler can safely curb the wild spirits that are now urging him on, he will realise that the enlightened discipline and strict morality of the Catholic Church is of more value to a State than irritating officialdom or soulless materialism."

Snobby high-brows in Eden Terrace

In May 1928, Clr. James Casey, at a special meeting of the Limerick Corporation, revealed a very glaring piece of snobbery of the worst type. The report said his statement will be read both with amazement and bewilderment.

He stated that because of the opposition of certain people in the Eden Terrace district of the city (North Circular Road), the ground landlord had lodged an objection to the building of the Utility Society houses there.

Were it not for that objection, Clr. Casey said the first sod of the foundations for the eight houses was to have been turned today by the Mayor. The matter was not going to rest there.

"The plans had been approved both by the Corporation and the Government, and everything was going smoothly, until the people of that aristocratic district got the idea into their heads that a municipal housing scheme might detract from the beauty of the place.

"Some of those people were so busy they wrote to the landlord, who was in Spain, directing his attention to the fact that the houses to be erected would be occupied by working men. The result was the objection.

"I know some of them," continued Clr. Casey, "a few high-brows in their Garden of Eden, but we are not finished with them yet."

There was a proposal before the meeting that the Corporation should acquire a private road in that locality for the edification of the people in Eden Terrace.

Clr. Casey, in indignation, said they should mark their protest against the action of those people by refusing to acquire that road until they came to realise that they were not superior to everybody else.

Support for Clr. Casey came from Clr. Dalton who added: "it was the cruellest thing he had ever heard of and should not be tolerated. It was a case of twopence halfpenny looking down at twopence and they are nothing else only a lot of twopences. No wonder the working man was turning Bolshevist when such scandalous treatment was being meted out to them."

It was agreed unanimously, as a protest, to adjourn the proposal to acquire the piece of roadway referred to.

In the same issue of the Leader it was reported that the Corporation were finding it impossible to sell all of the newly-erected cottages in Farranshone. It was said that people could not afford the deposit of £50 and it was decided to reduce this to £5. In the same year a local builder said that five-roomed houses could be built at a cost of £300 to help relieve the overcrowding in tenements throughout the city.

Cries of the drowning at Castleconnell

The wooden footbridge at Castleconnell, linking Limerick to Clare, is a well known landmark, but in 1910 agreement had been reached between Clare and Limerick County Councils to build a bridge to take vehicular traffic across the Shannon at this point. Both bodies would share equal costs, estimated not to be more than £3,000 each, but the objections of the land owners at each side of the river was holding up the project.

A letter-writer to the Leader wondered was the scheme dead or was it just slumbering "until other drowning cries re-echoed from the Shannon rapids."

"Last year we read columns from the able and fluent pen of Mr. W. F. Lee, hon. sec. Bridge Committee on this grand project and by this time many people thought they would be enjoying a circular drive through nature's beauties, crossing the lordly Shannon at Castleconnell by a useful and artistic bridge."

The writer instanced some of "the absurd and ridiculous reasons of the objectionists (from those with mansions on either side of the river): the pillars of the bridge would frighten the fish down river, the proposed structure would spoil the lovely bit of scenery as viewed from their windows; they were mischievously led to believe that their places would be invested with tramps; how could they tolerate the noise or smell of a motor car or the sight of a load of turf crossing from Clare tens of yards in front of their mansions, etc., etc.

"Are these aristocrats, who have been lucky enough to enjoy lordly seats on either side of the river, going to succeed in blocking the industrial advancement of our country? Such astounding audacity from even these presumed lords of the soil can scarcely be realised."

Another stumbling block was the question of the actual site of the bridge. A report said that the Clare County Council would request the Bishop of Killaloe to intervene in the dispute and call together the bridge committee and "once and for all end the bitterness which had been created in the locality of Castleconnell and Clonlara by this vexed question of opposition sites."

A report in April, 1910, said that a representative meeting about the bridge issued a statement "that it is publicly known that some selfish parties in the locality are doing their utmost in an un-national, un-Irish and unprogressive manner to cajole the landed proprietors not to give the necessary land for the approaches to the bridge at any cost. That such low and mean action is deserving of the condemnation of every true lover of his country, and that we, as representatives of the people of Castleconnell will take the strongest measure in our power to defeat the shabby tactics of those few anti-progressives.

"That we respectfully appeal to Miss Rich, Colonel Ruttledge, Colonel Vincent, and Colonel Massy Westropp not to pay the slightest attention to those would-be obstructionists who only represent their own selfish desires, and who, because the site was not selected to run into their doors, have mischievously tried to start an agitation against the kind and popular work of the site selection committee."

The report was signed by a large cross-section of Castleconnell people, acting under the presidency of the Lord Bishop.

The Limerick No. 2 Rural District Council passed a resolution earnestly hoping that the bitterness which had been created in the locality of Castleconnell and Clonlara on the vexed question of opposition sites would be resolved under the presidency of the Bishop of Killaloe.

Sadly, the project eventually fell through and Castleconnell would have to wait another 30 years before a bridge was built across the Shannon, albeit a wooden pedestrian structure, constructed by Army engineers during the Emergency.

A tranquil scene in Castleconnell in 1910, the year of the agitation for the building of a vehicular bridge across the Shannon, which had been passed by Limerick and Clare County Councils.

The old lady and County Library fire

A fire which started in a small sweet shop near Sarsfield Bridge early morning on Tuesday, February 22, 1944, had devastating results. Spreading to another nearby shop, both premises were destroyed in a short while despite the efforts of the Fire Brigade. The nearby County Library then caught fire, resulting in a large quantity of books being lost. Also destroyed were copies of famous paintings which formed the basis of the recently introduced county exhibition. Some 2,000 books were saved from the fire by members of the Fire Brigade.

The following day Fire Brigade members were mopping up amidst the debris when an elderly lady approached unconcernedly with a book under her arm. She asked one of the by now grimy firemen "would you change this for me please!"

"But ma'am," exploded the weary fireman, "can't you see the place is burned down?"

"Oh so it is," observed the lady, taking notice of the havoc for the first time, And then recovering herself, she replied: "But when will it be open again?"

Sorrows of a tenor

When Enrico Caruso died in 1921, a friend recounted how on one occasion the world famous tenor confided in him the sorrows that accompanied his fame. "When I was unknown," he said, "I sang like a singing bird, careless, without thought of nerves. But now my reputation is made, my audiences are more exacting. Here I am today bending beneath the weight of a renown which cannot increase but which the least vocal mishap may compromise me.

"My audiences, well disposed towards me, as they are, have to pay such high prices to hear me that they imagine I am a unique singer, and I appear before them stared at and envious.

"Imagine my state of mind when the curtain rises, for the human voice has its weaknesses. Like everyone else I have my cares and troubles and climate and temperature affect me. But the public never thinks of that, but demand an artist as perfect as they imagine me to be.

"That is why I am the unhappiest of men. I compare myself to a great parliamentary speaker before an important interpolation. When the moment arrives he may be sad, weary, ailing and he longs for repose. But his friends await him, his enemies rally round. His interests bid him speak.

"A tenor is much worse off, for alas he is compelled to sing."

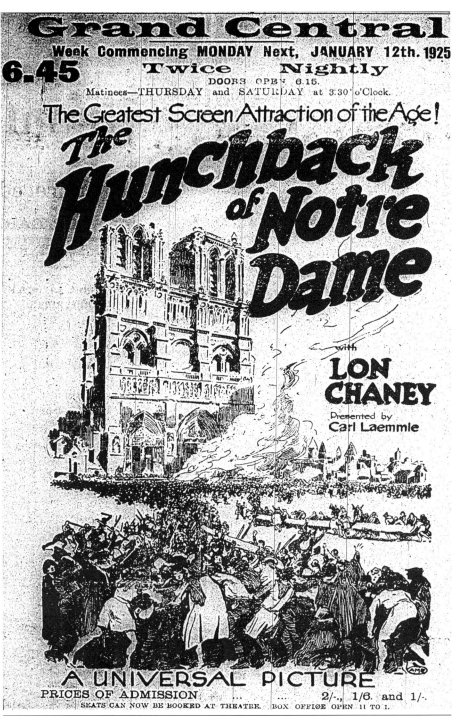

Execution of a spy

Mossie Hartnett, a native of Knocknadiha, Tournafulla, was an officer in the Irish Volunteers. Later he served as a member of the Limerick County Council and in 1976 he published a series of articles in the Leader of his thrilling experiences during the War of Independence.

It was a tough time for the Volunteers in West Limerick in the early years of formation. The people in general looked on them as madmen. They thought with the poor equipment it would be childish to engage the British Army and the armed police. The big farmers gave no support whatsoever, their only support coming from the small farmers and labourers. Well-to-do shopkeepers derided their efforts and were hostile to them.

On St. Patrick's Day, 1916, Mossie, who was captain of the Company, with Lieutenants Leahy and Sullivan, marched the battalion the eight miles from Tournafulla to Newcastle West to take part in a parade in the Square. Instead of being greeted by cheering crowds, they were assailed by soldiers' wives and friends (it was the height of World War I) who besides hurling verbal abuse, also threw rotten eggs at the Battalion.

Mossie recorded many of the great engagements that happened in the county during those stirring days, and his description of the secret burial of Captain Liam Scully, killed in the famous 6-hour attack and destruction of Kilmallock R.I.C. Barracks in 1920, was particularly poignant. Mossie made the arrangements for the lying in state at O'Gorman's farmhouse, close by his own place. The slain volunteer was laid out in a volunteers officer's uniform owned by Mossy. Under cover of darkness, on a balmy summer's night, his comrades shouldered the coffin to Templeglantine Cemetery and the remains were interred in a family grave specially opened up for the purpose.

Following the success of the attack on Kilmallock Barracks, it was decided to form a small full-time fighting force to devote its whole time in the fight against the enemy. And so was born the famous Flying Column of the East Limerick Brigade I.R.A., the first such flying column to be formed during the War of Independence.

Mossy's account of the discovery of a spy in their midst and his subsequent execution makes gripping reading. In this period (1919-1920), many young men "on the run" moved from county to county and from Company to Company. They were usually vouched for by their officers but it was an arrangement that carried definite risks of infiltration by the enemy. In this way a dangerous spy infiltrated into the ranks of Mossy's Company and it was some months before he was discovered.

Mossy takes up the story:

His credentials looked impeccable and he stayed in my house for a month. He surprised me by taking rather too much spirits, a thing foreign to the habits of an I.R.A. man on the run. He also engaged in a flow of very unsuitable conversation, especially in the presence of a saintly priest who had given us lunch in Abbeyfeale. I felt disgusted and succeeded in bringing the meeting to an end as quickly as possible.

But no suspicion of whom we shall call "A" had yet entered my head. Early in March, 1920, however, our intelligence received information that led to the arrest of "A" as a suspected spy.

I was told to find accommodation in our district for the suspect and that he was to be guarded day and night. Four senior officers from the Kerry Brigade brought him to East Limerick and following a search, were astonished to find a large sum of money in a secret pocket under his armpits, and also some documents, written on code, which they were unable to decipher.

I now met up with "A" again under very different circumstances to our previous meeting. We all tried to act as naturally as we could in the circumstances. The prisoner got a plentiful supply of cigarettes, we played cards with him and accompanied him on walks.

It was decided to hold a court martial and after several hours deliberation no verdict was reached, but the court decided to sit again if any new evidence were found. There was the question of the coded documents and here the prisoner gave us no help. I suppose if we were bad enough to have tortured or terrorised him he might have spoken, but such were not our methods.

The documents were eventually deciphered in Cork revealing beyond doubt that "A'"was an enemy engaged on espionage. The court sat again and the unanimous verdict was that he was guilty and he was sentenced to death by firing squad.

With few feelings of sorrow, I saw the prisoner being driven off in a pony and cart to the place of execution in the early hours of the morning. Scouts and guards were placed in a wide circle round the field where the execution was to take place.

Fully realising his terrible predicament and visibly trembling, the condemned man clutched his rosary beads in his hands. Near the place of execution, a priest heard his confession, then he shook hands with his executioners and admitted his crime.

Retiring in the early hours of the morning two of the guards tumbled into the bed in which the executed man had slept. When settling down to sleep the front door gave a loud bang and immediately they jumped out of bed holding drawn revolvers. It was just a sudden gust of wind which had caused the door to bang but it underlines the frightful tension under which men lived, even slept, at that time.

Stevie and the new pyjamas

The scourge of tuberculosis was rampant in 1951 and at a meeting of the City Council in April, Clr. G. B. Dillon asked was it true that there was a marked increase in the number of T.B. patients being treated in the sanatorium in the City Home.

The City Manager, in reply, said there was nothing to be alarmed about as eight new bedrooms had been recently opened which was the cause of the increase in the figures. "And we still have a waiting list of six. At the moment our T.B. section is packed out."

Clr. Stevie Coughlan said there was a good deal of jealousy between city and county patients in the T.B. section lately because the latter were provided with new pyjama suits. The city patients' pyjama suits were in rags in some cases.

Manager: "You should see my pyjamas (laughter). The trouble is that the county authorities had their pyjamas order attended to before us. There is a certain delay in getting such supplies at the moment, but the city patients will be able to have theirs very soon. Meanwhile I should like to tell you that our patients are clothed cleanly and comfortably even now."

Clr. Pa O'Connell said with Clr. Glasgow they inspected the City Home recently and found a vast improvement, particularly in the tuberculosis section. Speaking in Irish, Cllr. Glasgow said he thoroughly agreed with Cllr. O'Connell.

St. Mary's Cathedral bell-ringers c. 1950.

Mysteries of Shannon Airport air crashes

The first major air disaster at Shannon Airport, opened in 1939, occurred in December, 1946, when a constellation, Star of Cairo, crashed on Inis Mac Nachten Island near the airport. Thirteen passengers died in the crash.

Two years later a Pan-American clipper, the Empress of the Skies, crashed while attempting to land on the main runway. The clipper, a Lockheed constellation, blew up after striking the ground, and 30 passengers were killed. The only survivor was Marc Worth, head of the Lockheed firm stationed in Limerick, whose wife was waiting to greet him at the airport.

The plane crashed on a hilly portion of a farm owned by Mr. Moylan at 2.34 a.m. Rescuers were beaten back by flames which were said to have reached a height of 100 feet following the crash. The plane had some time previously set up a new flight record of 5 hours 11 minutes from Gander to Shannon.

On Sunday, September 6th, 1954, a KLM constellation "Triton" came down in the adjacent mud flats with the loss of 29 lives. Just three minutes had elapsed since the plane took off from the airport.

The Leader reported that it took two hours for news of the disaster to come through, even though the crash happened just two miles from the airport. Navigator of the plane, John Tieman, staggered into the terminal building covered with mud. He had swum and struggled over a mile and a half of water and mud to bring the news that the plane had crashed.

There were 46 passengers on board and a crew of ten. Twenty-eight were rescued but one died afterwards. It was reported that those who died in the plane were overcome by petrol fumes before they could escape. Survivors said that while they were in the plane fumes made them groggy and that probably a number of the passengers fainted and were drowned in the rising tide.

A heroine of the crash was Miss Elizabeth Snyder, a 25-year-old American woman, one of the passengers. She told pressmen that when petrol fumes filled the plane a man put a cigarette to his mouth. "Before he could light a match I knocked the cigarette out of his mouth. He did not realise what he was doing."

Captain of the plane, Adrian Viruly, said "that if Miss Snyder had not acted so quickly the plane would I believe have been blown to bits."

In the aftermath of the crash, a meeting of the Limerick and District Branch of the National Union of Journalists condemned "the false and malicious reports published abroad arising out of the recent crash of a K.L.M. plane at Shannon Airport." The meeting called for the appointment of a Public Relations Officer at the airport.

The statement said that "Shannon was one of the greatest and most important centres of its kind in any part of the world. It would not merely be a pity but something of a tragedy if it should have its good name in any way tarnished.

"The recent crash of the K.L.M plane gave rise to certain comments and suggestions clearly calculated to prejudice and damage the interest of the airport.

"The favourite place Shannon occupies in the appreciation of flying men, travellers and air companies everywhere was won solely on its merits."

The meeting called on the Minister for Industry and Commerce to make information available to the press in cases such as the recent crash and in other instances where authoritative fact rather than speculation should be at once given to the public. It recommended the appointment of a public relations officer, a functionary that is to be found at all other international airports.

Just six years later, in 1960, another appalling crash occurred when an Italian airliner came down just a few minutes after taking off, bursting into flames at impact and eventually coming to rest in Clonnaghan cemetery, situated just a mile from the end of the runway.

Twenty-three passengers survived the crash due to the fact that they were in the tail section of the plane which remained largely intact but like the 1954 crash, 29 perished.

A Leader reporter was quickly on the scene and reported dramatic accounts of the crash. "I arrived at the scene of the disaster at 2.30 a.m. and flames from the burning fuselage of the ill-fated plane were still shooting to the sky, brilliantly lighting up the surrounding countryside. I encountered stretcher bearers carrying bodies to the ambulances. The grimmest scene was that of two men digging under the wreckage trying to extricate a body. It took them two hours to release it."

John Lonergan, an airport worker who resided at Sixmilebridge, gave a graphic description of the crash, which took place at 1.34 a.m. on Friday, February 27. "I was just about to go to bed when I heard a terrific explosion. I then looked out and saw the sky over the airport all lit up. I got into my car and drove to help the fire crew. I brought John Enright with me and when we arrived we could hear people crying and moaning and some of them appeared to be terribly injured."

Two well known hurlers, Liam Moloney and Patrick Lynch, who had been visiting the airport with some friends, drove parallel to the ill-fated plane as it took off. Mr. Lynch described the crash: "The plane never seemed to lift more than fifty feet off the ground. The next thing we saw it dipping down behind the hill with flames coming from the wings. It then crashed with a great explosion and we were first to reach the scene and set about helping the injured, as did the airport rescue services. I picked up a little boy and passed him to Liam Moloney who then passed him on to Miss O'Dea. He was alive and well."

The injured were ferried to Ennis, Barrington's and the Regional Hospitals. The Bishop of Limerick, Most Rev. Dr. Murphy, visited the survivors at the Regional and Barrington's, where he proffered sympathy. The Italian

Ambassador also visited the injured.

One of those who died was an Italian granny who was on her way to visit for the first time her grandchildren in New York.

Six months later a jet fighter bomber made a miraculous landing at Shannon. It had been in collision with another fighter at sea, which went down with its crew of three off the west coast.

The B47 giant six-engined US fighter landed with one engine of the plane hanging off and two others damaged. The crew escaped injury and the landing was described by an air worker as being "miraculous."

The following year, Friday, January 28, 1961, there was another serious crash at the airport when an Irish Air Cops training plane struck some trees about two miles from the airport and crashed in flames. Four of the crew were killed, the only survivor being the pilot, Captain James Liddy of Dublin. One of the dead, Geoffrey Colum O'Donoghue, was from Kilmanaghan, Abbeyfeale.

The horrific spate of crashes continued unabated and just seven months later by far the most devastating crash at the airport occurred in the early hours of the Sunday morning of 10th September, 1961. A Douglas DC6 President Airlines plane, with 83 persons on board, came down within seconds of becoming airborne, into the mudflats of the river. There were no survivors of the chartered flight carrying employees of a German steel firm on a trip to America.

Within minutes all emergency services in the airport went into action and a rail line was erected to the site of the crash by the Board of Works the next day. One girl survived the crash and was attended by the airport M.O., Dr. Flynn, but she too died shortly afterwards.

Mrs. Sarah Donlon, Rineanna South, recounted the moment of terror when she heard the ill-fated air liner flying directly over her yellow washed thatched cottage, which, with the house of Mr. and Mrs. Thomas Donlon, is in line with the flight of aircraft leaving the runway not far away.

Frank Thompson, with the aid of twelve employees, worked day and night to coffin the victims for their return to their home towns in Germany, Austria and Switzerland. A wealthy Austrian hotel owner was among the victims. The crew of six were described as being the most unlucky on the plane as they had changed from another aircraft on landing at Shannon and were happy and cheerful taking the "holiday" craft the remainder of the journey home.

At the inquest it was stated that visibility was poor at the time and it appeared that the pilot, though instructed by the control tower to turn right at take off, in fact turned left. After the take-off variations in the engine were heard by members of the airport staff and it appeared to some that the plane was coming in instead of going out. The crash occurred two miles from the airport.

It was the third fatal air crash in Shannon in just over a year.

On a par with the mysterious Aer Lingus Viscount crash off Tuskar Rock in

1968 was the air tragedy of 1958 in which a KLM super-constellation went down off the Galway coast. The plane, "Hugo de Groot" had left Shannon at 4 a.m. on 14th August with eighty-five passengers and a crew of eight on board. Everything seemed perfectly normal at take-off with ideal weather conditions, but soon after heading out from the Irish coast radio contact was lost. This was not unusual for the time, but after a silence of five hours, with no contact being made with the plane either here or in Gander, a search was mounted off the west coast involving ships and planes.

The worst fears were realised when the first bodies were picked up 120 miles out to sea that afternoon and the grim search went on for several days. Only thirty-four bodies in all were recovered, most of whom were interred in Galway, where two rows of graves stand in mute testimony to one of the country's greatest air mysteries. Frank Thompson and staff had worked around the clock identifying and coffining the bodies.

One of the puzzling features of the crash was the fact that no SOS signal had been received from the plane, and it was presumed that whatever happened, the crew members in the cockpit didn't have the opportunity to raise the alarm as they tried to wrest control of the stricken aircraft.

Experts, from examination of the wreckage, deemed that there had been no explosion and ruled out any question of collision with a guided missile. The inquiry could not come up with any concrete answer as to the cause of the crash, but did add a theory that some defects could have led to an engine "over speeding" which could have caused the plane to plunge into the sea.

A rescue boat recovering bodies from the mudflats following the crash of the Douglas D6 in 1961.

County folklore: laying the chairs

"Eamos" was writing in the 1920's about an old County Limerick custom called "laying the chairs." In several districts, every night before retiring the chairs are placed in a half circle around the hearth on which the fire is left burning, but is what is known as "banked up." The chairs are supposed to be occupied each night for one hour after midnight by the deceased members of the family, as the following story appears to prove:

There is a certain family living near Adare who were in the habit of conforming to this custom, and some years ago a member of the family, finding he could not sleep around the mystic hour of midnight, bethought himself to find solace in a smoke.

Finding he had no matches he proceeded to the kitchen to obtain a light at the fire, but on taking hold of one of the chairs (which formed a circle round the hearth) he found to his surprise he could not move it. Seizing it with both hands, he endeavoured to forcibly remove it, when he received a blow on the head and was knocked senseless.

On another occasion another member of the same family was out late on All Souls' Eve, and on returning home he found a candle lighting on the table as he thought for him.

Taking hold of the candle he proceeded to undress and having quenched it went to bed. Immediately he heard a dreadful din from the kitchen as if all the furniture was sliding or being bashed about, and lighting a match he proceeded to the kitchen to see the tables and chairs slide against the walls in their opposite positions. Lighting the candle he replaced the articles of furniture in their original positions, and having quenched the candle again, retired but the same din was then heard again. Rousing his mother, she immediately asked him if he had quenched the candle and he said of course. "You quenched the candle left lighting for the Holy Souls" and told him to relight the candle. This he did and there was no more disturbance.

The shanachie who related the above incident said he had the experience of sleeping in the house of an old couple in Adare who practised the custom of "laying the chairs." But from one hour after the mystic hour of midnight a terrible racket was heard from the kitchen, as if all the furniture was being broken.

Questioning his hostess on the matter she replied": "Oh, they're there every night, we take no notice."

He did not accept her offer of another night's repose.

In praise of a reformatory

"The scene outside the courthouse, as the lads were being driven away, was extremely pitiable. The mothers and friends of the youthful offenders kept up a continuous cry and followed the car for a good distance."

This was a report of the sad culmination of a court case in 1900, when two young defendants were sent to a reformatory for five years after being found loitering in an enclosed premises in Robert Street for unlawful purposes. The boys had previously been apprehended for stealing tins of condensed milk from a nearby factory.

The boys cried bitterly in court on hearing the sentence and asked to be forgiven this time, but the magistrate refused to alter the decision.

The youngsters were evidently devoted play-goers and they admitted that their attempted larceny was designed to provide money to gain admittance into the National Theatre at Charlotte Quay.

After sentence was passed, the chairman spoke eloquently of the advantages of a reformatory, saying "in this institution, which is decidedly less objectionable than the poorhouse, they will be taught trades, and this advantage could with the strict moral supervision exercised in such institutions, fit them to take an honourable and independent position in society when their period of detention has passed."

The Leader, commenting on the case, said: "the pangs of separation are as keen in the case of the poor as in that of the rich, but the distracted parents can, at all events, console themselves with the reflection that the youngsters themselves will be removed from the influence which tempted them to criminal paths at such an early age in their lives."

Around the same time, three other boys, having been charged with taking a purse from a shop, it was suggested by the prosecution that they be whipped for their crime, and their parents, who were present, assented to the suggestion.

Judge Adams, however, said this punishment was old fashioned and barbarous. He did not believe the Irish people would like to see this archaic discipline used any more. The boys were sentenced to terms in a reformatory.

The use of the birch to punish young offenders was the cause of discussion in a city court case in 1916. There was divided opinions as to the use of this form of punishment, usually twelve strokes, with some advocating its introduction. It was still used in England as a deterrent but there was no power to do so here.

A Leader editorial said where fines on parents for their children's misdemeanours would cause hardship, the use of the birch in these cases should be considered. "If that could be done with success, youthful offenders will be thankful in later years to the magistrates and others that they will grow up not as criminals but as decent boys and men respected by all."

Attempted suicide:
a criminal offence

It was not unusual through the first half of the century to read of those attempting to commit suicide being prosecuted. In 1918, a young domestic girl, aged 18 years, working in the city, was charged with attempting to commit suicide by drowning herself in the Docks. She pleaded guilty to the charge.

Mr. Gaffney, C.S., said the girl could not be drowned as she was a good swimmer and had no desire to commit suicide.

Judge Law-Smyth: "I suppose she found the water too cold (laughter).

Mr. Gaffney said an element of romance was sought to be introduced into the case but the police, on investigation, refuted this.

The girl's mother, in evidence, said her daughter was of an excitable nature and was easily upset.

Mr. Gaffney: "Perhaps she was excited by a Kinema picture."

His Honour: "There would be danger in that."

He asked the accused if she went to many picture shows and she replied "No Sir."

The accused had been unemployed for some days and the judge upbraided her mother for not looking after her. He asked Mrs. Gibbons: "What are you prepared to do? She requires protection, and what are you going to do for her? The letters I have here tell against her."

Mrs. Gibbons: "I met the young man myself and he said he never promised to marry her."

His Honour: "She doesn't say so in her letters. She called him 'my loving pal' (laughter). I will give her the benefit of the doubt on this occasion and you will have to look after her."

The mother, on being further questioned, said that another daughter had attempted suicide because she was frightened by her father. "But she did not go into the water at all."

The accused was let out under the Probationers First Offenders Act in her own bail and the mother's surety of £20 to behave herself for 12 months.

The same year a man named Richard Allen was charged at the City Police Court with unlawfully attempting to commit suicide. The heading of the report said it was "a very serious case." The sergeant stated in his depositions that on going to the prisoner's house the wife of the accused reported to him that the man had attempted to hang himself, and she showed the sergeant a piece of rope which was hanging on a cross bar on the door. The sergeant arrested the accused, who subsequently stated in the lock-up "that he was sorry he didn't finish the job."

The prisoner, who it was alleged had been drinking, was remanded for eight days.

John McCormack dies

The death of Ireland's greatest tenor, John McCormack, was marked with an obituary in the Leader on Monday, September 17, 1945, which said the death took place the previous day in his home in Booterstown, Dublin. For over thirty years, the obituary went on, Count McCormack won international fame as a tenor and through him his native land had, during his long years on tour, an unofficial ambassador of great worth. Limerick, was one of the first places in Ireland in which he made a professional appearance before going to Milan in 1905, receiving a wonderful ovation here. When he won world fame, he always made it a point to include Limerick in his Irish itinerary.

His earnings at one time were put at £200,000 a year. But he left at his death something less than £15,000. Sir Compton McKenzie, author, was quoted as saying McCormack was a man who had fun with money, having laid out £70,000 in four years trying to win the Derby. In his 300 acre castled mansion (Mooreabbey) in Monasteravin, fourteen servants looked after his comforts and famous guests from all over the world stayed there.

During the past year he was giving special coaching to Mr. Christopher Lynch, and, as a matter of fact, had expressed his willingness to accompany the young Rathkeale born tenor on his forthcoming tour of America.

McCormack had been bestowed with many honours from the Church during his career and at the Eucharistic Congress in 1932 sang the Panis Angelicus in front of a half million people at High Mass in the Phoenix Park.

"It was inevitable that a singer of his ability should be besieged by Hollywood to sing in a film, but Count McCormack, who had little ability as an actor, for a long time resisted the most tempting offers. Finally, when he had acquired an Irish residence at Monasteravin, he accepted an offer to sing in a film 'Song of My Heart' but insisted on the film being made at his residence.

"For his songs in this film he was paid the munificent sum of £100,000, but the film was so successful that he was persuaded to make another, 'Wings of the Morning', which was also a big success." His generosity was recalled when in 1915 he purchased one hundred thousand Abdulla cigarettes for the use of the allied troops. 60,000 were sent to the Expeditionary Forces and the rest to the Red Cross centres.

An example of the world-wide adulation he received was exemplified when in 1925 he got a hysterical reception in the Albert Hall with patrons, from all over the world, screaming for repeated encores. "Indian ladies in gorgeous saris, appreciative Americans, Irishmen with their love of their pet country-man, Australians with their coo-ees of joy, helped to make up one of the most wonderful audiences in the world. They wouldn't let Mr. McCormack go. They screamed so loudly that had to come back again and again and give more encores. Extra policemen had to divert traffic so great was the crowd that waited for Mr. McCormack outside the theatre and they had to clear a passage to enable the tenor to make a speech from the steps."

Boherbuoy Band
attacked by Healyites

In the 1940's a correspondent was writing of the Boherbuoy Band and the time when its members were attacked while on parade. The band was an out and out supporter of Parnell and played at all the great rallies of the Irish National Party. When "the uncrowned king of Ireland" died in 1891, the Boherbuoy travelled to Dublin to play at his anniversary the following year, and for some years afterwards.

In an era of great political agitation accompanying the Parnell split, proclamations were made from time to time that no bands were to parade the streets. On one occasion, a great Parnellite rally was taking place and crowds lined up outside Cruise's Hotel to parade to the O'Connell Monument. While the band could not march, the cor. wrote, "see what happened" and went on to describe how Tom O'Brien, bandmaster, with his coronet, and George Dillon, with his euphonium, were seated on a sidecar, one on either side, and headed the parade on its way to the Monument.

In 1894, Bryan O'Donnell, Mayor, and Mr. Patrick McDonnell, father of Dr. C. McDonnell and dentist Joseph McDonell, presented the band with beautiful uniforms, which were made at Cannocks.

Shortly afterwards, on St. Patrick's Eve, 1894, the band, thirty-two in number, decided to show off the uniform. They paraded from their bandroom, quaintly called "the castle of comfort" down Nelson St. (now Parnell Street), Wickham St., High St., Mungret St., Broad St., with the intention of wheeling left at Clohessy's Corner into Charlotte Quay and back up the centre of the town.

All went well until Baal's Bridge was reached but as the correspondent said "boys oh boys, did trouble break out." The Healyite faction, which was very strong in St. Mary's Parish (a group of Parnell supporters had broken away from St. Mary's Fife and Drum to form their own No. 9 Band), gathered en masse on the other side of the river and let fly with a fusillade of stones at the Band as it paraded along the Quay.

Such was the attack that nearly all the windows in Geary's factory (then situated on the quays) were broken. A group of Parnellites, who were accompanying the Boherbuoy, then made an attempt to rush Baal's Bridge but were repulsed by the police. A further attempt was made to rush Mathew Bridge again by the Parnellite party, but they were again beaten back by the police. Quaintly, the report said "that nothing then happened until we arrived back at the bandroom.

"This uniform was greatly admired in Dublin at the Parnell anniversaries" the correspondent added, but did not state its condition following the infamous attack by the St. Mary's Healyites.

Boherbuoy band c. 1940s

Shoot-out at Doolin

In 1926, what was described as a remarkable truce between antagonist parties in the Doolin district, near Lisdoonvarna, was described by Supt. Feeney at Ennistymon in opposing the granting of occasional licences for the sale of liquor at Doolin coursing meeting on October 6. Supt. Feeney said that certain parties had a series of squabbles. They had, however, called a truce, and were now making preparations to fight their differences out on the day of the coursing meeting.

The Supt. added "that a large farm in the Doolin district, about 2,000 acres, had been divided up at a time when the great majority of the people were of a certain political persuasion. But many of them have changed sides since the General Election, with the result that the parties have since been fighting each other. A series of tussles have taken place and there have been three or four big boxing matches. One of them nearly proved fatal.

Now a truce has been called to give the contending forces an opportunity of collecting all available forces to fight out the issue at the coursing in Doolin."

Dr. Daly, solr. for the applicants, said he did not think the trouble anticipated would arise. Learning that the Superintendent would have sufficient forces to quell any disorder, the Justice granted the application.

In 1968 St. Michael's Rowing Club eight crashed into Sarsfield Bridge and were extremely lucky to escape with their lives. Tony Tyne, at stern of Limerick Boat Club training tub, helps to pull one of the crew aboard. The crew was comprised of young local Gardaí, including Ben Sullivan, later to become a double Scott gold medalist for bravery.

Gold in Ballybunion

In the 1920's the little hill of Knockaroe, beside Ballybunion, had suddenly become famous because of the efforts of two foreigners, who had started to dig on it for some hidden treasure supposed to be buried there for centuries.

A German Jew and a Hungarian named Barna came into the Ballybunion district some time ago and carried on the trade of hawkers, etc. Being attracted by the legendary tales of the people of the countryside about a huge treasure being hidden on the top of Knockanore Hill, they started to excavate an old lis or fort, which is on the highest point of the mountain, and employed a number of men at the work.

A huge pit has been opened, some 50 feet long and 40 feet broad, and each day during the past week the work of digging and shovelling has proceeded.

On the spot is some sort of a cairn, and locally the place is known as the "leacht", which, of course, means a monument. Local storytellers relate how a number of men attempted on a former occasion to unearth the buried treasure, and had succeeded in reaching a large flag with an iron ring on it, when some large birds, resembling turkeys, flew out, and that while the treasure hunters were watching them the earth caved in, and try as they would, they could not afterwards find the flag.

Huge crowds of people were reported to be visiting the scene of operations every day and interest seems to be growing in the matter.

. . . . and also in Bulgaden

The Kilmallock correspondent struck gold in April 1924 when he scooped the story that the whereabouts of a treasure throve had been discovered in Bulgaden. "For days," he reported, "the roads leading to Bulgaden were utilised by cyclists, pedestrians and vehicles, all bent on one objective; and if you should stand by the way and be not impressed or enthusiastic about the idea, you were hailed with the cry: "Are you not going to Klondyke?' as they sped on at a quick a pace as possible as would betoken the urgency of their mission".

The correspondent continued: "And for days and nights men delved into the soil where the treasure was supposed to lie, but chiefly by night, aided by the moon's pale beams, or, when occasion required, by artificial light; indeed the night is considered the most propitious time for such an enterprise.

"But what," asked the Kilmallock correspondent, "was the origin of the project? It was no more or less than that two or three men had dreamt that gold lay concealed near Bulgaden Hall, the residence of the first Lord Carbery."

In their eagerness to discover the treasure, the prospectors may have damaged or destroyed an archaeological site, for the place of the digging was a circular mound. The correspondent concluded that the dreams of the prospectors were finally shattered when a large stone, 9 feet long and 4 feet wide and 2 feet thick was uncovered. Other large stones lay beside it. Since there was no way of lifting the central stone the diggers reluctantly abandoned their quest.

MANY DEATHS

Ravages of 'flu

UNDERTAKERS KEPT BUSY

THE mortality rate in Limerick during the past fortnight, when the influenza epidemic was at its height, was very high. The funeral undertakers were kept very busy and staffs had to work overtime turning out coffins. Funerals reached a peak when on the 22nd of this month fifteen funerals were held. About 95 per cent of the deaths were of people whose ages ranged between 70 and 50 years.

The virulance of the attack has now subsided and the big majority of sufferers are at present convalescing, Staffs, however, are still very depleted.

The following statistics showing the number of funerals in Limerick from 11th, to today, January 24, shows the huge mortality rate: 11th: 2 funerals; 12th, 5; 13th, 5; 15th, 13; 20th, 7; 22nd, 15; 23rd, 14 and today, 24th, 1, making a total of 90 for twelve days. The average number of deaths for a full month during a normal winter is 60, or 15 per week.

DEATHS

GILLIGAN (Limerick), Jan. 17, 1951. At her residence, Peter's Cell House, Agnes, wife of Christopher Gilligan; deeply regretted by her husband and family. RIP. Remains will be removed to St. Mary's Church this Wednesday evening at 7 o'c. Solemn Requiem Mass tomorrow (Thursday) at 10 o'c. Funeral immediately afterwards to Tralee Cemetery.

GRIFFIN (Limerick) Jan. 16, 1951, at the City Home, John Griffin, 2 Little Glentworth Street. Deeply regretted. RIP. Funeral tomorrow (Thursday) from St Michael's Church to Mount St Laurence Cemetery.

HYNES (Limerick), January 14, 1951, at her son's residence, 97 Ballinacurra Weston, Ellen Hynes; deeply regretted by her loving sons, daughter-in-law and family. RIP. (American Papers please copy).

O'SULLIVAN: at his residence, Waller's Well, on Monday 15th, William (Sprite). Fueral tomorrow from St Michael's Church to Mount St Lawrence Cemetery. Deeply regretted by his wife, brothers, sisters and relatives.

O'Connell Street, 1930s.

The Arch Confraternity of the Holy Family jubilarians 1970.

Massacre in Dromkeen

The dawn of the 1920's saw the War of Independence being intensified, and the British Government saw fit to let loose on the land the infamous Black and Tans and Auxiliaries, the former to augment the armed police force, the latter to strengthen the regular military forces.

There was hardly a district in the city or a town in the county that remained untouched by the troubled years and the newspapers carried regular reports of the actions.

One of the country's biggest massacres of the Troubles, as they were to become known, took place in Dromkeen on 3rd February, 1921, when a well planned I.R.A. ambush at Dromkeen saw eleven of a British convoy comprised of three regular R.I.C. men (from Clare and Galway) and eight irregulars (all from England) being shot dead. It was a combined effort between East and Mid-Limerick Brigades of the I.R.A.

The ambush took place at a point between Dromkeen and Pallas, which was three miles away, on a straight section of the road, 300 yards in length. Up to forty riflemen from the combined brigades were reported to have taken part in the ambush, which took place at 1 pm when the convoy of two lorries containing thirteen RIC and Black and Tan personnel was halted by a barricade formed of farm carts carts drawn across the road. Under a deadly hail of fire, most of the convoy were shot dead, but several RIC men offered stubborn resistance when they took cover behind the wheels of the lorry before eventually being shot. The driver of one of the lorries, who happened to be the district inspector, and another policemen, escaped through the nearby fields and they were the only survivors of of the ambush. One IRA member was reported to have been shot, not seriously.

A few months later tragedy struck many families in the county when six I.R.A. men were killed in an engagement with the British at Lackelly in East Limerick and three Auxiliaries were shot dead in Oola which led to the arrest of eight I.R.A. suspects.

Full coverage was given to the five-hour battle for the Newcastle West R.I.C. Barracks which was left a smoking ruin by the I.R.A., and the reprisals that followed in which women and children had to flee the town; the terror in the Boherbuoy district in Limerick when the police, alias the Black and Tans, ran amok smashing in windows, doors and burning houses, and all the incidents of the war occurring in the county and city.

"Limerick Horror. Appalling Triple Tragedy. Mayor, ex-Mayor and Another Shot Dead." These were the headlines of Monday, 7th March, 1921. This assassination got world headlines and became known as the "murder of the two mayors," when in the early hours of Sunday morning, 6th March, British Crown Forces broke into the homes of the Mayor of Limerick, Ald. George

Clancy, and Cllr. Michael O'Callaghan, and with their faces blackened, shot dead both men in front of their families. The "Another" shot dead was Volunteer Joseph O'Donoghue who died in the same circumstances.

The funeral of the victims was reported in the Leader, (with the thick side of the column rules turned to give a melancholy look of mourning to the page), as being the biggest in the history of the city. "Never, in the history of Limerick, it is probably safe to say was a public funeral so thoroughly representative and truly expressive of profound and universal sorrow and sympathy as that which accompanied the remains of the murdered victims." Mayors from all over the country and Dail representatives were all in attendance. The previous month, the Lord Mayor of Cork, Ald. McCurtin, was shot dead in similar circumstances and the Limerick City Council adjourned as a mark of respect. And almost every issue carried news of Cork's Terence McSwiney during his 73 days hunger strike and the world waited and eventually heard of his death.

No part of the city or county escaped tragedy during these years. Two young boys from Thomondgate were shot dead on February 20, 1921, in appalling circumstances in Blackwater, a few miles from the city. At the military enquiry it was alleged that the boys kept running after being ordered to stop by a military patrol but a witness said that the victims, when they were surprised by the lorry passing along the road near the river, put up their hands and notwithstanding were shot dead. The boys were Cecil (17) and Aidan (15) O'Donovan, of Thomondgate. The president of the inquiry said he was extremely sorry for the death of the boys.

A shooting took place in Limerick, off Chapel Lane in William Street, on February 1st, 1920, when an R.I.C. Sergeant named Wellwood was shot and seriously wounded. Such incidents were to be repeated many times during the next two years. The Bishop of Limerick, Dr. Hallinan, at 12 noon Mass the following Sunday in St. John's Cathedral, condemned the outrage and said that those who committed such crimes did no good to Ireland. "These outrages were quite extraneous to and were not connected with the national movement."

How wrong he proved to be was borne out by the subsequent happenings of the next two years.

A diversion during those troubled years was the happy day, when Eamon de Valera, of whom there was constant reports of his tilts with British premier Lloyd George, and Limerick woman Mrs. Clarke (nee Daly) the widow of patriot Tom Clarke, were granted the Freedom of the City. Thousands turned out to greet them and the city was en fete for the ceremony.

Another diversion took place in 1920 when sensational reports came from Templemore stating that statues and crucifixes in the home of Thomas Dwan, started to bleed. The town was in an extraordinary state of excitement with crowds and invalids coming from all over the country following the report of a miracle when a soldier who had a serious leg injury in the First Word, walked home smartly unaided after kissing a crucifix in the house.

The first execution in Limerick since the 1880's took place in the New Barracks (later Sarsfield) when Thomas Keane was executed when caught in possession of arms on June 4th, 1921. Four days later, Galbally men Patrick Maher and Ned Foley were executed in Mountjoy for their alleged part in the shooting of two R.I.C men in the rescue of Sean Hogan at Knocklong. It was stated that Maher had nothing got to do with the rescue and Foley was present but was unarmed.

A dastardly crime and one which it was said hastened the Truce, took place in Castleconnell on Sunday, April 17, 1921, when the proprietor of the Shannon Hotel (now owned by Hickey's), Denis O'Donovan (grandfather of Des O'Malley T.D.) was shot down in cold blood when he refused to divulge the names of men who just before had been involved in a shoot-out on the premises in which two constables died. Surgeon Cripps, who was on a fishing holiday in Castleconnell at the time, was so horrified at Mr. O'Donovan's shooting that he wrote a strong letter to his brother Lord Parmoor, who read it out in the House of Lords. After a heated debate, he and Lord Cecil crossed the house as a protest and later William T. Cosgrave stated that it had a salutary effect on Lloyd George, who shortly afterwards initiated the Truce.

The whole country breathed a sigh of relief when the Truce was announced on 11th July, 1921. "Truce. Mr. De Valera addresses the Irish People," ran the local headlines.

On the run-up to the voting for or against the Treaty a Leader editorial urged the people to accept it, and in the same issue Dr. Fogarty, the nationalistic-minded Bishop of Killaloe, who had been targeted by the Black and Tans, saw the portents of more terrible strife in the disunity and acrimony in the debates in the Dail if it was turned down. "No man or group has the right to lead the country into a ruinous war against the considered judgement of the nation." He was referring to renewed war with the British if the Treaty was not accepted, but he and the country were not to know that despite the acceptance of the Treaty, a bitter Civil War lay around the corner. After enduring the hardships of the War of Independence, people despaired as the country was plunged into another war which was to leave a bitter legacy for the next half century.

Joy in Newcastle West

Newcastle West was the centre of memorable scenes of religious piety and fidelity in May 1930, when the Golden Jubilee of the Confraternity was celebrated by 15,000 worshippers. The local correspondent waxed lyrical in describing the scenes in the town:

The sun was passing down a brilliant summer ray on a town gay with bunting – on a people full of joy. On every street triumphal arches, rich in tracery, were to be met. Altars festooned with roses adorned almost every house. Dead walls were brought into objects of beauty, decorated as they were with evergreens and sweet scenting blossoms. Niches were transferred by artistic hand into grottoes – the whole presenting a sight long to be remembered.

Banners were suspended across the streets bearing such legends as "Jesus, Mary and Joseph help us." "God bless our Archdeacon (others mentioned bishop and pope), "Hail Christ the King," etc.,

The Limerick train brought in some 1,500 passengers, the town had already "surrendered" to the hosts who had arrived earlier. Joy was in the hearts of the people and little wonder, seeing that they were celebrating an event that took place fifty years before: the establishment of a battalion of God's army known as the Confraternity of the Holy Family.

In the procession jubilarians were given a place of honour and accommodated in motor cars, and as they passed they received the secret congratulations of the immense crowds. The singing of the hymns was inspiring. There was a hallowed silence all round creating a profound and mysterious awe. Led by the men of the Limerick Confraternity, the *Tantum Ergo* was sung and the ear was stunned as the multitude joined in at the Sport Field, where the ceremonies were taking place.

The Newcastle West choir sang delicately, their sweet cadences being wafted over the great expanse by a gentle breeze. As the Bishop, Most Rev. Dr. Keane, was being vested for the ceremonies, a dead silence prevailed broken only by the chirping of the birds.

Fr. Whelan, C.Ss.R., director of the Limerick Confraternity, gave an inspiring sermon, in which he said: "Were the foundations of this confraternity 50 years ago the work of man, it would have crumbled away and passed out of sight. Truly, this was the Lord's doing."

At the Consecration, "the sound of the sweet tongued bell brought a dead silence as the vast gathering on bended knees and with bowed heads awaited the Elevation of the Host."

Advertising style 1950

It's a job for . .
THE
Gaeltacht
CLEANERS - LIMERICK
Ring 793 (Private Branch Exchange). We Collect and Deliver.
24 HOUR CLEANING SERVICE
EXPRESS SIX HOUR SERVICE IF REQUIRED
Sponging and Pressing While You Wait

The Gaeltacht Cleaners, half a century after the insertion of this Leader adv., are still going strong with branches at William Street and Lower Gerald Griffin Street.

Bishop O'Dwyer: 'a very queer man'

"The country was electrified. The letters were first published in a provincial newspaper and the word spread like wildfire. Fabulous prices were being offered for copies of the paper."

These were descriptions of what happened in the aftermath of the publication of the letters of Bishop Edward Thomas O'Dwyer, Bishop of Limerick, in reply to Sir John Maxwell, Commander-in-Chief of the British troops in Ireland, in May 27th, 1916.

General Maxwell, in the month following the 1916 Rising, had written to Bishop O'Dwyer asking him to curb the activities of two priests in his diocese, Fr. Tom Wall and Fr. Michael Hayes, who were nationalistic in their outlook and actions. The General mistimed his appeal badly, as the Bishop, like most of his fellow countrymen, was appalled at the wholesale executions of the Irish leaders following the Rebellion.

The following is an extract from one of the Bishop's letters of reply, missives that were to become some of the most famous in the history of correspondence in this country: "You appealed to me to help you in the furtherance of your work as military dictator of Ireland. Even if action of that kind was not outside my province, the events of the past few weeks would make it impossible to have any part in proceedings which I regard as wantonly cruel and oppressive . . . . You took care that no plea for mercy should interpose on behalf of the poor young fellows who surrendered to you in Dublin.

"The first information which we got of their fate was the announcement that they had been shot in cold blood. Personally I regard your action with horror and I believe it has outraged the conscience of the country . . . . Altogether, your regime has been one of the worst and blackest chapters in the history of the misgovernment of this country."

The Bishop, in one fell stroke, had cast aside his tarnished image following his opposition to the Plan of Campaign and the Irish Party policies. He was now a national hero with letters of congratulation pouring into his palace in Corbally. Padraig O Conaire wrote his short story, "Anam an Easbuig" based on the Bishop's celebrated stand and a ballad, "O'Dwyer and Maxwell" did the rounds and proved very popular:

> And you think that I forget my country's martyred dead–
> The brave, the pure, the high-souled lads, whose blood you've foully shed,
> But here's your answer – I may share the fate of those who died,
> But I'll not be the first O'Dwyer to take the tyrant's side.

It came as no surprise when it was announced that the Bishop would be granted the Freedom of Limerick in September of 1916. Newspaper reports on the conferring were censored by the authorities, with a big line draped across the heading stating same. The conferring was not without acrimony, with Cllr. Matthew Griffin accusing a member of the Council objecting to the conferring at a previous meeting because he felt the bishop did not give the support that he ought to the Irish Party. The Mayor intervened and Mr. Griffin retorted: "You may as well, Mayor, try and stop the rays of the sun as stop me" (cheers from the gallery). "If His Lordship had advocated or supported the so-called Irish Party he would not be getting the freedom of the city that day," Mr. Griffin said (applause).

He went on to say that the writings of His Lordship had infused a new spirit into Ireland, and little did Maxwell think when he crossed swords with His Lordship of the metal he was dealing with (applause). His Lordship was a true Irishman and he hoped he would be long spared to guide the people (applause)

Dr. O'Dwyer, with all the adulation now coming his way, had his feet firmly on the ground and stated: "Popularity is a new experience for me, and I must be on my guard against its fascination."

The Bishop's letters, four in all, proved of inestimable propaganda value to the national cause and like the executions of the leaders of the rebellion, helped turn the tide of national opinion. At the Commission of Enquiry into the Rising in London, Mr. Birrell said Dr. O'Dwyer was an enemy of the Nationalist Party and described him as "a very queer man."

Leader condemns Rising

National opinion in the immediate aftermath of the Rising was anything but sympathetic to its perpetrators, as the following extracts from an editorial of the Leader of the time conveys:

"The public mind of Ireland is but slowly recovering from the stunning blow of horror inflicted upon it by the insurrection in Dublin on Easter Monday. That wholly insane enterprise had in its very element of sadness and tragedy, that there is not a man of the Irish race the world over capable of realising facts but abhors and condemns with vehemence the 'mad campaign' as the most Rev. Dr. Kelly, Bishop of Ross, aptly described it.

"The solitary redeeming feature in connection with the whole uprising is that the outbreak was the work of a small minority, most of whom were themselves more innocent, if well-meaning, dupes of others, and that it is denounced by none more loudly or more vigorously than by the vastly overwhelming majority of the Irish people themselves both at home and abroad.

"Further executions as a deterrent are wholly unnecessary, for apart altogether from the disastrous failure of the insane attempt made by the insurgents the feeling and opinion of Irishmen at home and abroad may safely be relied upon to prevent any repetition of the madness that marked Easter Week, 1916."

An Irishwoman living in London, in the same edition, wrote condemning the Rising, believing in the justice of Home Rule. "I am sorry that some of my misguided countrymen have in open rebellion played into the enemy's hands," she said.

Passengers taking the air on the decks of the Titanic in Queenstown (Cobh) before the last fatal leg of the journey to America.

Limerick people in world tragedies

Some of the great tragedies of the century, including the San Francisco earthquake, the sinking of the Titanic and the Lusitania, all had their share of Limerick people involved.

The San Francisco earthquake of 1906 took 700 lives, destroyed 28,000 buildings and left 300,000 homeless. Most of the city lay in ruins.

There were several Limerick people in the city at the time of the earthquake and afterwards several poignant letters they sent home describing the disaster were published in local newspapers.

Michael Daly of Kilscallen, Abbeyfeale, survived the tremors and wrote to say that there were people from every county in Ireland there at the time. Fr. John Power, Kilteely, contacted his sister in Old Pallas to say he was safe, and P. O'Brien, Mitchelstown, heard from his two brothers that they too were alright.

Stephen Dineen, a member of the well known city family of bakers, and who resided in Lansdowne Park with his wife Hannah for many years afterwards, was there and wrote a poignant letter to his mother telling of his miraculous escape. "It is impossible for me to describe the awful calamity, or for the heart of any man to conceive in the least degree the terrible scenes that have been witnessed here for the past few days – the dead and the dying. San Francisco is a thing of the past. They are just now burying a lot of people in the hill alongside me."

Stephen described his narrow escape from death: "In the early hours of Wednesday morning (April 18, 1906) the earthquake struck and my bed went up and down like a ship at sea. With the house on the point of collapse I made the front door but it was jammed. By a superhuman effort I opened it and ran onto the street. I did not know where to stand. If I stood in the centre of the street I would be electrocuted and I was in danger of houses falling on me on the sidewalk."

Stephen lost everything in the fire that followed, all he had left in the world were photographs of his father and mother and other members of the family.

Another Limerickman, Thomas O'Riordan, address not stated, wrote to say that when the 'quake struck he made up his mind that his last hour had come, "but dressed myself quietly and jumped two stories to the ground, landing safely. Skyscrapers, 20 and 30 feet high, were lying in ruins, and men, women and children were running around in their nightgowns. I can't describe the scene of ruin and desolation."

Thomas said he always had the idea "that 'Frisco would be burnt to the ground, and some people here say that it is a visitation of Providence, for I guess this town was one of the most scientifically erected on earth."

Canon Vance of Rathronan, Ardagh, heard from his son: "The fires were the most serious, but with all the water mains broken, there was little the fire brigade could do and they started to dynamite buildings which seemed only to add to the flames. Many victims were pinned under beams and fallen houses, and as the flames worked towards them, and no human help could avail, the soldiers had to shoot them."

The Leader, in its lead story on April 17th 1912, reported that several Limerick people had perished in the sinking of the Titanic on April 14th, including (from the city) Nora Keane, Nellie O'Dwyer, Daniel Keane, John Kennedy, Rosemary Place, Watergate; T. Morgan, and Patrick Lane from Clare Street. From the county, Patrick Colbert, Kilconlea, Abbeyfeale; Patrick Dooley, Patrickswell, Bruff; James Scanlan, Rathkeale, died.

Those lucky to be rescued included Bertha Moran and Mary Madigan from Askeaton.

As seen from above list, it was reported that Nellie O'Dwyer of High Street, Limerick, perished, but was later reported safe. "The news was greeted with great joy by her people and the citizenry in general," reports said. Nora Keane was later reported to have been saved. John Kennedy, also thought to be lost, was later reported to have survived.

Another survivor, Englishwoman Mrs. Dick, stated that seven of the rescued died and were buried at sea and that the ship's band played "Nearer My God To Thee" on deck before the sinking.

Three Clare passengers had a providential escape. Patrick Tracey, Cratloe, and Daniel and Miss Mary Sullivan had travelled into the city to book their places on the ill-fated ship but changed their minds and booked instead for its second crossing.

Mr. Fogarty, proprietor of the Theatre Royal, announced that he would give the theatre free for one or two nights to those wishing to put on performances for raise funds for the dependants of the disaster. A Mr. Organ replied suggesting that the Limerick Operatic Society should repeat their recent staging of "The Gondoliers." Fr. Devane, vice-president of St. Michael's Temperance Society, took up the offer, saying that they would put on a show, *The Rebel's Wife,* playing to a full house for one night. After the first act, the Boherbuoy Band played a selection of Irish airs.

A memorial service was held in St. Mary's Cathedral which was packed out. The Band of the York and Lancaster Regiment, numbering 65, played during the service and numbered Chopin's "Funeral March," Handel's "Dead March from Saul" and the hymn "Nearer My God To Thee" amongst their repertoire. The collection was got up for the survivors of the disaster and the Bishop said: "There is room for an exercise of general feelings awakened by the thought of the widespread bereavement and privation unexperienced in the history of maritime disaster."

The Chronicle carried a statement by some of the survivors which claimed that Captain Smith committed suicide before the ship went down. "His fellow officers tried to wrest the gun from him but he broke away and he shot himself on the bridge by putting the barrel of the revolver into his mouth. The chief engineer also committed suicide by the same means. Three Italians were shot to death by officers in the struggle for the lifeboats."

At the inquiry in England, of which details were published, the excessive speed of the ship was blamed for the disaster, being unable to avoid the collision with the iceberg.

The horrors of World War II were brought nearer home with the sinking of the Lusitania off the coast of Cork on May 7th, 1915. Two Limerick people miraculously survived the sinking: Patrick Hanly of Lisnagry who had harrowing stories to tell of the sinking, and Mrs. Cox, who lived in America.

While the casualty list reached a dreadful 1,924 lives lost, the Chronicle in its report chose to make its top heading: "Mr. Vanderbilt (the American multi-millionaire) had been feared lost." The jury in the inquest returned a verdict of "wilful and wholesale murder."

The German press, while lamenting the loss of civilian life, said it was all Winston Churchill's fault, for "conjuring up this cruel warfare which is the curse of mankind." The report went on to claim that the Lusitania was a legitimate war target, having 12 5.m guns on deck, and "was more strongly mounted than any German armoured cruiser."

When the news of the disaster became known in Limerick a sensation prevailed amongst the citizens, and the telegrams posted in the Chronicle window were read by a stream of people, which constantly increased as the startling news became known. "Needless to say, the deepest indignation at the outrage and sympathy with the innocent victims was expressed throughout the city," said the report.

The strange case of Maurice Lenihan's portrait

On February 23rd, 1927, a startling claim was made by Harriet Patricia Lenihan, with an address at York Street, Cork, to the effect that a painting of her father, Maurice Lenihan, the eminent historian and former Mayor, which had been offered as a gift to the city, had been rejected by the Mayor, Paul A. O'Brien.

In a letter to the editor, Miss Lenihan wrote:

Dear Sir – In a recent number of your paper I notice one of your correspondents asks how is it that the portraits of some men who in the days past had given up their entire lives and their entire brains in the service of their city and in the service of literature are not put up in Limerick halls. My father's name is mentioned.

As historian of Limerick, in America and Australia his name is honoured and alive. Education in his day had not reached the stage its occupies today. It cost my father six years' tremendous concentration and labour to write that history, which, perhaps he might have spent in a more remunerative manner.

When in Limerick some weeks ago, I offered as a gift, from my sister and myself, the very valuable and historical painting by the famous Irish artist, Harvey, to the city, as we are the only two members left of a once large family.

I saw the Mayor, but received the reply that there was no one now alive in Limerick who remembered my late father. Apart from the historical value of the exquisite painting by Harvey, in every city in the world the portraits of men who were an honour to their country and city are hung. My father lies in a neglected grave in Mount St. Laurence Cemetery. There were few men who bore more honours. He was Mayor and High Sheriff of Limerick, a Fellow of the Archaeological, Antiquarian, Arts and Letters Societies; an honoured and life member of the Royal Irish Academy.

But, better than all, he was a fervent and practising Catholic, and as his biographer said (the late Dr. Riordan), his life was blameless. His painting, with many more valuable paintings of our family, lie neglected and rotting in a damp room in Limerick, but such, Mr. Editor, is life. – Yours, Harriet Patricia Lenihan, (his daughter), 6 York Street, Cork.

Several letters appeared following this startling claim by Miss Lenihan. In an age when non-de-plumes were used to hide the identities of letter writers, "Maolmora" wrote in to say that it was strange why the Mayor did not take up Miss Lenihan's generous offer of such a valuable gift. "Paintings from the brush of artists like Harvey – whose picture of the Limerick Piper is world famous – are not easily come by and are eagerly purchased by English and American dealers, who pay huge prices for the works of the masters. The Mayor's plea that no one of the present day world remembers the historian is absurd. One might as well refuse an oil painting of Gerald Griffin, or Catherine Hayes, or Sarsfield, or any of our famous Limerick sons for the same futile reason.

"A great many people, still living, and not necessarily very old or very middle aged, can vividly recall the personality of Limerick's distinguished historian. The present writer remembers in his boyhood Mr. Lenihan visiting the Christian Brothers School in Sexton Street and he has a long way to go yet for the old-age pension.

"If Mr. Lenihan had lived in any other city but Limerick his genius would long ago have received the recognition is justly deserves. But such is life. I'm afraid the apathy has fallen heavily on our shoulders.

"I think Miss Lenihan's offer should have been placed before the Governing Committee of the Free Library with a view to having the painting displayed in the art gallery."

The Mayor took advantage of the columns of the Leader to reply to the accusations:

Dear Sir – Two of your correspondents are responsible for directing my attention to Miss H. Lenihan's letter of the 23rd inst. It is many months since Miss Lenihan interviewed me. If I rightly recollect she was then anxious that I should exercise my influence in helping her to get certain concessions. Incidentally, she referred to a painting of her father, reminding me at the same time that he once occupied the Mayoral Chair. It was then I said that very few, if any, of the present generation remembered him, and it would appear that one of your correspondents seems to share a similar view (he was referring to a letter which claimed that if the average young Limerickman was asked to know who was Lenihan or John Francis O'Donnell his face will look as stupid as the pursuits he follows).

I am satisfied from Miss Lenihan's letter that the painting was offered as a free gift. However, I don't think that the matter was made sufficiently clear to me at the interview. I informed Miss Lenihan that I would like to see the painting and submit it to members of the Corporation, but up to time of writing I was never afforded an opportunity of seeing the picture. – Paul A. O'Brien, Mayor.

The most hated man in Limerick

The man crowds loved to hate in early 20th century Limerick was the proselytiser Dr. Joseph John Long. For several years local newspapers carried regular reports of his harassment and assault by unruly mobs, who used follow him through the city streets. He was boycotted regularly by the city jarveys, who refused to take him on board for fear of retribution. He was under constant police protection. "How dare you come among Catholics" was one of the regular taunts thrown at him by the crowd, and "Dr. Long's auld mother keeps a soup kitchen in hell" was one of the favourite taunts of children when following the missioner.

In an age when divisions in the city between the two main religions were very marked, the doctor, a graduate in medicine from Trinity College, had been sent down from the Dublin Mission to Limerick in 1897 on the behest of the Irish Church Mission to Ireland. A native of Southern Ireland, he was a member of the Church of Ireland.

Dr Long (at rear) with his assistant, Mr. O'Hare, evangelist, and Mrs. O'Hare, dispensary nurse.

He opened a Medical Hall in Thomas Street, where he treated destitute people in particular mostly free of charge. However, it was generally believed by the Catholics that his true mission was to convert these misfortunes to the Protestant faith and this was borne out when it was revealed in a court case that he was a paid agent of the English based "Irish Church Mission to Roman Catholics" in Limerick.

One of the doctor's most bitter adversaries was Father Tierney of the Redemptorist Order of Mount St Alphonsus who in 1900 vehemently denounced the doctor at the weekly meeting of the Men's Confraternity.

"Men of the Confraternity, stand up on your feet, raise up your hands, and say after me, 'I protest in the sight of God, against the attack which has been made by the bigots of Limerick upon our religion. I promise never to attend myself and to prevent whom I can from attending.' This man is the hireling agent of the Irish Church Missions, the undying enemy of the Catholic Church, and they would set up outside this church their gallows and triangle, would drag us from our convent homes, scourge, burn and hang us without mercy. Proselytiser, souper, that is your name, and that is your calling."

Following this harangue, up to forty members of the Confraternity at once took up positions outside the Mission in an attempt to prevent Catholics from entering, with a priest riding up and down with a dog-whip in his hand to stop would-be entrants. The Catholic Bishop, Dr. Edward Thomas O'Dwyer, announced that any Catholic entering the Mission was guilty of a mortal sin so grave that no priest in Limerick could pardon it, declaring it to be a reserved sin, with the culprit being obliged to go the bishop himself for absolution.

Fr. Tierney entered the dispensary shortly after his attack from the pulpit, and ordered all Roman Catholics to leave. "This house is a souper's house, all Catholics must leave" he shouted to the terrified patients, some of whom rushed out. Dr. Long ordered Fr. Tierney out of the building and all sorts of rumours swept the city that he had assaulted the Redemptorist resulting in hostile crowds surrounding the building with police protection eventually having to be provided.

An incident in Thomondgate concerning Dr. Long eventually led to a series of questions in the House of Commons. In 1901 Dr. Long brought an action against Fr. Edmund O'Leary a curate in St. Munchin's for trying to prevent him attending a patient in Thomondgate and inciting a crowd to riotous behaviour. The magistrate, Mr. Hickson dismissed the charge, condemning the proselytising activities of Dr. Long at the same time, and allowed Fr. T. R. Shanahan. P.P., St. Munchin's to harangue the doctor in the court. After the court case, crowds tried to attack the doctor and it was with the greatest difficulty that he was escorted to his home by police.

The case, and the continuing harassment of the doctor, attracted much publicity in England, and the replies of Mr. Wyndham, Chief Secretary for Ireland, to questions in the Commons, proved unsatisfactory to many and he was much criticised in the English press.

A few months later a report stated: "For the past couple of days the principal topic discussed by everybody in the city is the prosecution of Dr. Long by the Corporation, for having obstructed the streets on 10th August last. The facts of the alleged obstruction are well known. To put it shortly, Dr. Long sat on a hackney car, the driver of which refused to accept him as a passenger, and the doctor refusing to dismount, a crowd collected."

The court was packed on the day of the trial with many of the city's Catholic clergy in attendance. Evidence was given that even though the driver

A Limerick family converted to Protestantism by Dr. Long who had to be spirited out of the city to start a new life in Canada with other converted families.

of the hackney car took the horse from out of the shaft, Dr. Long refused to leave the car. An immense crowd gathered to watch and evidence was given that George's Street (now O'Connell Street) was blocked and portion of William Street, by the huge group of onlookers to the drama.

The same year four young men were charged with harassment of the doctor and throwing bags of flour, one of which hit his wife, in Sarsfield Street. Mr. Hastings, for the defence, asked Dr. Long: "Are you ashamed to admit that you are paid by a proselytising institution known as the Irish Church Mission to Roman Catholics?"

Dr. Long: "I am not ashamed in the least, I am proud of it."

Mr. Hastings said he had the greatest respect for Protestants and he was not there to prevent Dr. Long, or any man like him, walking the town. But the people of Limerick and Ireland had suffered too much for centuries for their faith, and their feelings were very strong on the matter. Dr. Long was endeavouring to interfere with the religion of the people, and trying to bribe the poor Catholic children. He appealed to the bench to give as little sympathy to those people as possible, and try and put an end to this system of souperism, which he believed was only supported by peculiar people and old women (applause).

Mr. Hickson, magistrate, summing up, said there was little doubt but there was harassment, but even though he was a Protestant himself, he trusted that those responsible for Dr. Long being here as a paid official for doing what he considered was despicable work, would take such means as to remove this sore from their midst: it only disturbed the harmonious feeling that existed between the different sections in the city (hear, hear, and applause). He then dismissed the case against the defendants.

In another celebrated case, Bishop O'Dwyer accused Judge Boyd of the Circuit Court of having Dr. Long as a "paid agent." The case concerned a young girl named Violet Hegarty whom Dr. Long was trying to take into his care. He claimed that the father had given permission to take the child from the city's St. Joseph's Reformatory where she was under detention. Judge Boyd was trying the case, a fact which the bishop questioned as regards to his impartiality. The Judge denied that Dr. Long was his agent and refused to enter into any correspondence with the Bishop.

Things had changed little two years later and in a report of February, 1903, the Leader said: "Dr. Long would again appear to be in need of Advertisement if his coffers are to be kept replenished from English sources. At all events, the statement is made that as he was attending a 'patient' on Friday afternoon in Browne's Lane off Carey's Road, he was attacked by a number of boys and pelted with stones and mud. The attack does not seem to be of a very formidable character, as it is stated that the doctor produced a notebook as if to take down the names of his assailants. He then proceeded on his way without further hindrance."

The same year a letter was received by the Corporation Hackney Car committee from Dr. Long complaining that he was refused a "fare" by jarveys Michael Ryan, Michael Doyle and John Hare. The complaint got short shift, the committee being of the opinion that Dr. Long had his remedy in the Petty Sessions. The determination and resiliance of the doctor was beyond question and his name kept cropping up into the next decade as the following report in May 1911 indicates:

"Dr. Long Again! An Audacious Attempt and a Dismal Failure" were the headlines announcing the latest episode on the ongoing story of the Limerick Medical Mission:

The redoubtable Dr. Long made his latest attempt last night at "saving souls" in the city. About nine o'clock he went to St. Mary's Convent and audaciously demanded that a young city girl named Grace Kersley, aged 16 years, who had been for a long time in Mount St. Vincent Industrial School, be delivered into his care. He was accompanied by the girl's mother and a policeman.

From information given to our representative today at St. Mary's Convent it appears that this young girl, Grace Kersley, was in the industrial school for the last twelve years. Her mother was a Roman Catholic and married a Protestant. At the marriage the child's father consented to have the children brought up as Roman Catholics, and the children were accordingly baptised and brought up as Roman Catholics.

About two months ago Mrs. Kersley went to Mount St. Vincent and demanded possession of the child. She then stated to the nuns at Mount St. Vincent that she was a Roman Catholic. She then got possession of the child, who has since been under the influence of her mother and Dr. Long.

Early yesterday the child ran away and again sought admission at the Mount, but it appears that her time in the industrial school had expired and the nuns could not keep her. So she was sent to St. Mary's Convent where there is a school for such children.

At about 9 o'clock last night Dr. Long, accompanied by the mother and a policeman, came to seek admission to the convent, but they were refused. On their return back they were greeted with boohs and hisses from a large crowd that had assembled outside the convent.

This morning an employee of Dr. Long and the mother again visited the convent and demanded the child. The child positively refused to leave, and being questioned as to her religion, she said she was a Roman Catholic and did not want to be anything else. The child refused to go, and the parties left, being again jeered and shouted at. The child said she would not go back to the mother any more.

Almost thirty years after he came to Limerick, Dr. Long was still making news when in 1926 he made an appeal at the Circuit Court to have his dispensary at 47 Thomas Street exempt from rates. His solicitor, Mr. G. Cullinan, claimed the premises were used for the purpose of the Limerick Medical Mission of the Society for Irish Church Missions to Roman Catholics, the primary object which was to afford cheap or gratuitous medical assistance to the poor.

Mr. Hugh Moran, City State Solicitor, disputed this when opposing the application, contending that the dispensary was for the purpose of advancing the doctor's own religion and was used as a cloak and trap under the guise of a charitable medical institution.

Under questioning from Mr. Moran, Dr. Long admitted that when patients were assembled in the dispensary a religious service was conducted first with hymns being sung such as "There is a Green Hill Far Away." Mr. Moran also produced a booklet, "Ireland for Christ" in which Dr. Long stated that the dispensary was still flourishing despite the efforts of priests over a period of twenty-seven years in attempting to stop people from attending. "1,178 patients paid 4,385 visits to the dispensary last year, which is an increase in the previous year. 3,823 of these visits were by Romanists to receive medical aid and listen to the words of Christ Jesus, despite the fact to do so has been made a reserved sin, from which the poor Romanist cannot receive absolution from his priest, but most go to the Bishop himself" the statement added.

After much more interesting debate, Judge McElligott held that the premises, a substantial part of which was held by Dr Long's assistant, Mr. O'Hare, were clearly used for the purposes of religious propaganda and accordingly he dismissed the appeal with two guinea costs against the appellants.

Kilkee in Victorian times.

Letters to the Editor

The following is a random selection of letters to the Editor of the Leader through the century:

Undressing in Kilkee

Dear Sir – Reading a letter in a recent issue of our paper prompted me to write on another aspect prevailing at Kilkee, namely, mixed bathing, and undressing on the strand. The visitor to Kilkee is told that mixed bathing will not be allowed on the strand. Can the Improvement Committee tell anyone where else female relatives can be taught to swim, except on the strand? I am going there every year and cannot find a place to teach swimming. I know several male friends who cannot get their wives to go out on the strand principally on account of this foolish restriction.

Another ridiculous bye-law is about the prohibition of undressing on the strand. Surely there would be no reason for this if the Committee provided sufficient decent bathing boxes. It is nothing unusual to hear of ladies waiting up to two hours for the use of one, and if every person was to use the battered wrecks there at present we would have plenty of moonlight bathing. Anyone undressing on the strand is not doing it from lack of modesty, but solely to get finished bathing as soon as possible.

I have no wish to discredit Kilkee – in fact I would not enjoy a holiday else-where – but now that there is such keen competition for visitors everywhere the Committee should be alive and strong and provide a portion of the strand where a man can teach a lady to swim.

Every year we hear of people going to the Isle of Man, Tramore, Youghal, and other seaside resorts and coming back with glowing accounts of how visitors are catered for there. You never hear the same of Kilkee. Surely there must be something wrong. Thanking your for insertion. – NEPTUNE. 1919.

Limerick's choosy women

Dear Sir – I would like to take this opportunity to write about women's attitudes to men at dance halls in the city. I have gone to a lot of dances in the Republic of Ireland and I have found Limerick to be the worst.

As I write this note I am in the balcony of a Limerick dance hall. As I look down I can see men asking women to dance, but only to get refused. One woman might say "Oh, he was drunk" – just because he had a little sweat on his forehead. All kinds of men were getting refused, regardless of looks.

I would like to ask the women of Limerick what they look for in a man when they go dancing, if they are not going to dance? I fully understand that a lot of people, both men and women, are allowed in dancing under the influence of drink, but this does not condemn them all.

The women of Limerick seem to think of themselves as all beauty queens the way they seem to pick through the men. Well, I can say from experience from going to dances in Ireland that Limerick women are no better than those of any other county. I think they are even lacking in certain things, such as manners and politeness. This I can say from having visited all of Limerick's leading dance halls.

I would like to finish up by giving two women's attitudes. I asked one why she had refused a good looking chap a dance. She replied: "I didn't like the song that was being played!" – a Limerick girl's attitude. I travelled to a nearby county and asked a good looking girl why she had not refused anyone a dance. Her reply was: "I came to enjoy myself, and one cannot be choosy these days."

I would like some more of these girls to come into Limerick and teach the city girls what dance halls are for.

R. WITHERS, 65 Portland Estate, Limerick. September 22, 1973.

Loyalists in Castletroy Golf Club

Dear Sir – New Year's Eve Night (1949) was a memorable one at Castletroy Golf Club. The diningroom, which is of spacious proportions, had been very artistically decorated for the occasion. A wireless set had been plugged in and all eyes and ears were centred on the "music box" a couple of minutes before midnight.

When "Auld Lang Syne" came on, members and visitors took to the floor and the ceremony of ushering in 1950 was brought to a close by "God Save the King." I would venture to state that Castletroy had the unique distinction on being "out on its own" in the Republic on this occasion by playing the "National Anthem" of the very small minority.

Are we going back into the dim and dismal past? Or is the spirit of Ireland dead in this club. Signed: "Your Putt, Sir." Jan. 1950.

Fishy Deel story

Dear Sir – In an article in "Records of Big Fish" in your issue of 7th inst., K.H. mentions a trout of $13\frac{1}{2}$lbs. caught in the River Deel in 1897. It seems a pity to spoil a good story but it is a genuine "fishy" one and many another man, including myself, has had his leg pulled. I knew Jack Studdart of Arleman very well – a boy of my own age at the time, and when I congratulated him a couple of days later he told me he thought he could get away with it.

If K.H. will refer to the record from which he culled this gem he will see it mentioned simply as "trout caught half a pound under a stone" and not $13\frac{1}{2}$ lbs. The stone is still in the River Deel! – W. J. MASSEY, Stoneville, Rathkeale, Co. Limerick. 7/3/'53.

Demolish King's John's Castle!

Dear Sir – I must request space in you valuable journal to express disagreement – I nearly said disgust – with the letters which have appeared in your columns in recent weeks objecting to the taking down of that old ramshackle called the Tholsel in Mary Street. I do not see the object of preserving that old building. We Irish are too sentimental, too prone to look at the past.

When the new Corporation has been elected, the first thing they should do is issue an order to have all such eyesores removed. For example, the authorities of St. Mary's Cathedral should be compelled to take down the front of the old Exchange and to substitute it with a nice ornamental railing.

I would also suggest that King John's Castle be demolished because the high walls prevent the air and sun from entering into the workingmen's dwellings inside them.

Then, as I am at it, I would propose the removal of the Treaty Stone. It is a menace to modern day traffic, and as all Irish statesmen are united in wishing to coax the Six Counties to join us, it is only like showing a red rag to a bull to flaunt it in front of Orangeman on visits here. Also it is an affront to English trippers, whom we are trying to encourage to come and visit, to confront them with an object of Saxon guile.

I do not wish to be taken as proposing that the Treaty Stone be destroyed but I do suggest that it be removed to some nice, retired spot like the Manchester Martyrs' Memorial where it would not be in the way of annoyance to anyone. – Yours indignantly, "PROGRESS." 29-8-1934.

Shortly after this satirical letter was published, the facade of the historic Tholsel in Mary Street, a building dating back to the time of the Viking era, was demolished by the Corporation. – Author.

Teddy Boys

Sir – I read with interest the letter from "Ratepayer" in last week's Leader and his criticism of the teddy boy menace in the city. I, personally, agree with everything he said and I have every reason to. I am a school girl, aged 16 years, and I have every reason to complain about these pests and their behaviour in our city streets.

I was returning home recently after school, accompanied by three girl chums, when we noticed a group of teddy boys assembled at a prominent street corner. As we were about to pass them they exchanged dirty remarks about us, accompanied by cat-calls and wolf whistles as we passed them. by. This is not the first time we have been insulted by these ruffians, who seem to own the street, as far as I can make out. I am sure if the people who lived in Edwardian days could only see their "off springs" of today they would turn in their graves with shame. Yours sincerely, "SCHOOL GIRL," May, 1960.

Humiliating Dues

I WOULD sincerely like to see the reading of Christmas and Easter dues from the altar being stopped. It is very humiliating and is a form of class distinction. It is very easy for a well-to-do person to give £10 and in contrast a poor person 50p. I came to Mass to hear the Word of God, not what Mr. or Mrs. gave to our clergy. I feel very strong about this all the time. I know it has been stopped in a lot of places. I should be treated in confidence and not read out for everyone to hear. Abolish this practice immediately and it is up to a person to give what he is able. JOHN O'ROURKE, Clogher East, Kilmallock. Jan. 1972.

'Leader' lashes
Noel Browne and 'Times'

In the May 5th, 1951, issue of the Leader, the editorial (Con Cregan was editor at the time), lashed into Noel Browne, who had just resigned as Minister for Health in the Coalition Government. The Minister had tried to introduce the Mother and Child Welfare Scheme which failed to get the imprimatur of the hierarchy.

The editorial thundered:

Dr. Noel Browne, late Minister for Health, is neither to be envied nor congratulated by his new admirers. By his defiance of the Bishops he has got applause that clearly should set him examining his conscience. He has at one stroke become the darling of every bigot, anti-cleric, and pro-Leftist in the country. Those who desire the continuance of Partition look upon him, too, as something of a heaven-sent deliverer.

Just after his resignation the ex-Minster said: "As a Catholic I accept the rulings of their Lordships, the Hierarchy, without question." But this is precisely what he stubbornly refused to do, and his mulish attitude in that connection made his resignation or his dismissal inevitable. Surely he must agree that the bishop had not merely the right but the duty to pronounce as they did. The course he took establishes that he either lacks sound balance of judgment or is in some way susceptible to influences for his good.

Many years have elapsed since the late Tim Healy denounced The Irish Times as "the bigot's dustbin". That paper deserves the appellation today just as it did then. In heart and spirit it is still the same as of old and it never misses an opportunity of having a fling or providing ample scope for someone else to have it at what it recently referred to as a "certain grey eminence" meaning the Catholic Church.

The Times, in something like a war-whoop of delight, commented "that the most serious revelation from what happened was that the Roman Catholic Church would seem to be the effective Government of this country."

For one thing, this shows that in this country there is an undesirable clique that could be very dangerous and which would need to be watched and countered. It also indicates that a certain amount of very bitter and unreasoning type exists here.

How fortunate this country is in having such an authoritative body as the Hierarchy to keep it right in matters concerning moral principles. In this connection it is worth remembering that the only stable and authentic institution the world has today for true guidance and direction is the Catholic Church.

This may not be very agreeable to the Irish Times or those for whom it speaks, but it is nevertheless an unassailable fact.

The empty chair

After sixteen years in League of Ireland football, Limerick A.F.C. won their first national trophy when annexing the League of Ireland Shield in 1953. There was justifiable pride in the achievement and a grand banquet was held in Cruise's Hotel with all branches of Limerick sport being invited and present. Except one. The G.A.A. During the course of the after dinner speeches, the soccer club was lauded on its great achievement with several of the speakers reiterating Limerick's proud place in the sporting map of the country. Chairman of the soccer club, Justice E. O Riain, in the course of his speech, said: "I am glad to say that we have here the representatives of all other sporting bodies in Limerick. There is one absentee whom I very much regret. My directors were very anxious that this function should be fully representative of all sections of sport in Limerick. With that end in view I sent, personally, a letter in Irish to the chairman of the Limerick County Board of the G.A.A.

"I posted the letter myself and it should have been delivered in the ordinary course of post last Monday. And as I did not receive it back, then I assumed that it must have been delivered. I regret that I did not receive a reply thereto. I regret very much the absence of the chairman of the Limerick County Board of the G.A.A. at this function because I feel that it would make this function fully representative of all sporting bodies if he had attended. As I have said, I regret his absence, but I don't think we could have done any more. We invited him, and we are sorry he did not attend."

Chairman of the County Board at the time was Canon Punch of Mungret. –Author.

William B. Fitt is one of the few Limerick firms that has done business in three different centuries. In 1926 they were advertising in the Leader the sale of the contents of Glenstal Castle following the departure of Sir Charles Barrington and his family to England.

Ranks social 1967.

Dromcollogher:
city of the dead

The greatest Limerick tragedy by far of the 20th century took place in Dromcollogher on Sunday, September 5th, 1926, when the final death toll from a catastrophic fire during the showing of a film in a local hall was to reach 48. "Between 50 and 60 presumed dead. Limerick Fire. Appalling West Limerick Calamity. Shocking Occurrence at Dromcollogher. Disastrous Blaze at Picture Performance" were some of the grim headlines the following day. The film being shown was Cecil B. de Mille's "The Ten Commandments"

Not alone Limerick and the country in general were shocked by the terrible tragedy, but the disaster made headlines throughout the world and elicited international sympathy. Amongst those who sent messages of condolences was the King of England, George V: "The Queen and I are distressed to hear of the terrible catastrophe in Dromcollogher, resulting in the grievous loss of life. Please assure the families of those have perished, and the injured, of our heart-felt sympathy on the affliction."

The hall in which the pictures were shown was situated in the centre of the village over a large general meal and flour store, the property of Mr. Patrick Brennan, merchant. The length of the room was 50 feet by 15 feet. The walls of the building were of stone, and that of the structure was composed of timber, which, on account of the summer weather, was in a highly inflammable condition. The roof was of corrugated iron. The only way of entering or leaving the hall was by means of a narrow wooden staircase, or ladder, on the outside of the building, which led to a doorway, which was 3 feet wide and 6 feet in height.

One of the main witnesses to the build-up of the tragedy was local civic guard, Sergeant Long who told a reporter that about a quarter of an hour after the performance started he observed a film on the table near the door to be ablaze. "There were several other films on the table and I extinguished one of the nearby candles and I made a grab at the blazing film and pulled it off the table. At that moment a civilian came rushing along and struck the blazing film with his cap which had the effect of spreading the flame and igniting the other films. Just then the alarm was raised and there was a stampede of the people in the hall towards the entrance which was a narrow door-way just three and a half feet. wide, with a stairs leading to the entrance."

Other witnesses recounted how when the film caught fire, there was a blaze, just like a flashlight. "The flames spread quickly and there was terrible panic, with many rushing for the only exit. This was closed and when it was opened many simply threw themselves down the stairs to the ground. Some man inside the hall shouted and said that everything would be alright, and that the people

Mourners say farewell to the Dromcollogher fire victims.

should get back to the rear of the hall. Those who took his advice were soon cut off from the only exit.

"Many made it to the safety, but the terrible heat now added to the trials of those remaining. There were trapped as far as that exit was concerned, and in their fury to escape turned their attention towards the windows. Men and women and children were thrown down in this rush and trampled on. Men fought wildly for the windows. Those that could wrenched the bars from their fastenings, but, after all, only a small number succeeded in saving their lives in this way."

Many of the victims, particularly children, were trampled in the panic and mad rush for the door, with many more trapped in the fire, which quickly took hold of the wooden floor which eventually collapsed, and cut off any means of escape.

There were many scenes of heroism during the rescue attempts, not least Thomas Buckley, an ex-school teacher, who helped many people to escape but who himself perished in the flames, as did James Quaid in the same circumstances.

Fr. O'Callaghan, C.C., St. Patrick's, Limerick, later the Bishop's secretary, lost his mother in the fire and Rev. Bro. Brendan O.F.M., suffered a devastating loss when both his brothers, their wives, and two of their children died.

Some families were practically wiped out in the tragedy (all from Dromcollogher), and these included Jeremiah Buckley, N.T., (brother of above mentioned Thomas), his wife, daughter Bridie, and servant Norah Kirwin; Mrs. Joan Barrett and her two children; Mrs. Daniel Collins and her daughter Kitty; Mrs. Daniel Fitzgerald, her son and daughter; Mrs. Florence McAuliffe, her son and daughter. Mrs. Jeremiah O'Brien, and her daughter Nellie; Mrs. Turner and her two daughters.

Another victim was a London-Irish girl, Nora Mary Hannigan, aged eleven, who was visiting relations with her mother in Ireland. The *Star* reported that her father, when he received a telegram stating "come at once, Nora is dying", lapsed into unconsciousness and it was several hours before he could be revived. A neighbour said that Nora was the prettiest little thing "with the sweetest manner I have ever known, with a glorious mass of deep auburn hair."

For those lucky enough to escape (there was approximately 150 attending the performance) and the spectators who watched helplessly at the raging inferno, it was an experience of traumatic dimensions as the heartrending cries of despair of those trapped could be clearly heard above the crackling of the flames.

Reports on the burial of the victims (two more were to succumb to their injuries) in the churchyard of St. Bartholmew, said that there was scarcely a house in the locality that had not lost someone. "Dromcollogher presented the appearance of the city of the dead. People find it impossible to realise the awfulness of it" said the report.

The President of the Free State, Mr. Cosgrave, attended the Requiem Mass that morning, the celebrant being the Bishop of Limerick, Most Rev. Dr. Keane. When the bishop asked the congregation to kneel down with him in prayer for the victims, many broke down and sobbed uncontrollably.

At the inquest which followed the tragedy, the jury recorded that "We find that all the persons who lost their lives in the cinema fire of Sunday night, September 5th, did so from asphyxia and burning caused by a lighted candle falling on the exposed films on the table, which ignited the hall. We find that the operator, Mr. Dowling, was guilty of negligence in having the films exposed on the table, and we find that there was carelessness on the part of Mr. Forde in having a lighted candle on the table. We tender to the bereaved relatives our heartfelt sympathy and pray God to give them strength to bear their affliction."

The fire was the subject of editorials in all the dailies, with the Irish Independent stating "There are some things too deep for words. This thing must never happen again," while the Cork Examiner was quoted: "The tragedy is a sad reminder of the urgent necessity for some better system of regulating and licensing cinema halls."

The Daily Telegraph commented: "Sympathy in face of such an over-

The burnt-out shell of the grain store under the hall in which the fire occurred.

whelming horror will certainly be evoked from all corners of the world. By establishing its melancholy pre-eminence as the scene of the most far-reaching cinema disaster ever suffered in these Islands, Dromcollogher has won for itself a tragic kind of fame. We may hope at the same time that this fire, by its very frightfulness, will burn into the minds of local authorities even in the most remotest rural districts the imperative necessity of taking stringent precautions where cinema performances are licensed There are some things too deep for words, too deep even for tears. This thing must never happen again."

At the conclusion of the inquest proceedings, the Guards took Forde and Downing into custody, and with the owner of the hall, Patrick Brennan, were charged with manslaughter. At the Central Criminal Court in Dublin, on Friday, December 15th, the jury returned a verdict in which they found Brennan not guilty, but could not agree in the case of Forde and Downing. They were acquitted later.

A relief fund was opened almost immediately and one of the first to contribute the then substantial sum of £100 was Will Rogers, the famous American, described as the highest paid entertainer in the world, who was playing in London. He also offered to come to Dublin to take part in an entertainment in aid of the victims, a suggestion which was acted upon. On Wednesday September, 10, he appeared with the No. 4 Army Band and Miss

May Doyle, soprano, in La Scala Theatre, Dublin, and £400 was raised from an attendance estimated to be 2,500.

Other early contributors to the relief fund included the President, Mr. Cosgrave (£75), Jameson & Co. (£250), and the Jam Sahib of Nawanagar (£200). When the fund closed the following year, December, 1927, over £16,000 had been donated for the relief of the dependants of the disaster. The total number of children left dependent amounted to 53. "Out of the funds, a Celtic Cross will be erected over the graves of the victims and a modest sum will be set aside for annual Masses for the repose of the souls of deceased, all of whom were Catholics," the report concluded.

A sad addendum to the tragedy appeared in the Leader in 1929, written by the Newcastle West correspondent:

"Rumour has it that the man who was more or less responsible for the terrible disaster in Dromcollogher had died, under tragic circumstances somewhere in the Australian backwoods. His life was tragic and a little sympathy must be felt for the unwitting medium of the terrible holocaust.

"His mind must have been in a terrible state of unrest at the thought of the sorrow that was caused through his honest attempt to make a living, which in other ways, might be denied him. He was not capable of holding his own where muscle and sinew and bone was needed. In life he had sympathy; in death he will have a prayer, even from those who suffered terrible sorrow because of him innocent instrument of fate."

By extraordinary coincidence, fifty-five years later the same amount of victims who died in Dromcollogher (48), perished in the Stardust fire in Dublin.

Dr. Keane, Bishop of Limerick, blessing the coffins.

Limerick's 1931 wedding of the year

"No social event of recent years in Limerick was the occasion of great a display of public interest, or so remarkable a manifestation of popular goodwill."

So opened the report of the wedding of Thomas E. O'Donnell, solicitor, and Miss Margaret Doris Roberts, only daughter of Dr. James Roberts, at St. Joseph's Church, in September, 1931.

The report went on to say:

The marriage of this youthful couple was not only an event of interest to the families immediately concerned; somehow or other the general public fastened on to the occasion for an expression of the sentimental and romantic ideals that, at whatever age, lie deep down in all of us.

The youthfulness of the pair, their remarkably good looks; apart from either of these blessings, their popularity: all combined in striking the imagination of the public.

Long before the bridegroom, blond and handsome, arrived at the church, every seat in the edifice was packed. As the bride, beautiful and gracious, accompanied by her father, passed up the aisle, a subdued murmur of admiration went through the congregation.

Outside many hundreds of well-wishers and spectators had witnessed the arrival of bridegroom and bride. Here was the ideal wedding, and every youthful heart, and many an aged one, thrilled to the occasion. Mr. W. L. O'Donnell was best man; Miss Creina Byrne, cousin of the bride, and Miss Paula O'Donnell, sister of the bridegroom, were bridesmaids.

The tremendous interest taken in the city in the happy event was manifested in the huge crowds which attended the ceremony. No more remarkable demonstration of goodwill has been witnessed in Limerick for many a year.

The bride was dressed in oyster satin with a head dress of pearls and orange blossoms, and she wore a long tulle veil. The bridesmaids wore blue and beige, with velvet caps.

After the ceremony, the bride and groom left the church with the benisons, spoken and unspoken, of everyone who was present.

The bridegroom was a well-known figure in Irish rowing, having stroked the Limerick Boat Club Senior Eight to the highest honours, that of the Senior Eights Championship of Ireland. Members, as a token of esteem to their popular captain and stroke, formed a guard of honour with their oars.

Curraghchase: the burning of a mansion

On Saturday, December 20th, 1941, the three residents of Curraghchase House, Kildimo, had retired for the night. The trio were Mrs. Isobel de Vere, widow of Robert Stephen de Vere, and her two maids. The magnificent residence, described as one of the finest in the country, was home in the previous century to the poet, Aubrey de Vere, whose family had been in possession for 200 years. Among the many notables who had visited the mansion was the poet Tennyson, who had stayed there for a five week duration.

At about 1.40 a.m. the electric bells in the mansion went off and roused the sleeping occupants. On investigation it was found that a fire that emanated in the library had taken hold and the three occupants were forced to flee for their lives.

The flames quickly caught a grip on the building and the conflagration

Joan de Vere and her husband Martin Wynne-Jones in happier days when the mansion (background) was fully functional.

spread rapidly. Neighbours and estate workers ran to help but they were powerless in the face of the terrible blaze. The report went on: "Rivulets of flames spread with baffling rapidity through the ground floor and aided by a strong wind quickly shot up to the other storeys. Tongues of fire were soon licking at the roof and smoke was billowing through the windows, the whole conflagration throwing a blood-red glare across the night sky.

"Within a short time the whole building was engulfed in a searing mass of roaring flames and clouds of smoke. The roof, alight from end to end, collapsed with a rending of timbers amidst showers of sparks and falling debris."

Further graphic descriptions of the fire went on to say that it was 4 a.m. when the Limerick Fire Brigade finally arrived on the scene and by that stage the residence was completely afire. It was found that there was no water supply available except the pipe-line in the house which had already been cut off. Helpless in face of this unexpected contingency, the brigade members directed their efforts to salvaging what articles of furniture that could be removed with safety from the ground floors.

The Rathkeale cor. wrote: "Priceless art treasures and many antiques and articles of historic value were among the valuables lost in the fire. These included an ivory chess table once owned by Marie Antoinette and a massive statue of Moses, said to be one of only two to be found in the whole world.

"Scores of people from the surrounding districts came on Sunday to view with evident regret the smouldering walls which were all that remains of the historic mansion. Sincere sympathy goes out to Mrs. de Vere, who is a most charitable and kindly woman, and who has done much to alleviate distress in the area as she has been most generous in giving poor people free access to her woods to obtain firing."

The original owner of Curraghchase was Vere Hunt, an officer in the Cromwellian Army. This name remained unchanged until a descendant, Aubrey de Vere, the most famous of that family, assumed by royal licence the surname and arms of de Vere.

Aubrey had left a poignant recollection of the mansion: "My earliest recollections are of our Irish home, Curraghchase, and I always see it bathed in the summer sunshine. It was not once as it is now. At the bottom of the lawn there now spreads a lake, but at that time it was rich meadowland divided by a slender stream with fair green hills beyond.'

The facade of Curraghchase House, the skeleton of a once great mansion.

JUNE 2, 1926

A FIRST CLASS SERVICE

All Orders receive personal supervision from the Proprietor, and nothing is overlooked in Quality, Economy and efficiency. A first class service is afforded by

CHRISTOPHER THOMPSON,

40 THOMAS STREET, AND 43 ROCHE'S STREET,

TEL - 272   ## LIMERICK.

Thompson's Funeral Undertakers were founded in 1909 at 43 Roche's Street and in 1922 moved to its present site at 40 Thomas Street. On the death of the founder, Christopher, in 1961, his son Frank, who had joined the firm in 1938, took over as managing director and with his son John has carried on the great tradition since.

When dancing was an occasion of sin

The import of foreign dancing to the country in the 1920's and 30's was the cause of much comment, particularly from the clergy. The Bishop of Limerick, Most Rev. Dr. Keane, writing to the adm. of St. Michael's Church in Limerick, said he had been much surprised at reports of extraordinary happenings at a public dance hall recently. "They recall rather the revels of pagan Bacchantes rather than the proceedings of a Christian community. There is an increasing danger of the demoralisation of our people and it is time the law was invoked. Public opinion must express itself in no uncertain fashion and heads of families must not allow any of their families to attend the places of entertainment concerned. The old penalty of social ostricisation might be applied to the owners of the hall."

Dr. Keane, Bishop of Limerick.

In 1925 the Rathkeale cor. cast derision on local fox trot dancers, saying that not satisfied with wriggling on the dance floor like a rattlesnake or sick monkey, the latest fashion is to puff smoke into your partner's face while the band plays "Doodle Doo Doo" or "Booby Boo Boo".

The cor. went on to say that some little snobs act in this manner just to show their contempt for a gathering to which they would not bring their own sisters or sweethearts. "There was a time we had in Ireland women − real women − who would not hesitate putting these 'dalteens' across their knee and administering a well deserved spanking," the irate cor. concluded.

A paragraph headed, "Evil Dance" revealed a lively gathering in Sligo in the 1930's. "The assembly that took place on this night was nothing better than a saturnalia" said Judge Gleeson at Sligo Circuit Court, in giving a judgment in a case for assault in 1933 which arose out of a dance at Muingwar, Co. Sligo. It was stated that practically all the 200 people at the dance were under the influence of drink.

In the early 1950's, a rather bemused Chronicle correspondent wrote to say that as yet, he has not quite assured himself that he participated in a gyration entitled "the Hokey-Pokey", which a large gathering indulged in at the TWA dance in Cruise's Hotel, and appeared to thoroughly enjoy.

"This import from the jungle of South Africa has a terrific vogue at the moment, and for sheer paganism it outdoes the 'Conga.' It was alright to have people insisting that you put your left foot in and your right foot out and in the interim, shake them all about, but at least one dancer refused flatly to put his left hip in and his left hip out – not even to please a very charming partner. However, the function was a great success."

Films and plays also came under scrutiny from the "Vigilantes", an *ad hoc* group formed to guard the morals of the citizens, with some instances of films being burned publicly. The most celebrated case was the play, "Biddy" at the Lyric which had to be taken off after two nights (see separate story page 73)

Following Bishop Edward Thomas O'Dwyer's death in 1917, his successor, Dr. Hallinan, was just barely installed when he took up the cudgel on his perceived immorality of films. His complaint was that an announcement of a film taken of his ordination, "Episcopal Ordination of Most Rev. Dr. Hallinan" was wedged between two sensational titles of pictures "in an adv. of a place of amusement (not named), the location and proprietor of which was unknown to me."

Bristling with indignation, the bishop decried using the film of the ordination as a means of making money, "thus gathering in the coppers of the curious and thoughtless." But it was from the moral viewpoint that Dr. Hallinan reserved his main broadside:

"The consecration of a bishop is one of the most solemn and sublime of the religious functions of the Catholic Church. I need not dwell on what certain sensational titles of films symbolise. Anything better calculated to lower the religious and moral tone of the spectators of this entertainment than his combination of piety with profanity, of sublimity with vulgarity, it is hard to imagine. And this is the kind of pabulum with which the minds of the rising generation of Irish boys and girls are being daily fed in these institutions called picture palaces.

"I would wish that the managers of the schools in the city visit their respective schools and warn the children against patronising them and I request the clergy to use all their opportunities, in the pulpit and confession, to explain to the people the dangers connected with them."

Record salmon at Castleconnell

The Chronicle in 1902 carried a report of a monster salmon landed by rod and line by Mr. F. Milburn on the Doonass stretch near Castleconnell. The fish, reported to be fresh-run from the sea, was 50 inches in length and 30 inches in girth. The verified weight was 54 lbs. and was claimed to have been the heaviest salmon landed by rod and line on the Shannon.

The cor. added that the national record was held by Michael Maher who on the Suir in 1874 landed a salmon of 57 lbs. in weight. His lure was a fly which he had tied with various feathers gathered in a nearby farmyard.

A report from Castleconnell in the 1920's showed the wonderful salmon fishing which was quickly drawing to a close with the advent of the Shannon Scheme and the consequent lowering of the water levels of the river. General Corry killed two salmon at Newgarden, 32 and 35 lb.; on Prospect, Colonel Leathem one, 20 lb.; on Doonass, Major W. Gough, six, 40, 12, 30, 14, 14, 22l b.; on Worldsend, Colonel Roche-Kelly, one, 20 lb.

What was stated to be a record salmon captured in nets in the Upper Shannon was landed by the Abbey Fishermen in 1925. The fish, which was captured at Corbally, weighed in at 62 lbs. and was displayed at Mrs. McInerney's fish store in Lock Quay. It was put hanging outside the front door and elicited no amount of curiosity from passers-by.

The good old days in Castleconnell . . . playing a salmon that weighed in at 43 lbs.; no names given of the anglers or gillies on the postcard.

A remarkable West Limerick woman

On Holy Thursday, 1938, there occurred the death of a remarkable woman named Nellie Doody. A native of Tournafulla but who spent her last decade in Abbeyfeale, many stories have been told of the amazing piety of the deceased especially of her self-mortification and her extraordinary perpetuation of pilgrimages to holy wells.

One of the stories, related by the Abbeyfeale correspondent shortly after Nellie's death, concerned a woman who lived near the holy well at Killenagh, a few miles from Abbeyfeale. Seemingly one of her best cows became hopelessly stuck in a marsh and neighbours found it impossible to rescue her. Seeing Nellie approach the well on one of her customary pilgrimages, the owner of the cow ran towards her and begged her to pray to Our Lady that the cow might be saved. Nellie only said: "You must be pleased whatever is God's will." So saying, she knelt down to say an Ave and before she was finished the cow withdrew from the swamp unassisted.

In her younger days Nellie worked as a farm servant but getting on in life, and in poor health, she was no longer able to work and lived on the kindness of her friends, most of them poor. She never stayed long with any of them and then tried to repay their kindness afterwards.

Most of her life was spent in mortification and she spent most of the day and night in prayer. She was a daily communicant, refused to eat any flesh meat, and never broke her fast before 12 noon each day. Her mind seemed to be in constant touch with the location and atmosphere of the ancient Irish monastic institutions and keeping them alive seemed to be an important part of her life's mission.

She generally went barefoot and any boots, clothes, money or food she got were given away to those whom nobody knew better than she were most in need of them. A woman who once gave her a pair of boots enquired when Nellie wasn't wearing them, what happened them. Nellie replied that there was a poor widow who badly wanted a pair of boots to go to Mass and she gave them to her.

She lived a life of severe self-denial and mortification, although it was easy to perceive from the pale, sallow appearance and languid movements that she was anything but physically well. Often in this weakened condition she would walk miles on pilgrimage to wells and shrines in bitter, cold, weather, and in her bare feet. She slept but little in the humble homes where the people did what they could to make her few hours amongst them comfortable, but comfort was not for Nellie. Because she usually spent a good part of the night in prayer, she generally elected only such places where she knew this devotion of hers would not be resented, or any disturbance her prayers might cause.

At night-time, the deceased would walk for miles in the countryside for no other reason that she considered the privilege of attending Mass in the morning required some little sacrifice.

She was buried in Teampall na Glantine Cemetery on Good Friday, 1938, in a plot donated by the parish priest, Rev. John Kelly.

"Her whole life was wholly absorbed in the one idea of serving God in her every action and the world about her supplied her only with occasions for further self-denial and mortification," the cor. concluded.

An old style bedroom suite which could be had from McCarthy's, Thomas Street, in 1950. The firm is the oldest surviving business in Limerick, having been established in 1830.

Carry-on at the Markets Field

The rugby correspondent in 1927 (M.J.M.) said he had many complaints from different patrons of the Markets Field about the growing commercial and musical enterprises that were taking place in the stand. He stated "that it is rather depressing to have to open one's weekly notes with an invective on an old disease, but so many spectators have come to me complaining about the carry on in the stands that I must bring the clubs' attention to it."

One man complained: "At the recent match between Garryowen and Young Munster which I attempted to view from the stand I had to put up with a banjo solo, a fiddle trio, a ballad entitled 'The Dingle Puck Goat' a banjo duet, a melodeon entr'acte, and a persuasion to purchase two different species of apples.

"In between these delightful interludes I saw some snatches of rugby, but until some effort is made to make rugby matches purely games and not amateur talent contests or musicians and monologue merchants, I am not attending.

"The general trend of the other spectators remarks goes to prove that the programme of musical interest presently being offered are not a huge success, and we must again ask the clubs to either omit the present programme or else to introduce honest vaudeville, or, for instance, the Army No. 2 Band, to distract the spectators.

"And while we are at it, another correspondent states that the barbed wire is as effective as ever, and so much balls are being punctured that he is thinking of taking shares in a football factory".

The victorious Munster team being cheered off the field after their historic win over the All-Blacks in 1978.

Mother Teresa
refuses honour

In May 1993, Mother of Teresa of Calcutta refused the freedom of the city of Limerick. The world famous Nobel Peace Laureate would not accept the honour because the matter had become political amongst city councillors.

Willie O'Dea had made the offer on behalf of the Corporation but as the decision had to be unanimous, there was controversy in the Council on the matter.

Co-ordinator of the nun's visit to Limerick was Nora Bennis, who stated: "It is diabolical for Limerick. They (the city council) need to explain to the public what has happened. It is not up to me to say," she added.

In turn, Mrs. Bennis was criticised for the £10 fee which was being charged to those who wanted to see Mother Teresa in the Limerick Inn. "We have world renowned speakers including Mother Teresa addressing the conference and the £10 is just to cover costs," she said. A report said that people of little means who wished to see Mother Theresa could not afford the £10 or the price of the taxi to the Limerick Inn.

As it transpired, Mother Teresa's visit was cancelled because of a fall she received a few days beforehand, in which she broke three ribs.

Ironically, the City Council decided to go ahead with the granting of the Freedom of the City to Mother Teresa and in a meeting which only lasted two minutes, Mayor John Quinn proposed the motion and Cllrs. Frank Prendergast and Cllr. Gus O'Driscoll jointly seconded.

Queried whether or not those who paid £10 to attend a conference, at which Mother Teresa was to be the guest speaker, would get their money back, Mrs. Bennis replied: "It was made quite clear to people who paid the £10 that it was a conference fee, not money to see Mother Teresa. Anyway, it is not a matter for the Limerick Leader to be probing whether or not people who wanted their money back, would receive it," she sniffed.

Nora, a member of the Solidarity and Women Working at Home Movement, was in the news again when in January, 1995, she called for a boycott of the sex shop, Utopia, about to open in Ellen Street. "I would encourage people to boycott this filth." She put the question to Mr. Bellamy, the shop's owner: "Will he guarantee there will be no more rape inside and outside marriage?" Mr. Bellamy replied that his shop didn't sell sex, it sold adult toys and no-one under 21 was admitted.

The shop opened on Monday January 15, without any protest, but Nora and the Solidarity movement confirmed that they were conducting a 24 hour fast and day of prayer in their homes "so that the shop will fold up as quickly as possible."

She added: "As the Lord said, there are some evils so diabolical that only prayer and fasting will get rid of them."

Reporters and photographers waited patiently for the first Utopian customer to arrive but were disappointed when no-one showed up: there were no early morning callers. "We are not going to have too many people coming in with you lot around," said Mr. Bellamy. Gardai called to view the premises and were satisfied that the law was not being broken.

The previous month Nora was in trouble with Fianna Fail's Jack Bourke, who described her criticism of Bertie Ahern's first public appearance with his partner, Celia Larkin, "as looking for cheap publicity." Nora had stated that "Mr. Ahern, as a public figure, had a responsibility to reflect the ethos of the nation. People of this nation clearly stand by the bond of Christian marriage," she stated.

1940 # A NEW PIANO FOR £5!

This was in 1940, and sixty years on, Savins are still giving good value for money.

Royal wedding in Limerick

"Hundreds of viewers watch British Royal Wedding in Limerick" was the heading in the Leader in May 1960. The occasion was the wedding of Princess Margaret and Mr. Anthony Armstrong-Jones and while the age of television had dawned, it had yet to come Limerick way except for a few electrical shops who managed to show some pictures from the BBC.

"Hundreds of necks were craned in Patrick Street, Bedford Row and Upper William Street today to view television sets, placed in the windows of different shops, in efforts to catch glimpses of the royal wedding.

"The reception at times was fairly good and viewers were able to see portions of the procession from Westminster Abbey. The majority of viewers, strangely enough, were men, but the women had taken over the major vantage points. At least two dozen women kept watching continuously throughout the morning and up to lunch-time their shopping bags were still empty. In Bedford Row the viewers graciously made way for an old lady who expressed a desire to see the wedding 'of her princess' ".

London was en fete for the occasion and there were remarkable scenes of enthusiasm as the procession passed by.

There was general excitement the following year throughout the city and county with the opening of Telefis Eireann, the first television station in the country. On Sunday, December 31, 1961, President de Valera broadcast to the nation and officially inaugurated the service. Few households had purchased TV sets, "biding their time" to see how things went. Consequently, hundreds of people gathered round the windows of a number of electrical firms in the city on New Year's Eve to watch history being made.

"Talk of the Town" was complaining in 1963 that the news programmes were too much Dublin orientated and sniffed that Dickie Rock's wedding was shown while Brendan Bowyer's ("an international star") was not.

Diana you were wonderful

Record queues formed at Limerick City Hall in September, 1997, to sign the condolence book as a mark of respect on the death of Princess Diana, who died in a car crash in Paris. A second book had eventually to be opened in an attempt to alleviate the queues. "Diana you were wonderful;" "we will miss you Diana" were some of the poignant signatures in the books.

Laura Moore, of Murroe, who "idolised " the late Princess and who had a roomful of souvenirs of Diana, was extremely saddened. "She hugged everyone, from the old to the very young. She could chat to a super star one night and the next day talk to homeless teenagers in London. If she found something funny, she would giggle. When she was sad she would cry," she said.

"I started my scrapbook collection back in 1981 when Diana and Charles got engaged. It was my intention to follow her progress from being Lady Diana to her one day becoming the Queen of England."

The Princess had been described as "the queen of people's hearts," and a Corbally man was on a business trip to London when the news broke. "I went down to Kensington Palace where there was so much flowers that the smell hit you right away. It was overpowering. It was very silent, everybody was soft spoken. Candles were burning but nobody sang songs or hymns, they were just in a state of shock. The atmosphere was very eerie, but very moving," he said.

Parteen historian Donal O Riain had a letter from his friend in Chicago P. J. O'Dea, who had met the Princess in Chicago the previous year and had received a letter from the Princess before she lost her title: "The Princess will forever hold deep affection for all the people she met and the many who waited to greet her. Her Royal Highness sends you her love and very best wishes."

Limerickman Jim O'Brien, manager of Jurys, was in Paris at the time of the princess' death and described the atmosphere around the scene of the accident of very sombre and awfully sad.

Patricia Fehilly wrote: "Throughout the county and city this week, people have been expressing shock and sadness for the woman whose dazzling beauty, elegance and simple humanity transcended all our anti-monarch feelings."

A 1950's Glin Castle Wedding with the bride, Miss Rachael G. FitzGerald, younger daughter of the late Knight of Glin, and Madame FitzGerald. Bridegroom was Mr. Michael M. W. Severne and best man was Mr. Timothy Parker; bridesmaids: the Hon. Fiola FitzGerald, Lady Rose Blyth, Miss Susan Dennis, the Hon. Melissa Wyndham-Quin; train bearer the Hon. Amanda Birken.

Tragedy in St Mary's Park

There were huge headlines in local newspapers on January 23, 1960, announcing the death of five members of a family in St. Brendan Street, St. Mary's Park. "Death of five in City family due to carbon monoxide," was the grim heading announcing the deaths of Mrs. Mary O'Donoghue and her four children from fumes from a burning fire in the grate. Three of the family survived, including the father, James, children Geraldine and Annette, and they were being treated in Barrington's Hospital.

At the inquest Mary Markham of St. Munchin Street said she was sent for about 1.50 a.m. and when Jimmy O'Donoghue answered the door after the third knock I asked him what was wrong and he could not talk but just muttered "upstairs" and I helped him to the front bedroom. There were five children in the bed with the mother, Mary, in a kneeling position at the foot of the bed but I could not say whether she was dead or alive. She felt quite cold.

"There was a cot beside the bed and the baby, Frances, was dead in the cot. Geraldine was at the foot of the bed beside the window. She was alive but appeared to be very dizzy. Patrick was next to her and he also was dead. Angela was on the other side of the bed and was alive. On the inside of the bed at the top was James, and Marion was on the outside of him. Both were dead.

"The husband James was in a daze and kept repeating "Mary, Mary, Mary." Fr. O'Connor arrived and Jimmy and the two surviving children were taken in his car to hospital."

The findings of the post mortem revealed that death was due to carbon monoxide from the fumes of the banked-up coal fire, which had been burning in the bedroom grate. Dr. Hickey, State Pathologist, said the children were well fed and well nourished. A rider was added by the jury at the inquest that the Corporation examine the chimney and if necessary, other chimneys in the housing scheme.

It was reckoned that 10,000 attended the funeral in St Mary's and there were unprecedented scenes of grief when the coffins were put into the three horse-drawn hearses and many people were seen to weep openly. Three of the coffins of the children were covered with swansdown and they lay side by side in the third hearse. Blinds in business houses and private houses were drawn as a mark of respect and thousands lined the route of the funeral to the cemetery. Canon Patrick J. Lee was celebrant at the Requiem Mass and he also officiated at the graveside. Amongst the public representative attending were the Mayor, Ald. John Carew, T.D., and many other public representatives.

Ald. Steve Coughlan was writing to the Mayor calling for a special meeting of all public bodies with a view to launching a testimonial fund for Mr. O'Donoghue and his two surviving children.

The statues that moved a nation

The mid-eighties saw the start of the moving statues syndrome. First off the mark was Ballinspittle in Co. Cork and like the country at large, bus loads of curious travellers from all over Limerick made the journey down with many reporting back that they had seen the statue moving and more startling claims that other saints could also be seen with her.

In August, 1985, reports came in from Mountcollins that a statue of the Blessed Virgin had been seen to move. In the following months there were reports of the same phenomenon coming from Cahermoyle and Manister.

Many people from the county and Clare travelled to Limerick to view the statue at Garryowen, near the Markets Field, following reports that some people had seen blood coming from one of the hands of Our Lady. The Rosary was recited several times each night as hundreds converged on the shrine. There was an unconfirmed report that a young lad in a wheel chair jumped out in front of the shrine shouting "I'm cured, I'm cured,' which caused great excitement. It was found out later that it was a hoax and that he and his pal had borrowed the wheelchair in order to perpetrate the hoax.

In the county, Foynes was one of the top attractions when it was reported that Our Lady's statue had been observed moving. Cratloe was also proving a huge draw with crowds visiting the shrine there and reports of people having seen movement. Cahermoyle and Manister, two of the first to report the phenomenon, drew constant crowds of believers, and the curious.

The Prior of the Dominicans in Limerick, Very Rev. Killian Dwyer, said that the attitude of the Church to the phenomenon of moving statues bordered on the "sceptical." "These alleged happenings had a tendency in provoking numberless counterfeit imitations. As soon as one incident is reported, another is recorded elsewhere, triggering off a reaction that tends to escalate to the confusion and bewilderment of ordinary people," he said. Fr. Matt O'Shea of the Oblate Monastery at Cahermoyle said he "was impressed by the extreme reverence and goodness of people praying there."

A Leader Editorial said the alleged sightings "tended to trivialise religion in the media and amongst the community and have yet to be supported by established fact. The case has yet to be tried let alone proved."

A Blackpool man, John D. Vose, however, was a believer, and spent months touring the country and interviewing people and said he himself had a strange experience in Kilfinane Church when he saw the Statue of Our Lady change into the agonised face of Christ. He also claimed that children in the village playing football "saw a vision in the sky, with several different colours," and got their mothers' permission to talk to them. "I believe in it implicitly."

He said he had great faith in Our Lady and added: "I am not a religious crank or do-goodie. I like my pint. I do not believe any of the people I interviewed were having me on." He said he would be publishing a book, "The Statues That Moved a Nation" in the near future.

Golf in Ballybunion:
50p a round

Spartacus, in the Leader on April, 1972, said he had met a very angry golfer and part of his anger was based on the assumption that Good Friday is not a Bank Holiday.

But the powers that be in Lahinch Golf Club said it was.

It appears that he went with a party of golfers to Lahinch on Good Friday to have a round of golf, with the green fees that are chargeable on Bank Holidays, Saturdays and Sundays being demanded, and incidentally, had to be paid.

The normal green fees charged at Lahinch are £1 on weekdays and £1.50 on Saturdays, Sundays and Bank Holidays. So, if Good Friday is, in fact, what is generally accepted as a Bank Holiday, he would appear to have no grouse at all.

On the other hand, this golfer told me that another group of golfers went to Ballybunion on the same day – and he reminded me that Ballybunion is rated as one of the best golf links in the world – and the members of that second party were only charged green fees of 50p!

He has sworn that Lahinch has seen the last of him and his numerous golfing friends as a result of the charge, and that in future they will all head to Co. Kerry links at Ballybunion, where, he considers, they have a much better idea of the fitness of things. As one who is aware of the amount that the tourism interests in Lahinch have done over the years to entice visitors to their locality, it surprises me that they were not more circumspect in their handling of that group of golfers, an immense amount of propaganda if it is be counteracted effectively in some sporting circles.

As a result, the Ballybunion Links should have a noticeable increase in the number of golfing visitors from this area during the coming season. And good luck to them.

The man who closed Ferenka

It was Mr. Nobody who did it! It was Mr. Nobody who closed Ferenka. Don't blame me. Don't blame the piano player. It certainly wasn't us. And surely that changes everything.

The cry is on the lips of the citizens. "Remember Ferenka". We should never be allowed to forget it that is for certain. I can still hear the cheers echoing around the Savoy. "We won't go back unless this, and that, and the other. Hurrah!"

"If they don't like it they can damn well close Feranka," someone declared, and hundreds of production workers cheered. They damn well did close Ferenka but I don't hear all the brave words and resounding cheers now.

"We will see this thing through to the bitter end," one of the union officials declared to the strikers. Well that official was as good as his word. We have now discovered what the bitter end is. And now we have to live with it.

When they (the whole lot of them did their bit in this dispute) found out that they had closed it they all looked at each other and wondered. There was an almighty clamour by everybody to explain how the plant could have been kept open and how if someone else did this thing and that thing it would never have had to close.

Well, I hope they are all happy now. Everyone stood by their principles. All those involved still have their honour. What a victory for everyone.

The union officials still have their jobs. The ENKA people still have their jobs. But thousands – many of whom were not even directly involved but were in the service industries – have lost their jobs.

We have taken millions of pounds, which the IDA put into the plant on our behalf, along with the £7 million which came into the region each year, and thrown it away.

They can say what they like. In the end, Ferenka is gone. Limerick has once again shown the world that it is a pitiable place devoid of intelligent life.

It is the innocent people who have been deprived of their livelihoods whom I feel sorry for. What kind of idiots are we at all? - SPARTACUS, L.L. 19-12-1977.

Ferenka, the tyre-cord manufacturing plant near Annacotty, opened in 1970 and became the scene of constant friction, especially between the different unions. At one stage, there was actually two strikes in progress at the one time. The factory eventually closed in 1977 with the loss of 1,400 jobs. – Author.

Greyhound in the bed!

At a meeting of the Clare County Board of Health in 1924 the chairman, Mr. J. D. Moloney, stated that he had paid a visit to the County Home at Ennis two days previously, and found a greyhound in a patient's bed in the harmless lunatic ward close by the fire. Lunatic attendant Flynn was called before the Board, and admitted that the greyhound found in the patient's bed belonged to him. He regretted that it had occurred and promised that it would not occur again, and that he would abide by the regulations.

Mr. McMahon said there were so many dogs about the hospital that you would need an extra attendant for them.

Mr. Kelly: Call it the Dogs' Home. The chairman added that he had also found that the linen had not been changed in the beds of the consumptive ward for four weeks and in the same ward he had found that dirty conditions existed. The place was filthy.

Mr. Kenny said that the house used to be like a first-class hotel but it was now in a shocking state, and required to be overhauled from top to bottom. There was so much red tape however that he supposed it would take a long time to effect reforms.

Chairman: Red tape is not responsible for greyhounds taking over a patient's bed.

LIMERICK LEADER, SATURDAY, JANUARY 19, 1940

DE COURCY'S SALES.

COUNTY OF LIMERICK.
MUNGRET.
SALE OF OUTSTANDING IMPORTANCE OF THE LICENSED PREMISES AND ADJOINING LANDS, KNOWN AS

"QUILLIGAN'S," MUNGRET,
ADJOINING THE LIMERICK CEMENT FACTORY,
To be offered for Sale by Public Auction
AT THE SALESROOMS, 7, GLENTWORTH STREET, LIMERICK,
On FRIDAY, FEBRUARY 9th,
At 12 o'clock, noon.
LOUIS DE COURCY has been favoured with instructions from J. A. Quilligan, Esq., to sell as above those extremely valuable business premises. The

---

1940 advt. showing de Courcy's sale of Quilligan's Licensed Premises in Mungret, now known as Shanahan's. de Courcy's was established in 1931 and has been one of the foremost in the auctioneering business since then.

Limerick M.P's not sound suffragists

In April, 1911, a large and enthusiastic meeting was held in the Athenaeum in support of the movement for extending the Parliamentary franchise to women. There was a great muster of ladies present and the eloquent addresses were listened to with the greatest attention. The hall was tastefully decorated for the occasion with shrubs and flowering plants.

One of the main speakers was Mrs. Sheehy Skeffington and she accused the M.P's for Limerick as not being sound suffragists: "The member for the City of Limerick, as they knew, was a strong supporter of their movement but the members of the county gave little support. Mr. Lundon, M.P., had informed her that the women of his division did not want the vote, and Mr. O'Shaughnessy, M.P. for West Limerick, was also opposed to women suffrage."

The speaker pointed out that the criminal, after a time, had the vote restored to him; the lunatic in his lucid moments could exercise the franchise, while the male child in time grew out of his ineligibility, but the woman was constantly banned. The battle for the vote had started 50 years previously and their efforts were fraught with great results. They were determined to press for the measure giving votes to women being enacted during this session of Parliament.

Miss Margaret Ashton M.A., highlighted the huge anomalies between the pay of men and women in the army clothing contracts. "The men were engaged at the minimum rate of 24s. a week, whilst the women received 3s. 8d. a week for the same work. Could any woman live on 3s. 8d. a week? The men were in a position to say we will vote against you if you don't give us a decent week's pay and they got it; but there was no power of that kind behind the women and they were obliged to suffer on starvation wages.

"They had been told that if women got the vote they would not know how to use it. Well, in reply to that she (speaker) would point out that the women who would get the Parliamentary vote had their names already on the register for Municipalities. They knew they could not become M.P's but the Bill before Parliament was a very wise and moderate measure entitling women only in a very small way the privileges that men enjoyed. She appealed to all women in Limerick to join either of the three branches that had been formed in Limerick, and resumed her seat amidst prolonged applause.

Lady Clarina proposed that a copy of a resolution pointing out the long denial of the vote to women be sent to the Prime Minister and that all Irish members of Parliament be urged to interest themselves now more keenly in the interests of Irish women than they have done on previous occasions.

The show of hands indicated that the meeting was unanimous in support of the resolution. The Mayor proposed a vote of thanks to Miss Ashton and Miss Sheehy-Skeffington, which was suitably acknowledged.

Decontamination Squad, A.R.P Section, Limerick Corporation, 1940. At rear, side-loader refuse collector lorry used for the decontamination equipment.

Stories of the Emergency

When war broke out in 1939, it was just sixteen years after the cessation of hostilities in our own civil war and bitterness and old wounds unhealed were still abounding. However, with the real possibility of invasion, old adversaries who had fought on opposite sides in 1922/23 buried the hatchet and were now standing side to side again as the country, from 1940 onwards, prepared for an invasion that it was reckoned could come at any time or from any quarter.

The question on everyone's lips was would the Germans attempt an invasion or would the British invade here to forestall a German landing as they had done in the case of Iceland? Whichever, it was felt the country's neutrality was no deterrent to either of these eventualities happening. As a consequence, many young men began to enlist and the period that became known as the Emergency had dawned.

The Newcastle West cor. reported in March, 1940, that the response to the call for men for the Defence Forces and for the Local Security Force appears to be gathering momentum and at a meeting of the West Limerick Brigade, Old IRA, a resolution was adopted calling on all Old IRA members to enrol immediately for service with the various defence forces. Ballyagran branch carried a similar resolution. All other correspondents reported a great response for enlistments: in Rathkeale 200 enrolled in the Local Security Forces: leaders were P. Roche, M.C.C.; J. O'Leary, B.E.; J. G. Power, manager Munster and Leinster Bank; R. Sheehy.

Volunteers had several options, either joining the regular army or the LDF (Local Defence Forces) or the LSF (Local Security Forces).

In the city in 1940 a special meeting was held at the O'Connell Monument in support of the campaign to organise national defence measures to meet any emergency. Ald. Dan Bourke, T.D., the Mayor, had summoned the meeting and was applauded when he said: "The whole country was united in its determination to safeguard its neutrality. There was grave danger that their neutrality would not be respected but if their young men joined the Army they could make it unprofitable for anyone to attack them. Those too old to join the army could give their services in other capacities, on the Local Security Force, Red Cross and A.R.P."

Mr. McCormack said no mother need be ashamed to see her son wearing the uniform of his country, and no sweetheart but should love her young man more because he was a soldier of Ireland (applause).

Notable local sportsmen to answer the call to arms were Mick Mackey, the famous Limerick hurler. The report said that Mackey would be available to play for Limerick in all important matches during the season. "If the team were to lose his services their chances of reaching the All-Ireland final would be very greatly reduced," a report said.

Paddy Griffin, Garryowen's star wing-forward, has also donned the uniform of the National Army and the County Board of Health was told at its meeting that several of its staff had joined up including C. Cleary, E. Cregan, M. Madden, F. Goodwin, P. Barrett and P. Coughlan.

The full effects of the war had not yet fully hit the country in the early years, and in 1940 the Athea correspondent was saying that the Christmas business in town was the best for many years but bemoaned the fact that so many were unemployed in the district and many families were in dire straits. "There were huge congregations attending the Masses with many familiar faces among them that had been absent for the past year. Here and there too were gaps caused by the absence of those who have passed the bourne during the year, people on whose mortal eyes will never rest again on this world of ours."

Early in 1941 the first effects of the war began to be felt in earnest here as essential commodities like flour, tea, coal, petrol, etc., which had to be imported, began to dry up and rationing was introduced.

From then on to the post-war years, a major activity was the pursuit, by fair means or on the black market, the above commodities plus cigarettes, bicycle tyres and dry batteries for radios. Tea and sugar were some of the scarcest and sought after commodities and many novel ways of stretching out tea were devised. It proved the No. 1 purchase in the black market.

Despite these privations, people were more united than they had been for a long time and borrowing and returning of such things as cups of sugar from neighbours were the norm. Some of the wounds of the Civil War began to heal as the populace found common cause.

It was an extremely difficult time for transport, all private cars were eventually put off the road, and trains with great difficulty ran on turf. Even the humble bicycle was in trouble with the scarcity of tyres and tubes and it was reported that cyclists were reduced to stuffing their tyres with grass in the absence of tubes. Water bailiffs had to use bicycles on their patrols and at a meeting of the Conservators it was decided to allow them each £2 a year for maintenance.

A simple method of saving petrol was reported by the Clare cor. when Mr. Flinn, turf contractor, Ennis, on arrival in Limerick with three lorry-loads of turf, attached two of the empty vehicles to one and towed them back home to Ennis afterwards.

With travel by car or bus practically non-existent due to shortage of petrol, Lord Adare showed great initiative when he put two stage coaches on the road plying between Limerick and Rathkeale. "A flourish on the horn, a swish of

the whip, the startled crack of horses' hooves on the road, the creak and strain of the harness and the initial sways of the coach and all were off to start the new service from Rathkeale to Limerick this morning (May 8th, 1941)" reported the Leader. Back had come the coaching days of the last century.

The coach drew up at Cruise's Hotel, fittingly the Bianconi's original stopping place. The service proved a huge success with Dublin tourists also availing of the facility. The coaches, "The Shamrock" and "The Thomond" contributed greatly to lessening of transport difficulties, and gave work to a considerable number of local people. It closed down for the winter months and Lord Adare was considering whether or not it would operate the following summer.

In 1943, according to "No. 7" in the Rowing Notes, it was not permissible to use private motor cars, and travelling to the Galway Regatta Shannon R.C. supporters had to disembark from the train at Ardrahan and cycle the rest of the way. Athlunkard veterans Tom Earlie and Willie Reid, were also doing the same but saved themselves a long cycle when Ned Connaughton of St. Michael's came to the rescue and took themselves and their bikes into the taxi he was travelling in.

The first prosecution of over-charging under the new regulations in the early forties came in Shanagolden when a shopkeeper had the misfortune to over-charge the local sergeant for his quota of tea. He was fined 10/- for his misdemeanour. At the same court, a farmer was fined for allowing noxious weeds to grow on his lands, a charge which was to be repeated many times over the next few years. There were many cases reported in court throughout the war, and afterwards, of black-marketing and several city shopkeepers and bakers paid heavy fines and even imprisonment were meted out to those found guilty.

Restrictions were numerous and even women's clothing came under scrutiny. In May, 1944, three city dressmakers were prosecuted for putting too many pleats in skirts. The restrictions were enforced to effect economies in the use of cloth. The defendants pleaded ignorance of the Emergency Powers Order and Justice Flood let them off with the Probation Act. However, he warned that for the future, despite the injured vanity of the ladies, the Order would have to be complied with.

Compulsory tillage was introduced and prosecutions followed for those who did not comply with the regulations with district judges berating those prosecuted for their lack of patriotism. "Till more, toil more" was the cry from the all those in authority, including bishops and government ministers. The Taoiseach, Eamon de Valera, speaking in Limerick, warned that the people might have to face starvation and he declared grimly that it was a crime against the community to allow arable land to remain untilled.

The Corporation were allotting plots of one-eighth of an acre on the outskirts of the city for those willing to grow their own produce. The unemployed would receive their seeds and implements free and those who were in a position to do so would be asked to make a small donation.

Top: Concrete pillbox still extant in Corbally which was erected on the banks of the Shannon as a river defence during the Emergency. Below: Defender's view of St. Thomas's Island from the inside of the pillbox.

In December, 1941, It was decided at a meeting of the Corporation to convert forty of the underground arches in O'Connell Street into air raid shelters. Four of these had already been converted and had met with the approval of the Department of Defence. The City Surveyor said that 1,200 would be accommodated in the shelters at a cost of £1,030. It was also proposed to erect 15 overground shelters, at a total cost of £9,000. Ald. James Reidy asked what arrangements were there in the event of having to evacuate the city.

Manager: I have made arrangements for a bus service to be provided in such an eventuality. He also stated that three centres, the Christian Brothers Schools, Sexton Street, the City Technical Institute, and the City Home would be food and rest centres and he also added that the five Parish Councils would operate these centres.

The severe shortage of every kind of commodity was exemplified when it was proposed that due to a scarcity of leather, that members of Local Defence Forces be supplied with boots with timber soles. "All available supplies of leather must be preserved for the army. The army have long route marches and wooden soles would be impracticable. Furthermore, it was pointed out that F.C.A. members use their boots when working on their farms, etc., and the wooden soled variety would do just as well." This report, by the Ennis cor., concluded by saying that "when needs must the devil drives" and it seems almost certain that boots with leather soles cannot be officially issued next year.

To add to the difficulties, a serious outbreak of foot and mouth disease broke out in the country in 1941 and quickly spread to Co. Limerick with cows being slaughtered in several areas. Many sporting fixtures were cancelled in the efforts to contain the disease.

The tea scarcity provided some practical jokers in Limerick with a rare opportunity for a good hoax. In 1942 early workers proceeding to business one morning were delightfully surprised to find a display card prominently hanging on a shop window which ran somewhat as follows:

"Tea! Unlimited quantity! 5d. per ounce!"

The discovery seemed too good to be true, but more than one observer did not wait to calculate that the price was obviously in excess of the Government controlled price per lb. At the risk of being late for work, several even turned back to tell their wives of the good news.

By the time the shop was opened for business many people had seen the advertisement and the startled shop-keeper was confronted with a huge queue and series of demands for tea. But alas for the hopes of the would-be purchasers, the shop-keeper disclaimed all knowledge of the advertisement, which was as much a surprise to him as to the shoppers.

By 1942 restrictions on the amount of newsprint a paper could have had its effect here when the mid-week editions of the Leader were reduced from eight to five columns.

An irate shopkeeper wrote in accusing wholesalers of holding back goods and selling them at excessive profit to certain purchasers who in turn sell them at prices well above the market. "Numerous small shopkeepers are thus deprived of a living and are barely able to keep their heads above water."

Even when the war was over, in September 1946 there was still huge scarcities and the Killaloe cor. reported that they were in a bad way in the town for the lack of cigarettes. "The nerve soothing weed was never so scarce in our midst and shopkeepers were besieged every morning and evening by women-folk in quest of same for themselves and their husbands, many of whom were complaining of headaches and loss of appetite, dizziness and sleeplessness due to the want of the popular cigarette. The menfolk eventually tried the pipe but they discarded the dudín the moment the belated cigarette supply arrived in town," the cor. concluded.

Despite the many restrictions and scarcities of World War II, the mundane matters of life went on in Limerick City and County. The big stores like Cannocks and Todds still had their sales and in 1942 men could buy a tweed coat for 75 shillings and raincoats for 35/-. In the early years of the war, Limerick Motors Works were still advertising Ford lorries for sale at £313.

The hunts were still meeting in 1941 and the County Limerick Hounds and Limerick Harriers advertised their places of meets. The Savoy was showing what was to become one of the great all-time classic films, Orson Welles' "Citizen Kane" and the Coliseum was showing Gary Cooper in "North-West Mounted Police." Butter (just before rationing) could be had at the market for 1s. 6d. lb., hen eggs 1s. 10d. doz. Chickens 10s to 14s a pair. Potatoes 6d. to 11d. per stone. Hay 50s. to 70s. per ton and calves from 35s. to 100s. each.

The first Muintir na Tire Hall in the country was opened in Murroe in 1941. It cost in the region of £1,400 to build and stood on spacious plot of ground in a sylvan setting. A very large gathering saw Archdeacon Nolan perform the opening ceremony. The same year, a committee of five was set up to investigate the scenes that accompanied the Rathbane v Friarstown camogie game at St. Patrick's Field.

Boundary extension was on the City Council's mind even back in the war years and a meeting of the Clare County Council condemned the move to have the city boundary extended as far as Parteen. The chairman of the Clare Council, Mr. Sean Brady, said the move would result in a huge loss of rates revenue for the county. He stated: "We (the council) should be prepared to oppose the proposal by every means in our power. He was satisfied that by doing so they would be acting in accordance with the unanimous wish of Clare people."

The war did not detract from the Faith of the people and the new church at Janesboro was dedicated to Our Lady Queen of Peace in December, 1942. Rev. J. Gorey C.Ss.R. delivered what was described as "an inspiring sermon."

The same year the death of Sir Charles Barrington Bart., formerly of Glenstal Castle, took place in Botley, Hampshire, at the advanced age of 95. Before leaving for England in 1923, he offered the castle and demesne to the Irish Government but the offer was declined due to the cost of upkeep. Sir Charles then sold the property to the late Right Rev. Monsignor Ryan who presented it to the Belgian Benedictine Fathers. Sir Charles was said to be one of the best of landlords and had a huge interest in the welfare of Barrington's Hospital, which his family founded, and it was this that bound him to Limerick during those years when he went to live in England. It was said he had the distinction of introducing rugby football to Ireland when attending Trinity College.

Cultural needs in these times were provided by such as the Boherbouy Band who played regularly during the war years in the People's Park and amongst their selections advertised were pieces by Bach, Gounod, Auber, etc. Conductor was D. McCormack, B.M. And it was the great era of the Gilbert and Sullivan operas in the Lyric Theatre presented by the pupils of C.B.S Sexton Street. Prof. King-Griffin waxed lyrical on a performance on the "Yeomen of the Guard" which he said "I would carry away with me many pleasant memories of many delectable moments when I sat enraptured by the beautiful voices of the boys."

All through the war Mary Harding in her syndicated column gave useful household hints during those frugal times. "Do not throw away your old net of lace curtains. Wash out the starch in them and you may use them for a host of domestic ways including boiling fish." She also gave the odd piece of medical advice such as the healing powers of salt. "A pinch of salt on the tongue, followed by a glass of cold water, will cure sick headaches, and a shallow teaspoonful dissolved in a cupful of hot water will relieve indigestion and dyspepsia; salt hardens the gums and whitens the teeth; by using very fine dry salt, as one would snuff for colds, hay fever may be relieved."

When peace came in May, 1945, it didn't mean the end of rationing and for a long time afterwards vital commodities were as scarce as ever. The effects of the war were still being felt in transport, and buses to destinations outside the city were few and far between. "People have become so used to queuing during the war years that they often queue for considerable time at the terminus in Sarsfield Street and when buses don't turn up, start queuing again so inured are they to waiting," said a report.

Five of the 100 young German children displaced after the war and brought to this country, were taken into homes in Ennis. Some of them, according to Miss M. B. Murphy, secretary of the Children's Committee, had never known what a home was, living in cellars and later refugee camps.

In 1946, with the world still trying to come to terms with the after effects of the devastating war, and with foodstuffs still extremely scarce, to compound matters record rains put the harvest in great danger. Matters were extremely serious and for once, the city and county was united as volunteers from the city, in their hundreds, plus the army, were taken out by army lorries and buses to assist in saving what remained of the wheat harvest. Volunteers registered in the offices of the Co. Limerick Committee of Agriculture in O'Connell Street.

"City Workers in Wheat Fields" were some of the headlines. The towns, too played their part and Newcastle West was to the forefront when it was announced that "Town Closes Down to Help in Harvest Work."

Many firms in the city sent their workers out to help in the harvest, Ranks, not surprisingly being to the forefront and it was stated by the firm that the workers would get their normal pay. Cannocks, also, said they would release some of their workforce and several other city firms said likewise.

The harvest crusade was dealt a severe blow when on Saturday September 23, a heavy downpour which swept across the south of the country, inundated the lands, and 700 volunteers from the city, who were to be transported out the country in six C.I.E buses, were disappointed when told that the trip was off. However, 200 eventually left but the continuation of heavy showers when they reached their destination put paid to all plans of harvesting.

"Their disappointment was great as they returned home saddened as they were imbued with the one desire to give all the assistance possible, even though they were labouring in far stranger surroundings. It was their golden wish that next Thursday (shops half-day) or Saturday afternoon (factory half-day) or Sunday, would be favourable as for most of them these were the only periods in which they could answer the nation's call."

There was one note of disharmony however: County Councillor Mr. D. P. Canty, at a meeting of the County Committee of Agriculture, said "he was really disappointed that the Limerick Corporation had not convened a meeting, if only as a gesture of sympathy to the County Limerick farmers. Other cities had done so but he was glad that the Limerick Chamber of Commerce and Employers Federation had taken action to assist in the crisis."

DECEMBER, 1940

TURKEYS
and GEESE
UNLIMITED QUANTITIES REQUIRED
Highest Market Prices Paid
CASTLEMAHON C.D.S.
LIMITED
CASTLEMAHON, NEWCASTLE WEST, CO. LIMERICK

'Phone—Castlemahon 3.   'Grams—"Creamery, Castlemahon"

Castlemahon Food Products were doing their bit for the war effort in 1940 as this Leader adv. shows. Sixty years afterwards they are still going strong, as they have been for most of this century.

---

de Valera speaks out against Shannon Scheme

In 1927, with the construction of the Shannon Scheme well under way, Eamon de Valera at a meeting in Nenagh spoke out against the scheme. "My Party (Fianna Fáil) would not have started on such a gigantic scheme as that, but would work on a scheme on the Liffey which would satisfy the people of Dublin and then train their own engineers, and later have it linked up into a grand general plan instead of bringing in Germans for work of that kind."

Despite Dev's criticism, the scheme was eventually brought to a successful conclusion and on Monday, 22nd July, 1929, President Cosgrave formally opened the sluice gates of the weir at O'Brien's Bridge to permit the flow of the Shannon into the Shannon Scheme head race canal. All the Saorstat's top dignataries and politicians were in attendance including Mr. de Valera, who was described as looking remarkably well.

There were regular reports of accidents in the building of the scheme At its height, the country's biggest ever building project employed 5,000. Amongst the fatalities were a young German fitter, Leobard Gernsperk, who was electrocuted when he tripped and catching a wire, which was live, he died instantly. Another German, a carpenter named Rudolph Wegel, was killed when he fell 33 feet from a ladder. Amongst local fatalities were Edward McCormack, John Street, who was killed trying to jump onto a lorry transporting him and fellow workers to Ardnacrusha, and Daniel O'Brien, who was killed when he fell under a locomotive on the scheme.

In September, 1927, great public interest was taken in the trial of 14 Connemara men (labourers in the scheme) at the Liberties District Court. They were charged with conspiring to commit a felony, causing grievous bodily injury and with damage to property.

The trial was a sequel to a fracas which took place in the Shannon Scheme hutments at Clonlara on Sunday evening, 4th September, when it was alleged the prisoners attacked fellow workers with sticks, stones and bottles.

The outbreak, it was stated, was due to a feud that existed amongst the workers and others, that the Connemaramen were the object of jibes and insults, because of their meagre knowledge of English.

The prisoners, who were marched from the County Gaol to the Courthouse handcuffed to each other, aroused much interest. During the hearing of the case remarkable evidence was given, one witness stating that the Connemara men "wanted to wipe out the civilised race." There was evidence that the fracas between the Connemara men and other workers lasted a half hour and two of the workers were badly beaten by the men from the West. Mr. Tynan, for the defendants, said that some of the men were running down his clients and may have been laughing at their lack of English.

Supt. Mooney said he regarded the case as very serious. If workers on the Shannon Scheme were to split into factions like that it would be impossible to say what damage it would do.

Justice J. M. Flood. summing up, said that there was little doubt but the defendants were under provocation but that could not be put forward as an excuse. He fined several of the defendants and discharged several others.

In the years preceding the opening of the Scheme, newspapers were full of articles from different sources about the perceived benefits of the project, and there was also reservations, and parochial jealousy: a letter appeared signed "a Clareman" to the effect that the Shannon and its power belongs of right to Co. Clare and that no one else has a right to touch it!

There was a feeling in Limerick, often expressed, that we were situated so near the Scheme that we should get the electricity cheaper than the rest of the country, which was later proved to be a fallacy.

Fr. Philip, OFM, told a packed audience in the Athenaeum in 1927 that £2,000,000 could well be earned by the workers in the scheme, which would go into every shop in Limerick and "I hope not too much of it will find its way into the public houses."

During the building of the scheme. Dr. Joseph Power, M.O.H., reported that there were 21 families, or 103 men, women and children, living in partitioned out-offices under abominable conditions in a farmyard at Blackwater, Ardnacrusha. He said that there were no sanitary conditions whatsoever, and open space near houses were used as lavatories and yard drains were choked and foul-smelling. The first houses in the city to receive electricity from the Shannon Scheme were in Corbally in 1930, followed shortly afterwards by Ballinacurra. In some rural districts, it took another thirty years before electricity from the scheme came their way.

Workers' sleeping quarters on the Shannon Scheme.

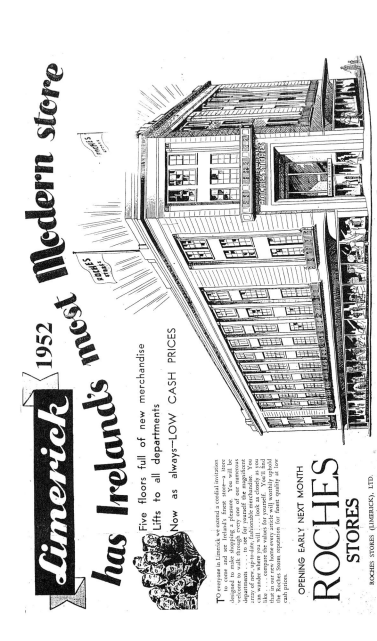

Roches Stores took over McBirney's Monster Draper House in the 1940's but the premises was burned to the ground in 1948. The fine new building as we know it now was opened four years later and as can be seen from the opening advt. of 1952, it has remained basically unaltered since. It is a splendid example of 1940/50 architecture and unlike many of the glass and plastic buildings that came afterwards in the 1960's and 70's, signalling the demise of O'Connell Streeet as an outstanding thoroughfare, the Roches building has stood the test of time.

Fear of the Red Menace hits city

In 1970 the Mayor, Stevie Coughlan, alerted the city to the dangers of what he called "The Red Menace." He appealed to parents and to all people in authority to alert themselves to the terrible danger that is in our midst. "There are amongst us left-wing extreme agents of a foreign power who are distributing insidious propaganda and seek to tear down and destroy our Christian way of life.

"Unless we act now to wipe out once and for all this most undesirable element that is fighting for a foothold in our city, there is a real danger that our apathy will result in a take-over of all authority and the suppression of the freedom that we enjoy, and for which so many Irish people have given their lives."

Several sources weighed in behind the Mayor in his anti-Maoist campaign, not least the Leader in an editorial, which thundered: "This is the Maoist movement which may well be regarded as a threat to the peace of the nation – a fact which can be realised only too clearly if one is to read some of the publicity material distributed throughout this city. The people of Limerick must wake up to the threat that is facing them and they must unite to run all those connected with such a movement out of the area before serious damage is done to the community as a whole.

"The Irish Revolutionary Youth Movement must be crushed and run out of the city without delay. What the Maoist advocates is nothing more than the dream of fools. Have we forgotten the slaughter and the slave labour that is so much part of life in Red China?"

Regular contributors to the letters pages like W. W. Gleeson and Daniel J. McAuley rushed into print. "Whack", as W.W. was known, was highly indignant that of all places, the Maoists had chosen his beloved St. Mary's Parish (Nicholas Street) to set up their propaganda book-stall (shots were fired through the window later on). He said only two of the City Council ("the rest must be Cistercians") at their weekly meeting saw fit to speak on the setting up of a Maoist bookstall in his beloved parish.

"It saddens me to think that a group of fellow-citizens, once Catholic no doubt, but now Dermot McMurroughs, Quislings, Fifth Columnists, anti-Christs, call them what you will, have set up in business calling themselves the Disciples of Mao Tse-Tung, whose avowed aim (in blood) is to make Limerick a second Poland, Hungary, or Czechoslovakia (that's what they think).

"Already the facade of their premises, once white, has been painted red. See for yourself, dear reader, I do not exaggerate. What's next?" wrote W.W.

Daniel J. McAuley said there was a time when the Irish Revolutionary Movement would not have stayed long in business here. "The Maoists must be crushed the same as the Communists crushed Christianity in China. They should be given the same reception here as Christians would get from Mao."

This was Stevie's golden era. He then turned his attention to what he described as the left-wingers within the Labour Party and attacked Barry Desmond. "Who does he think he is telling the people of Limerick what they should or should not do regarding the forthcoming visit of the South African team?" He also attacked Bernadette Devlin.

Moves were initiated to expel the Mayor from the Labour Party due to his outspoken comments, with the St. Mary's Branch making a statement "that steps have been taken to expel him." The Leader commented: "It is clear, however, that such a decision is most unlikely for Ald. Coughlan has been a constant poll-topper since he joined the party."

Cllr. Mick Crowe (fourth from left) with Greystones residents around 1970.

Back Garryowen
says Mary Ann Walsh

Mary Ann Walsh, described as having no fixed abode, was one of the characters of the District Court through the 1940's and 1950's, where she appeared in front of District Justices D. F. Gleeson and J. M. Flood on a regular basis charged with habitual drunkenness. She frequently used violence when drunk and faced regular charges of breaking windows and was noted for her fierce tongue. It was an era when practically all proceedings in the District Court were reported in local newspapers and Mary Ann's jousts with whatever judge was sitting were regularly recorded. In 1949 she was once more in front of the Justice. "I met a friend who plied me with whiskey, your honour," was her excuse when asked to answer the charge of drunkenness. "You're running out of excuses, Mary Ann," said Justice Flood. "A month in jail or a fine of 10/-."

Mary invariably took the jail sentence. The judges, when in benevolent mood, would sometimes leave her off with a stern warning to mend her ways to which her reply invariably was: "I will My Lord." But everyone in the court, including the judge, knew it would only be a matter of time before she was up again.

On one occasion, on the eve of a Munster Senior Cup Final, when Justice Flood dismissed her case she shouted out: "Up Guinness, and back Garryowen tomorrow!" to the amusement of the assembled court. Reputed to be of good stock, Mary Ann was regularly described as being a habitual drunkard; in today's terms she would be called an alcoholic or "wino" and her face, a criterion of her tragic lifestyle, bore all the hallmarks of her addiction.

Rumours of the war

A Leader editorial in 1940 was alarmed at the many fantastic rumours that were abounding in connection with the war then raging in Europe and gave an example of how rumours started.

A woman was crossing Sarsfield Bridge one evening and heard an angler shouting to another: "they're pulling down the docks." This was of course was meant to say that the fish were biting further down river. The woman hurried home with the startling intelligence and before the evening was out the town was awash with rumours that either invaders had destroyed the docks or that some sort of riot had occurred amongst the dockers and they were pulling up the quays!

When Mackey was king

"The All Ireland Champions. Limerick Team's Greatest Triumph. Joyous Scenes follow Homeric Struggles."

Thus trumpeted the headlines on the 1st October, 1934, to usher in Limerick's great hurling era when in the All-Ireland final replay the previous day they beat Dublin by 5-2 to 2-6.

The account said: "Limerick had a decisive victory over Dublin in the replay of the All Ireland final. The scenes of enthusiasm – the spontaneous and unrestrained outbursts of cheering that marked the close of the game cannot be adequately described. The Mackey's, Mick and John, were a tower of strength in those attacks and their exploits were a joy to witness."

It was estimated that up to 20,000 greeted the champions on their arrival at the Limerick railway terminus. A monster procession took place through the streets to the Imperial Hotel in Catherine Street. Along the route of the procession, which was preceded by a cavalcade of horsemen, the riders being decorated in the colours of the team, tar barrels and bonfires blazed.

Two years later, in 1936, Limerick won their fourth Munster championship in a row. They put eight goals past a hapless Tipperary with Mick Mackey the hero and went on to another all-Ireland success when on Sunday September 6th, they trounced Kilkenny in the all-Ireland final by 6-6 to 1-5. Banner headlines blazed: "Dazzling Glory of Limerick's Marvellous Hurling Display, Irish Champions and World Champions."

The report said that while the Kilkennymen played a great game, they surely "were not in it" in the dash, finish and superb artistry that have made the wearers of the green and white the unequalled combination that they have proved themselves to be. Limerick have shed lustre not only on themselves and their city and county, but on their country in general.

Mick Mackey, the captain and one of the heroes of the hour, said when interviewed: "The cheering of the thousands of Limerick people present gave us great heart and spurred us on to greater effort. We were carried away by a wave of enthusiasm and nothing could stop us. I'm very proud, Limerick is very proud of their world champions. Garryowen forever!"

Chairman of the county board, Mr. W. Clifford said "Ireland has never before, and may never again, produce such a team. All were wonderful and the captain was the brightest star of all."

There were unbridled scenes of joy and enthusiasm when the train bearing the victorious team arrived in Limerick. The train was long behind schedule due to the receptions accorded the team at the various stops along the route. At Castleconnell, home of the Limerick captain, the scene of enthusiasm was indescribable as the small station was invaded by excited crowds and bonfires blazed throughout the district.

Top: Mick Mackey crashes home a goal against Kilkenny in the All-Ireland final of 1936 and (right) a vigorous Limerick attack on the Kilkenny goal.

Limerick were described as the greatest team of all time, and this win was sweet revenge for defeats at the hands of Kilkenny in the finals of 1933 and 1935.

During the summer, Limerick toured America and went undefeated (hence the title of world champions). There was a film of the tour showing in the Lyric Cinema with the feature starring Shirley Temple and Lionel Barrymore in "The Little Colonel."

1940 was to bring further All-Ireland glory to the "greatest hurling combination the county has ever produced."

War time travel restrictions did not deter hurling fans from going to Thurles to see Limerick playing Cork in the Munster Hurling Final in July, 1940. Thousands travelled from the city and county by many modes of conveyance. It was a successful foray as Limerick beat Cork and neither did the restrictions deter 50,000 spectators from heading for Croke Park for the showdown with Kilkenny in the All-Ireland final.

The report on the final on September 1st said that the match was played at top speed, the display of field craft by both sides electrified the vast attendance. Limerick won their third All-Ireland Senior title in seven years, on the score of 3-7 to 1-7, and the minors also won, beating Antrim, for their first title in this grade

"Kilkenny Beaten by Two Clear Goals." "Limerick Submerges Kilkenny". "The Green and White on Top" were some of the headlines that trumpeted Limerick's great win. The report of the match inferred that Paddy Clohessy was star of the Limerick team. "Kilkenny attack fell on dangerous breakwater in Paddy Clohessy, who played the biggest part in subduing the Kilkenny attack." Mick Mackey played a captain's part in the win, inspiring his team.

Thousands turned out at the Limerick station to greet their heroes on their return from Dublin. "People Frenzied with Joy" was the heading.

Later that week the triumphant team was introduced to an enthusiastic audience at the Savoy Cinema. The City Manager, Mr. Berkery, said that he hoped this would be a forerunner and "that year after year we would have the same introductions."

There was no Savoy the following year as the holders of the All-Ireland got a ferocious trouncing at the hands of Cork in the Munster semi-final on the unbelievable score of 8 goals and 10 points to 3 goals 2 points. It would be another 33 years before Limerick would win another All-Ireland.

In 1944, Limerick led Cork by five points towards the closing stages of the Munster final in Thurles but the southerners pulled out all the stops and in a sensational finish won by a clear goal. Many novel methods of transport were used getting to the final in Thurles: sidecars, pony and trap, ass and car, and the predominant mode of transport was the humble bicycle. Supporters set out from all parts of the city and county by bike in the early hours of the morning and some snatched sleep in hay barns along the way.

After a lapse of 33 years, Limerick in 1973 at last regained the All-Ireland Senior Hurling title. At Croke Park, in wet and misty conditions, they defeated favourites Kilkenny by 1-21 to 1-14.

"Limerick Lay the Ghosts of Old" wrote Charlie Mulqueen. "The men in green did us proud and gave the thousands and thousands of supporters a day they will never forget. Limerick, for a time, almost joined the 'Cinderella' counties of the game. Now, thankfully, all that is far behind, hopefully for a long time to come."

Mick Mackey spoke on radio and said: "I am thrilled, we are all thrilled." The report said "he spoke for every man, woman and child in Limerick."

"Caman" (Seamus Kelly), the great Leader G.A.A. correspondent for many years was elated and said a grand feature of the Limerick display was their most effective ground hurling, a facet which proved the success of former Limerick teams.

Thousands converged at the railway terminus on the Monday night to welcome home the victorious team and there were scenes of great rejoicing. The train stopped at Castleconnell where in an emotional scene Mick Mackey presented Eamonn Grimes with a silver salver to mark his forthcoming marriage. It was a double celebration for Richie Bennis as his wife gave birth to a baby son earlier on in the week. The Liam McCarthy Cup was taken on a tour of the county and it was said it would be missing for many weeks.

Sean Murphy gave a graphic description of the crowds that turned out to see the conquering heroes saying that when the cavalcade reached St. Patrick's Road, his conservative estimate of the crowd was two million. "I was glad they were on our side," he added.

The Mayor, engine driver Mick Lipper, had driven the train with the team on board to the match and a group of nuns were seen on the platform in Portlaoise waving green and white flags.

Limerick reached the final again the following year but Kilkenny, with Eddie Keher unstoppable, gained ample revenge when they cut loose in the second half and won with 12 points to spare.

The hurlers next date at Croke Park was in 1980 and despite the star performance of Eamonn Cregan, who scored 2-7, most of the Limerick team played below par, and were well beaten by Galway in the end.

1994, and with a five point lead towards the finish, Limerick looked impregnable in the final against Offaly but like a sleeping giant the opposition shook themselves and went on a late scoring spree. In that fateful last five minutes Offaly scored two goals and

Mick Mackey triumphantly holds the McCathy Cup aloft following Limerick's All-Ireland win in 1936.

five points to run out winners by six clear points, one of the most bizarre finishes to an All-Ireland in its long history. Limerick supporters showed their appreciation, however of their team's achievements when it was estimated that 20,000 turned out to greet them on their return home from Dublin.

Two years later Limerick were back again in Croke Park, this time with Wexford as opposition, and hopes were high that the ghosts of '94 would be exorcised. But defeat was their bitter lot again with the Limerick forwards, especially in the second half, failing to click.

Limerickwoman witnesses shooting on the *Titanic*

Nellie O'Dwyer of High Street in Limerick made the journey to Queenstown (now Cobh) in 1912 to join the Titanic on its fateful maiden voyage. She was employed in Brooklyn, New York, for six years previously and had been on a visit home. Preliminary reports said that she perished when what had been described as the unsinkable ship sank after hitting an iceberg. She was, happily, rescued from a lifeboat by the liner *Carpathia* and afterwards gave a graphic account of the sinking of the Titanic to the Brooklyn Daily Times, reprinted in the Limerick Chronicle:

"I was dozing to sleep when the big ship seemed to jar. I was not frightened, but got up to ask the other girls what had made the vessel act so. Then it was still. You know, all day and all night there was the whirr of machinery and when it stopped it was queer. For the longest while, none of us could find out what was the matter, but then some young men who were on the vessel with us from Queenstown told us to go back to sleep. It was nothing. 'Ye foolish girls, go back to your beds,' they said to us. 'Sure the ship struck an iceberg, but it would take a power of icebergs to harm her.'

"So we, well most of us, started to go back, but the boys said they were going up on deck to see the 'berg, for the captain was going to bring it aboard. Of course 'twas fooling us they were. Some time later we could hear folk running around above and we went up the stairway to the upper steerage deck. Something was wrong, we could see that, but we were not frightened, really.

"But we could hear them shouting to get the life belts. We knew then something must be wrong. We girls and some of the women with us knelt down on deck and said the Rosary. Some ladies and gentlemen passed us from cabins and looked at us curiously. Boats were being lowered and people were being helped into them. Some were almost thrown in.

"Poor Paddy Lane, he was a fine young fellow, a little younger than I am, and when we were leaving the other side (Ireland) his folks asked me to please look after Paddy in America. When the boats were being lowered, Paddy knelt on the deck and prayed. Then he began to run around calling for the priest. And he started for the other side of the ship. I never saw him again. Paddy went down when the ship sunk.

"Then there was a sweet little boy. Oh! the grandest and most beautiful prayers that one could hear come from a child, do you know I think he was lost, for I don't remember him next morning in any of the boats.

"The captain treated everyone alike, whether they were from first cabin or the steerage. He acted angry only towards the men that were pushing forward. He kept us from panic, so he did. The Italian men were the worst. There was a poor fellow near where I was, and they could not get him back, and an officer shot him and he fell at my feet. I never heard the ship's band playing louder. Men were shouting, women were crying for their husbands and children to stay with them. I don't know how I got to the cabin above.

"I was among the last, and there was only one boat left. Yes, that is true about the old couple. I could hear her husband bidding her get into the boat, and the last I heard her say was "no, no, no." As we came along, the last thing that I saw was the priest waving his arms like as if it might have been absolving us all. The poor man was going towards the steerage.

"Do you know, we still had no notion that the ship was going down? We were a little afraid getting into the boats. That is all of them, men or women, were afraid, except the stewards. There was a queer look on their faces as they helped us along. I didn't understand then, none of us did. Now we who were saved know what that look meant. There was some trouble with the nurses. They were supposed to place lifebelts on the people. A few of them tried to escape, but the officers shouted at them, and they came back to their work.

"The poor girl that was to go into the boat just before me was afraid. She jumped and missed the boat all but one ankle, and a man at the oars grabbed her. She slipped from his hold and was drowned. I got afraid and an officer lifted me. Someone said 'careful there', and I was dropped into the boat. She was pulled away and I sat up to look at the big ship. It could not have been more than seven minutes before there was a terrible explosion. O God, be merciful to us all! The cries that came from the ship I'll never forget. I could see before the explosion just dimly the face of a woman who had six children on board. I think none of the little ones got up soon enough to be saved. The poor mother never left the ship.

"Then, those in charge began to give orders, keeping the boats a little apart. A little while after we could see one boat with a green light on it. Some man was giving orders in it. In our boat was a tall man with a moustache, and he seemed to have some way of giving of orders. We had sixty-five in the boat, and they started taking people out, and putting them in boats that had very few in them.

"Five or six Chinamen were found at the bottom of one boat. The way they were saved was by fixing their hair down their backs, and putting their blankets about them. They were taken for women when the boats were leaving the ship. Then they took some of the people from our boat, we had a sailor and an Italian stoker to row us.

"It was awful, so it was. The Italian knew no English, and he didn't seem to understand the sailor's telling him 'back water.' There was no other man now. So, to try and save the people, I took the oar from the Italian and the sailor and I rowed about as best as we could. Sometimes the green light I told you about on that one boat made me think now and then that a ship was coming and we were afraid it would run us down before we could be saved. We would often mistake a bright star, do you know, for the top light of the vessel. Towards morning we rowed over to the place where the *Titanic* went down, but there were only pieces of wreckage floating, except for the few life belts that poor souls had adjusted the wrong way before they left the ship."

The report went on to state that there have been varying accounts as to the air that the ship's band played as the vessel was sinking, but Nellie O'Dwyer declares without hesitation that it was "Nearer My God To Thee." She declares that her boat was not equipped with either water or provision of any kind. She knew the names of none of the persons in her boat.

"The awful period of sorrow aboard the *Carpathia* was relieved by Nellie O'Dwyer, who was an angel of mercy. Her robust constitution had been disturbed but little by the trying privations of the night on the open sea, and she went among the suffering survivors tenderly nursing them, making tea for them, and with the characteristic bouyancy of her Celtic heart, forcing a smile and cheering the forlorn with a word of comfort," concluded the report.

Lahinch around the time of the sinking of the Titanic with the Golf Links Hotel on the hill in the background.

The children that nobody wanted

Abandoned by their parents, and with Dublin and Limerick Corporations each denying responsibility for their care, that was the tragic lot of the five O'Donoghue children from Crosby Row in St Mary's in November, 1956. It had been noted that the maintenance of the abandoned children would be 15 shillings a week.

The pitiable story enfolded in Limerick Childrens Court before District Justice Gleeson when Inspector J. Foley of the National Society of Prevention of Cruelty to Children sought to have the children committed to a Limerick Industrial School.

A similar application was made in a Dublin Court the month before but Mr. Justice McCarthy refused the application and sent the children back to Limerick to be committed.

Limerick corporation solicitor Mr. W. W. Dundon opposed the application on the grounds that the place of abandonment was Dublin where the father resided.

The Justice adjourned the case until the following Friday when, he said, the Dublin Corporation could be represented if they so desired.

Four-year-old Brian O'Donoghue, one of the abandoned children, pictured in the People's Park in the early 1950's, before his father lost his job in Shannon.

Inspector Foley said that the children, the youngest of whom was an infant of 15 months, were parked outside the Court in a car.

"Their father, a native of Dublin, had been employed as a radio officer at Shannon Airport but in July last year he lost his job because of bad time-keeping. For failure to pay the rent, he was put out of his home in Limerick and had to transfer to Ballinacurra Weston.

"He then left to join his father in Dublin. While away, his wife was in receipt of Home Assistance for six or seven weeks when she decided to go to Dublin to get the father to support the children.

"The grandparents refused to take in the children and they were sent to St. Kevin's Home on October 3rd. The grandparents eventually decided to take them in, on the understanding that the mother would be with them, but she left for England and did not return. The father, he understood, had been in Scotland looking for work but was now back in his parents' home again."

Inspector Foley, continuing, said that he had phoned their Dublin office yesterday to have the father notified of the Limerick Court proceedings, but when their inspector called the door was slammed in his face.

"The children had no home now and were being pushed around. I have settled numerous disputes between the husband and wife."

Justice: The obvious thing to do is to issue a warrant for the arrest of the husband and wife. Nobody seems to have done anything about the people who are responsible: the parents.

The Justice said he would like to consider the facts of the case since a similar matter had already divided the Supreme Court.

Inspector Foley said he would arrange to have the three little girls placed in the Mount Convent until next Friday and he would try and get the boys placed in Glin. Up to to-day they had been in the female section of the City Home and he did not think it right they should return there. One of the boys was nine years of age.

A footnote stated that for the maintenance of abandoned children, the Corporation and State have to pay 15 shillings a week in respect of each child.

At the court the following Friday, there was considerable legal argument. The District Justice in Dublin had refused to make an order committing the children to schools in Dublin as he held that they were the responsibility of the Limerick Corporation because the parents had resided there.

Justice Gleeson said the case was a very difficult and troublesome one and even the Supreme Court was divided on the matter. Taking all the circumstances into account, he would hold that the residence of the parents was in Limerick and that the consequent responsibility would be that of the Limerick Corporation.

The five children, two boys and girls, whose ages ranged from one and half years to nine, were committed to Mount St. Vincent Orphanage, Limerick, and St. Joseph's Orphanage, Glin.

The children played in the court during the hearing of the application.

Stevie Coughlan,
Dev and the Jews

Of all the local politicians mentioned in local newspaper files of the century past, Stevie Coughlan stands out as the most colourful, outspoken and controversial. From his early days as a local councillor, agitation was his middle name. One of the first major controversies in which he was involved in came in February 13, 1952, when large headlines proclaimed: "City Council Repudiates Mayor's Letter To Sunday Newspapers."

Stevie, who was Mayor at the time, had an obsession that Limerick, which he claimed was the major centre of the dairy industry, should have a chocolate crumb factory. He maintained that with so much surplus milk in the county, there was a definite opening for such a factory. After years of frustration, which included a failed deputation to see the Fianna Fáil Minister in Dublin, he wrote a letter to the Sunday newspapers making disparaging references about An Taoiseach, Mr. de Valera.

In a highly conservative era, his criticism of The Chief was taken as a gratuitous insult, and the letter caused a sensation. At the following Monday night's

---

City Council meeting "the public gallery was crowded to capacity, but hundreds more were unable to gain admittance".

Fianna Fáil members of the Council were incensed.

"If you were behind the Iron Curtain you would tremble in your skin before you would dare address the head of the Government as you have," thundered Ald Dan Bourke, Fianna Fáil T.D. and former Mayor himself.

Stevie, well able to defend himself, riposted: "Are you comparing this country to the Iron Curtain. Thank God we have our freedom here."

The debate got highly personal with all of the Fianna Fail councillors lining up to have a crack at Steve and Ald. Dan Bourke being the chief protagonist. "We have watched you pitifully since you scraped into the Corporation. You were elected under very shady circumstances."

Stevie: "You are making a most serious charge."

Ald. Bourke defended the honour of The Chief at all costs, and went so far as to quote the Provincial of the Holy Ghost Fathers as describing Mr. de Valera "as eminently suitable for the high office of Taoiseach."

Kevin Bradshaw took up the cudgel on behalf of his Party, outlining what The Chief had done for the country, especially keeping us out of the War. Pointing his finger at the Mayor he added: "You took no hand act or part in any of the Emergency services."

Stevie: "I was lucky not to be inside de Valera's glasshouse in the Currragh."

The debate raged on, hot and heavy with all the councillors, no matter what their affiliations, condemning the letter, and some called for the Mayor's resignation.

One of the senior councillors, P. J. Donnellan, said: "You may have been over enthusiastic in trying to do your best for Limerick but I and all my associates condemn you." Pa O'Connell said as far as he knew Mr. de Valera never used an offensive word, even to an opponent and Mr. Finnan added "there was only one apology the people will take from you and that is your chain, Councillor Coughlan, ex-Mayor of Limerick. That's what I call you."

Ald. G. E. Russell was one of the few sympathetic voices and while admitting that the letter was not above criticism, he made an appeal for the motion of censuring the Mayor to be withdrawn. "Of any of the Mayors I have served under, Mr. Coughlan has done more than any to bring about more employment and to bring a little happiness into the lives of the poorer people."

The Mayor, defending his action, said it had been said that in insulting Mr. de Valera he had committed an unpardonable sin, but he (Mayor) said when he saw the way he had been treated and kicked about, in his fight for the factory and the unemployed, he decided to fight or die.

"I do not regret that letter," he added. "I fired that shot and have another up the breech if necessary. I owe no apology to anybody for trying to create employment in Limerick."

Stevie was now fired up and rounded on some of his tormentors like Fianna

Fáil's Kevin Bradshaw whom he accused of trying to join Clann na Poblachta and paid 30 shillings to the party funds. He accused another Fianna Fáil man, Gerry "Paver" Dillon of being a former Blue Shirt.

When a proposition was made that the Mayor should resign, the law agent intervened and said it was out of order. The meeting eventually decided unanimously to repudiate the letter.

During the course of the meeting, the Mayor had requested the Town Clerk (Mr. McHugh) to hand out samples of the famous chocolate crumb to the councillors, some of whom refused, with just a few sampling it.

Alas, this was the nearest anyone ever got to partake in Stevie's dream of a chocolate crumb factory: his valiant efforts, which were to make headlines in the Leader for several issues afterwards, coming to naught in the end.

In 1970, when he was Mayor again but a Labour T.D. this time, Stevie stirred up a hornet's nest regarding the incitement of the Redemptorist, Fr. Creagh, and the consequent boycott of the Jews of Limerick in 1904.

It was practically a forgotten blot on the history of the city, but in April of that year, at the annual conference of the Credit Unions of Ireland in the Parkway Motel, Stevie's blundering references to the incidents opened a can of worms that have reverberated down to this day.

It appears what Stevie (he was speaking for himself he said, not as Mayor of the city), tried to explain was that the usury of the Jews in Limerick justified Fr. Creagh's incitement and its tragic circumstances.

The Mayor claimed as a young boy he remembered the pogrom of the Jews which was started by Fr. Creagh. "Why did he do it?" he asked.

"I remember an unfortunate woman who was having a baby in the Vizes Field area and who was in bed when they (the Jews) came looking for 5/-, 10/-, or 7/6, scourging the unfortunate people.

"They took the bed from under the unfortunate woman – it is tragic for me as Mayor of Limerick to have to say this (at this stage of the proceedings the Mayor paused for some words and became emotionally upset before continuing).

"Father Creagh in a most courageous way declared war on the Jews in Colloney Street, which is now known as Wolfe Tone Street. The Jewish extortionists . . . ."

He was then interrupted with cries of "sit down, sit down," and cries of "be neutral mayor" and some slow handclapping.

After the interruption the Mayor continued: "Fr. Creagh acted as a Catholic and I say here and now that he took a very wise move and a very wise step when he created the bank with 170 members and as a result of his action we now have this beautiful credit movement here today."

The days following the convention, there was national condemnation of the speech with Ald. Gerald Goldberg, of Cork (whose family left Limerick for Cork after the boycott), to the forefront. "The Mayor's anti-Jewish remarks were intemperate and a misuse of high power." He intimated that he was going to table a resolution for a public meeting of Cork Corporation which wound up stating "it places on record regret that anybody should misuse high power to denigrate any section of the Irish people, whether Roman Catholic, Protestant or Jew, or any other minority." Ald. Goldberg said that the Chief Rabbi was "very upset" and added that Mayor Coughlan's claim that he remembered the Limerick pogrom was grossly misleading as the events took place 66 years before and the Mayor would not have been even born then.

The Credit Union Convention issued a statement disassociating themselves from the Mayor's remarks.

Jim Kemmy, chairman of East Limerick's Constituency Council of the Labour Party, stated that "Deputy Coughlan's statement in which he approves of and attempts to justify the pogrom involving the Jewish community in Limerick in 1904 has brought further embarrassment and shame to the Labour Party and to the City of Limerick."

Stevie later publicly apologised for his remarks in an exclusive interview with the Leader stating that "it was never my intention to insult any minority group and if I did this it was unintentional and I sincerely regret it. I am not anti-Semitic and I never was. I can say the same for my wife and family. When Jews were refused entry to the tennis clubs here my mother-in-law, Mrs. Nellie Hanley, heard of this and invited the Jews to play tennis at any time in the two courts in her house on the Island Road. Out of this came the Dalcassian Tennis Club and it was the Jewish members who were responsible for its foundation."

The Mayor was invited to appear on the Late Late Show to defend the speech, but declined.

When Mick Lipper displaced Stevie as Labour T.D. for East Limerick, there was much acrimony between them, eventually resulting in a court case. On Monday May 4, 1981, the District Court heard Stevie allege that he was assaulted by Deputy Michael Lipper, two months previously.

Stevie, in evidence said, he met Deputy Lipper in the hallway of the Mid-Western Health Board, was accosted by him and hit him three blows to the chest.

"He was shouting and roaring and he called me a 'tinker', said Stevie, and I told him to go easy as there were women present."

Deputy Lipper, in evidence, said Coughlan remarked that he (Lipper) was finished, all washed up and would soon be back driving trains. "I pray for Coughlan every morning," he added.

Evidence was given by Mid-Western employee Liam Wrenn about the alleged incident. The case was eventually dismissed.

Stevie died in December 1994 and there were nationwide tributes, with obituaries describing him as being a controversial, outspoken and colourful character.

An innocent victim of The Troubles

Charles Barrington succeeded to the title of fifth baronet and came into possession of Glenstal Castle and huge demesne running to 9,000 acres, on the death of his father, Sir Croker Barrington, in 1890. One of the country's greatest sportsmen, Sir Charles was accredited with being the first to introduce rugby football into Ireland (at Trinity College) having learned the game at Rugby College. He was also an outstanding oarsmen with Trinity.

In 1895 he married Mary Rose Bacon, daughter of the Premier Baronet of England and they had three children, Winifred, Charles and Fitzwilliam. Winifred, it was reported, was hugely popular, especially with the tenants of the estate with whom she mixed freely, and as a very young woman had done valuable war work in military hospitals in England. Theirs was an idyllic existence in Glenstal, with a staff of twelve serving in the castle, shooting parties coming over from England during the season, trout fishing from well stocked lakes in the estate, and a private nine-hole golf course laid out by Sir Charles himself.

Winifred Barrington

In 1919, when Winifred came of age, a glittering ball was held in her honour in the castle with many members of the ruling class throughout the county attending.

Winifred was on friendly terms with some of this set in the area, and later on this extended to include District Inspector Biggs, a member of the hated Black and Tans, and a marked man due to his intransigent treatment of local people especially if it was thought they had dealings with the I.R.A.

On the evening of Mary 14, 1921, according to a Limerick Chronicle report, Winifred and some friends went fishing on the Newport River beyond Kiloscully. On their way home, with Inspector Biggs driving, the car was ambushed on the approach to Coolboreen Bridge, just three miles from Newport.

The sequence of events that was to follow proved a salutary triumph for the I.R.A. but was to bring terrible tragedy to the occupants of Glenstal Castle.

"A Story of Shocking Occurrence" was the heading the following day as the full story of the tragedy unfolded at the military enquiry held in the New Barracks shortly after the affray.

Passengers in the car gave graphic details of the ambush, stating that they came under fire when they approached the bridge. "The car carried on for a few yards, and then stopped. Inspector Biggs, who was driving, had Miss Barrington alongside him and he appeared to be hit in the throat. Both left the car and the Inspector advanced about twenty yards and fell. There was interchange of fire between another officer who had also left the car, and the attackers, and Miss Barrington was seen to drop on the side of the road.

"About five or six men came up and when Inspector Biggs was identified several shots were fired at him where he lay. Miss Barrington, lying at the side of the road near the car, appeared to be shot, but being conscious, she asked for help and one of the attackers said he was sorry but another said it served them right."

Winifred was brought to a nearby house but died shortly afterwards from gunshot wounds in the chest. She had also received wounds to her leg. The castle and the area in general was plunged into great sorrow as the result of the tragic death of such a great favourite.

The funeral of Winifred, described in the Chronicle as "an amiable young girl" took place to Abington Cemetery on Wednesday, 18th May. The report went on: "Passing through the village of Murroe, all houses were closed and blinds drawn in all of the windows. The bell of the Catholic Church toiled mournfully until the end of the procession passed out of sight."

A former teacher of Winifred's in the National School in Murroe stated that when the corpse was laid out in a room of the castle, Winnie seemed to be still alive. The coffin was surrounded by the huge pink rhododendron blooms, for which the castle grounds was famous. It was also said that Winifred had been receiving instruction in the Catholic Faith from a nun in the convent in Cappamore.

People in the area braced themselves for what they thought would be inevitable sanctions in the area after the shooting, but on the instructions of Sir Charles, no reprisals were carried out. Sir Charles and his family left Glenstal for England shortly after the tragedy and while many believed this was as the result of the shooting of his beloved daughter, others formed the opinion that he could not afford to keep up the castle due to the greatly diminished estate brought about by the passing of the Land Act.

The Jewish Question

Of all the sermons that were ever preached in Limerick, that given by Fr. John Creagh, director of the Arch Confraternity, on January 11th, 1904, proved to be amongst the most controversial with far-reaching consequences that even to this day are still regularly recalled.

"The Jewish Question" was the standing heading given in the local newspapers in the many reports that followed through the ensuing months. The text of Fr. Creagh's sermon was printed in full in the Leader and in this he laid into the Jews, especially the community in Colooney Street. "They are the greatest enemies of the Catholic Church, they crucified Our Lord, and murdered the early Christians. They would kidnap and slay Christian children if they dared" were amongst the more blood-curdling of his claims

Fr. Creagh.

and in a further sermon, in which he took Michael Davitt to task for his defence of the Jews, he suggested, in so many words, a boycott of Jewish trading in retaliation for what he claimed were exorbitant lending rates that were driving poor people to the edge of starvation.

His sermons, and the harassment and assault on the Jewish community that followed (50 in all as claimed by the Chief Rabbi, the Rev. Levin) made news in the national newspapers in England and there were even comments in the German papers on the question, as reported in the Leader, which claimed that the article was a gross distortion of the situation. "Two or three families are completely ruined and fifteen others are only saved from actual starvation by the humane action of the local Protestants" claimed the German article, and the report also quoted the London Press as styling the persecution as "an Isiah Kisbenev." "Comment is superfluous" concluded the Leader report.

The "Jewish Question" was also raised in Parliament by Sir John Hennaway who asked the Chief Secretary of Ireland what steps are being taken by his

Majesty's Government to protect the life, property and freedom of tradition of the Jewish population in Limerick. Mr. Wyndham replied that the persecution of the small Jewish population in Limerick has engaged the most careful and anxious consideration of the Government.

Fr. Creagh's exhortations, however, got support from several quarters, the Executive Council of the British Brothers League having a letter published to the effect that "they offered their sincere thanks to Fr. Creagh for the noble work he has undertaken to prevent a class of undesirable aliens, who have received the hospitality of the Irish race, from demoralising the nation, and bringing misery through their born instinct of greed, usury, and arrogance."

A letter signed Joseph Banister from London claimed that two-thirds of the London Press, owned by Jews and others owned by pimps and sexual perverts, have been filled with hair-raising yarns of horrible outrages committed on the noble, industrious, law-abiding, inoffensive Hebrews of Limerick, brought about by religious hatred."

John Redmond, M.P., in a letter said "I feel sure the good sense of the Irish people will be sufficient to protect them (the Jews) from any wrong, but I have no sympathy whatever with the Hebrew community in Limerick."

The Dublin Express, described as the extreme Conservative organ of anti-Catholicism in Ireland, was taken to task by the Leader for what was considered a gross exaggeration in stating that there was an alleged attempt to wreck a Jewish shop. The Leader investigated the report and found that it was two drunks who passing the little shop of a petty Jewish dealer, Mr. Blond, merely took down one of his shutters which was partly open. "This is how the Express described the shop being wrecked, and is another attempt to colour the Semitic situation in Limerick," the report concluded.

The most celebrated prosecution and consequent imprisonment during the period of the "Jewish Question" was that of 15-year-old John Rahilly from Carey's Road who was imprisoned for a month for assaulting Rebbi Levin by striking him with a stone on the ankle. Passions were aroused by what many regarded as a severe sentence on one so young and at a specially called meeting of the Corporation it was unanimously decided "to adopt a memorial to the Lord Lieutenant requesting clemency" which did not succeed.

When Rahilly was released he was met at the station by a large crowd and chaired to his home nearby and made "the recipient of a silver watch and chain on behalf of a number of friends, as a token of their sympathy."

In an interview afterwards young Rahilly said a certain warder on his arrival in Mountjoy came to him and said "come here you Limerick Jew slayer.

"I reported him to the chief warden who asked me could I point him out, but I said I would not as it would be worse for me during the time I was to be in jail."

The period during the month of January saw the full thrust of the attacks on the Jewish community and on the 22nd of that month there were several prosecutions heard which merited the headlines: "The Jews. Today's Prosecutions. The latest phase of the Question."

Fr. Creagh departed for the Philippines in May, 1906, and the Confraternity presented him with a valedictory address in which it was stated that "we are buoyed up with a mighty hope that you will prove another noble warrior in the battlefield of Catholicity, holding aloft the saving cross as the living emblem of salvation on those desolate shores and by your zeal and undaunted energy in the cause of the Holy Church will take your stand as did those glorious Missionaries of our faith and country who so long ago fought and won victory after victory in their struggle over infidelity, and save countless souls from the thraldom and tyranny of Satan and his myrmidons."

Crescent College pupils early 1950's.

The Yank and the Eucharistic Congress

The country's greatest outpouring of religious fervour through the century was undoubtedly the Eucharistic Congress of 1932, its culmination in the Phoenix Park in Dublin being described as the greatest and most evocative gathering of the Faithful that was ever seen up to that time. The Congress commenced on Sunday, 19th June, 1932, and continued to the 26th. There was hardly a Catholic home in the country that did not join in the outpouring of religious emotion, and houses were decorated: statutes, holy pictures and all kinds of adornments were put in the windows of every home. Villages and towns vied with one another to see who could produce the greatest display.

The event proved a boon to all local correspondents and their Notes from all parts of the county were full of colourful descriptions of the efforts people were making to mark the occasion in fitting manner. The Rathkeale report said that much whitewashing and decorating was being done and related the following story of how deep the Eucharistic Congress had penetrated the spirit of the people:

A returned Yank who happened on an old woman as she was putting up a little flag to fly from her humble home accosted her, saying: "I guess, Mary, nobody will see your little flag in this out of the way place".

"Ah," replied Mary, "my little flag will be seen by a very great and noble visitor.

"And who might that be," said the Yank, "is this great and noble visitor you expect to see your flag?"

"God himself will see and admire it," said Mary, and the Yank held his peace.

"Kilmallock Gleanings" said that the motor car that does not carry the papal flag is the exception; big, growing palm trees were put in front of houses in Ballylanders and were illuminated at night. The Abbeyfeale cor. said that painters and decorators had been busy for the past month preparing for the great event and every house floats its papal and congress colours. "Never before for any ceremony of national importance have the people been so earnest in showing their zeal to be associated with a such an event of religious significance." The names of those going up for the Congress from Abbeyfeale were given and these included Dr. Phil McCarthy, Dr. William O'Connor, J. D. Hartnett, D. G. Hartnett, D. P. Murphy, J. F. Hanly, N.T.; J. O'Kelly, N.T.; Miss Fitzgerald, Ed. Eggleston, D. F. O'Connor, P. A. O'Connor, J. Moriarty, N.T.; D. M. Shanahan, B. O'Rourke, J. Collins, Justin McCarthy, etc.

In Foynes the cor. waxed lyrical in describing the village's manifestations. "Twelve lines of bunting spanned the street, the beautiful and profuse display of flags and buntings from every house made pictures which were striking and convincing manifestations of the great fervour and lively faith, surely an exhibition that is highly creditable to the villagers." The Bruree cor. said this "Old City of the Kings" was not left behind in the matter of flags, buntings, in honour of the great occasion and it never presented a more lovely appearance than it does now. 8,000 from Limerick left the Railway Station for the final day of the Congress and they joined many thousands of other people, many of them overseas, for the High Mass in the Phoenix Park. It was estimated that a million attended and thrilled to clearly hear the Pope's voice broadcasting a special message to the Congress from the Vatican. "And John McCormack's singing of the 'Panis Angelicus' will be remembered forever by all who attended."

The Arch Confraternity of Mount St Alphonsus were very strongly represented and were met on arrival at Kingsbridge by their director, Fr. Murray C.SS.R. "It was a grand sight, an inspiring manifestation of Limerick's undying loyalty to the Church of Limerick militant, and as the banner of the Holy Family was unfurled in the station, the words of the great Confraternity hymn came to one's lips:

Confraternity men to the fight,
And raise up your banners on high;
Jesus, Mary, and Joseph in sight,
In our battles their names be our cry.

All the streets, lanes, and alleyways of the city were festooned with all types of decorations and at different points altars and grottoes were erected. "All that is best in the womanhood of Limerick was represented in Dublin by the Confraternities of St. John's, St. Michael's, and St. Mary's," said a report.

In many parts of the city touching scenes were witnessed as those unable to travel to Dublin listened in on the radio and fell on their knees during the Consecration of the Mass and later when the Legate gave the Benediction.

The Windmill area decorated for the Eucharistic Congress in 1932.

Forgotten outrage: the riots of 1935

While the attacks on and boycott of the Jews in 1904 are well chronicled, another sectarian outrage took place in Limerick in 1935 which is a largely forgotten incident.

"Riots and baton charges in Limerick. Attack on property of Protestants. Military called out." These were the headlines on July 27th, 1935. With Catholics being attacked and burned out of their homes in Belfast in the rioting that followed the Orange parades of that year, feelings ran high here and mobs started attacking Protestant property, culminating in the burning down of Kilmallock Protestant Church of SS. Peter and Paul and damage to the houses of Canon Sackville Taylor and Mr. Frederick Amon.

When civic guards arrived on the scene the church was ablaze and the roof fell in. "There was nothing we could do save the building," said Guard T. O'Callaghan. The Kilmallock cor. said "there was a shock of horror in the town the following morning when only the walls of the church were seen to have survived the attack."

In Limerick, on Saturday night, July 20th, a mob estimated to be in the region of 200, started to attack Protestant owned shops and were broken up by repeated baton charges. So serious was the situation that Det. Sergt. Murphy decided to call out a detachment of the military from Sarsfield Barracks. The mob, considerably swelled, regrouped, and turned its attention on Protestant places of worship. A determined effort was made to set fire to the Presbyterian Church in Henry Street and one of the doors had actually been ignited before a mobile force of Guards arrived and scattered the crowd.

Attention was then turned on the residence of Canon Abbott in Barrington Street and despite his appeals, large stones were hurtled through the windows before the Guards again came on the scene and broke up the mob as they were about to turn their attention on the nearby St. Michael's Protestant Church. Rev. Fr. Moriarity, C.C., St. Michael's, a neighbour of Canon Abbott, also appealed to the crowd to desist in their attack, but he was ignored and again the Guards wielding batons came in and broke up the mob.

A crowd estimated to be in the region of four to five hundred regrouped outside the L.P.Y.M.A building in O'Connell Street, and attacked it. A window was then broken in Stewart's Chemist Shop opposite and when the crowd began to close in on the Guards, detectives drew their revolvers and some shots were fired in the air.

At this stage the military were called into action and in the height of the rioting, cordoned off O'Connell Street. The Guards made a determined baton charge and peace was eventually restored around 2.30 a.m. on the Sunday morning. Several incidents in the St. Mary's area were reported with four Protestant owned houses being attacked and in some instances the knockers being taken off doors and thrown through windows.

Besides the buildings already mentioned, the following Protestant owned premises were attacked and had windows broken: Stockill's, Catherine St.; Widdess, Roche's St.; Wickham's, Henry St.; Matterson's, Roche's St.; Lindsay Bros., Patrick St.; Masonic Club, The Crescent; Protestant Diocesan Hall, Pery Square; the Gospel Hall, Cecil St.; Goodwin & Co., William St., and Archdeacon Wallar's house, Mallow St.

Many arrests were made and a native of Northern Ireland, David McNally, who was described as one of the ring-leaders (which he denied) was eventually sentenced to three months' imprisonment for his part in the rioting as was local man Michael Tierney. Mary A. Healy was bound to the peace, testimony being given by Det.-Officer Brophy that she made use of the words to the effect that the "Protestants should be burned out". References to the treatment of Catholics in the North were heard from other sections of the crowd.

The Monday following the rioting, the Mayor, Mr. James Casey, and the city manager, called on the Protestant Bishop, Rt. Rev. Dr. Irwin, and on behalf of the citizens proffered sympathy, and said that in view of the possible serious repercussions on the hitherto harmonious relations existing between all classes of the citizens, a special conference was to be held in the Town Hall. The meeting was attended by representatives from all classes of the city and the outrages were condemned out of hand.

The rioting was condemned at Masses in various churches on the Sunday morning and in St Joseph's, Fr. Fitzpatrick said that the reason advanced for the rioting was because of the certain incidents, deeply regrettable, which had occurred recently in Northern Ireland. "We Catholics, deeply deplore these incidents, as do our Protestant fellow-citizens, but they do not afford any justification for giving to the ancient and historic City of Limerick the reputation throughout the world as another Belfast or Portadown." He appealed to the citizens to express their sympathy with their Protestant neighbours.

Fr. Kerr, rector in the Redemptorist Church, said that it was with a deep sense of shame and humiliation they had heard of the disgraceful scenes. "It is deplorable that any Irishman, and presumably any Catholic, should degrade himself so far as to adopt the tactics of the Orangemen who are at present subjecting the unfortunate Catholics of Belfast to fiendish persecution. If reports be true, the perpetrators of these outrages here reveal a very confused mentality, for it is said that while inflicting the wanton destruction of property they were crying 'Up the Pope'. How is it possible to promote the cause of God, of the Pope, or Ireland, by violating the commands of God and his Commandments."

At the Circuit Court, Justice McElligott said that he regarded himself as an adopted son of Limerick, a city which he had grown to love. "I had hoped that the atmosphere of peace and freedom which I have experienced here would last but this has now been shattered. I appeal to my Protestant friends to forgive and forget the gross injury done to them in the name of religion by an irresponsible, irreligious, worthless mob, who put human life in danger from their actions for many hours."

The editorial in Monday's Leader, while condemning the attack, hinted at the dark forces of Communism. "Those at the back of the hooliganistic display were certainly no friends of the Catholic Church or of Ireland. The only cause that could possibly be served by their conduct is that of Communism, which makes it a point wherever it can to utilise disturbances in order to create an atmosphere for the propagation of its hideous doctrines. It is well known that Communistic agents are ever ready to seek any opportunity and pretext for stirring up and keeping on disorders and outrages as a means of installing their pernicious poison into ignorant and uninformed minds likely to be misled by it."

Death of Donogh

Donogh O'Malley (left) Minister for Education, died suddenly in 1968 at the age of 47. A hugely popular and innovative politician, many people wept openly as the funerala cortege wended its way from St. Johns Cathedral. Journalist Gus Smith wrote "our tomorrows will be emptier," and Terry O'Sullivan in his column in the Irish Press said O'Malley was a true Prince of Thomond. "He will be remembered as the man who introduced free education," said another report. O'Malley was also an outstanding sportsman, having the unique distinction of playing senior interprovincial rugby for Munster, Connacht and Lenister.O'Malley is pictured here with Eamon de Valera, "The Chief."

Haughey speaks on morality

Charles Haughey, in 1975, was spokesman on health, and on a visit to Limerick said "it was a time of great crisis and the nation is not getting the moral leadership they need from the Government. There is huge unemployment and the Coalition will have to go abroad shortly and borrow massive sums to tide them over their difficulties," he said at a Fianna Fail gathering.

The following year Charlie, with his two sons Kieran and Sean, had landed at Shannon on their way to his new island purchase in Kerry when the taxi conveying them to Limerick crashed. His injuries necessitated a stay in the Regional Hospital of several days. It was stated

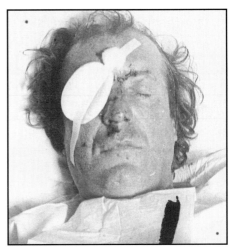

Charles Haughey in the Regional Hospital after his car crash on the way from Shannon.

that Mr. Haughey was accident prone, having been in another road crash the previous year and had several riding accidents.

As Taoiseach, Charlie visited Kilmallock, Bruff and Bruree in the Fall of 1980. Calling to the farm of Fianna Fáil T.D., Michael Noonan, he did not hide his views regarding "the beauty and elegance" of the ladies present.

"They were only trotting after you at the Curragh yesterday," he added with what the report said was "a devilish smile."

The Taoiseach was in "irrepressible mood," with plenty of witticisms such as when he was presented with a brass bucket in Kilmallock he quipped: "I must find out from the committee before I go back to Dublin if it is for the boiling of spuds or the making of poteen."

The Taoiseach visited the museum and former home of one of his predecessors, Eamon de Valera, in Bruree and was photographed sitting at the desk where the "Chief" used sit at school. He was followed by a crowd of up to 700 admiring supporters. Addressing them, he said "We were all in readiness for a General Election and well prepared to call Garret's bluff," a remark that elicited loud cheering.

The visit to Limerick proved a triumphant success and though tired afterwards, Charlie said he knew he would get a warm reception, but not to the extent he had received.

A reporter asked the Taoiseach to elaborate on his statement of calling "Garrett's bluff," but Mr. Haughey just smiled and said "what are you going to give me for Christmas?"

Dessie is kicked out of Fianna Fáil

Four years later it was a different story as an unsmiling Charlie came to Limerick following the expulsion of Dessie O'Malley from the party. Two of his fellow Limerick T.D's, Gerry Collins and Michael Noonan, were amongst the 56 Fianna Fáil Deputies who voted to expel O'Malley from the Fianna Fáil Parliamentary Party in May 18th, 1984. 16 Deputies voted against the motion including Willie O'Dea, who stated afterwards that "it was a hard decision for me to make, but I felt that the punishment did not fit the crime."

Beforehand, two former Mayors, Cllr. Tony Bromwell and Cllr. Clem Casey came out in favour of the expulsion but Jack Bourke, who was one of Haughey's strongest supporters in the city, said he was shocked at the proposed expulsion. "I personally didn't see anything wrong with what Dessie said on television or what was reported in the Sunday newspapers. It is a bad day for the Party and a bad day for Fianna Fáil. ''

Fianna Fáil's Cllr. Paddy Kiely refused to comment, but did say he did not know if Mr. O'Malley's expulsion would damage the Party locally.

The Taoiseach, Charles J. Haughey, had tabled a motion at the Parliamentary Party meeting calling for the expulsion of Mr. O'Malley due to his challenge to his (the Taoiseach's) handling of the Northern Ireland Forum Report. The voting went 56 for to 16 against.

Mrs. Pat O'Malley, wife of the expelled Deputy, said her husband's opponents had been waiting for this day. "A certain element will probably be delighted with the way this has happened. They will be glad they have finally got rid of him. But why have the Forum at all? The whole idea was to open up new ideas, otherwise it was a waste of money." She described the treatment to her husband as unjust. "He has devoted his life to Fianna Fáil and this is it. It is very disillusioning."

It took O'Malley's secretary one and half hours to open the many hundreds of letters of sympathy that poured into his office on the days following the expulsion. "It is incredible the support I have got" the Deputy said. He would not comment on the fact that two of his fellow Limerick T.D.'s had voted against him.

"FF Kitty Rattled at Church Gates" was the lead in the Leader in the weeks that followed when Eugene Phelan reported that the annual Fianna Fáil collection in the city was down substantially. There was no collections outside some of the churches and abuse was hurled at some of the collectors.

At a meeting later of the local Tom Clarke Cumann, a vote of confidence was passed in Mr. O'Malley and his policy on the Forum. "We support Mr. O'Malley's call for debate on party policy and do not want a dictatorship position in the party," said Mr. Dick Sadlier.

Bishop Empey joined in the chorus of defence of O'Malley. In a Chronicle report he said "young people are becoming disillusioned and cynical regarding politics. Again and again I hear them talking about a lack of integrity in political life and I find this to be both sad and frightening. Mr. O'Malley knew well what the consequences of his actions would be, yet he still took his stand. Such integrity, and it is to be found in members of all the political parties, is the antidote to this galloping cancer."

The following February Deputy O'Dea tried to heal divisions and made an impassioned plea to Des to join in welcoming their leader, Mr. Haughey, to a Comhairle Ceanntair Dinner in Cruise's. Haughey's right hand man, P. J. Mara, said they were going down to Limerick with "an open mind and open heart."

Even though he had an engagement to speak in Chicago, Des made his appearance at the dinner. Supporters of Mr. Haughey and O'Malley "tried to outshout each other at the function," the report said. Haughey said: "Those who came to see confrontation or disagreement are going to be disappointed" and when O'Malley spoke he turned to his adversary and said "welcome to my constituency", which was greeted by roars of approval from his supporters.

By the end of the month O'Malley was expelled from the Party itself. He had abstained from the vote on the contraception bill and was expelled "due to conduct unbecoming a party member." Several Fianna Fail members of the City Council threatened to resign from the party and there were fears of widespread defections. Cllr. Clem Casey said Des "should be spanked on the bottom and told to be a good boy."

Following the foundation of the Progressive Democrats in the months afterwards, Fianna Fail Councillors John Quinn and Paddy Clohessy were first to defect from Fianna Fail to join O'Malley's new party and in January, 1986, speculation was rife that former Mayor, Tommy Allen, was also about the join the party.

Chairman of the Workers Party in Limerick, Mr. John Ryan, referring to the new party, said: "manufacturers of soap powders have for years prospered by marketing the same product in new or greatly improved form."

There was consternation in Fianna Fail ranks when in the 1987 general election three P.D's were returned in Limerick: Dessie O'Malley and Peadar Clohessy in the East and John McCoy in the West. Jimmy Kemmy was returned as a Democratic Socialist. Two years later O'Malley and Clohessy retained their seats but Michael Finucane took the West Limerick seat for Fine Gael.

A rugby mad city

All through the century, there was hardly an issue of the *Leader* or *Chronicle* that did not have reference to rugby, a sport that since the time of the Occupation was played in all the original five parishes of the city.

Garryowen were the dominant team, not alone in Limerick, but in Munster during the late 1800's and early 1900's but in 1928 Young Munster stole a march over their old adversaries when they won the All-Ireland, the famous Bateman Cup.

There was unprecedented scenes of celebration at Limerick Railway Terminus when the victorious Young Munster rugby team, crowned all-Ireland champions, arrived back from Dublin bearing aloft the Bateman Cup. They had beaten the crack Lansdowne team in the final. Several city bands turned out and 12,000 well-wishers cheered the team to the echo.

"Never did Limerick in its palmiest days render such a welcome to any victors; the welcome was spontaneous, full hearted and sincere to a degree" said one report.

The procession was headed by a group of men with a banner emblazoned with big characters stating "All Cups Come to Limerick" (referring to the other national wins that season of L.P.Y.M.A in hockey and Limerick B.C. in the senior eights).

Tar barrels and bonfires lit up all the districts in the vicinity of Parnell Street and the Mayor, Cllr. J. G. O'Brien, said it is no parish victory but a victory for Limerick.

Through the ensuing years, Bohemians, Shannon, Young Munster all had their moments in the Munster Senior Cup, Shannon's three in a row being the outstanding achievement in the 1980's.

The 1990's saw Limerick clubs dominating the All-Ireland League. Garryowen started it all in 1992 and the following year in front of their 20,000 delirious spectators Young Munster were victorious against St Mary's in Lansdowne Road in a nail-biting finish. John Costelloe, in charge of the traditional mascot, a goat, had many adventures before he finally got his charge into the grounds. These included having to hail a coal lorry to get the mascot to the match when refused entry on the Dart. Fred Cogley was accused of bias in favour of St Mary's in his TV commentary which he strenuously denied.

Garryowen were to the fore again the following year and then the great Shannon run started culminating in a famous record four-in-a-row, a feat which earned them the title of the club team of the century, a superlative achievement, which will take some beating in the century that lies before us.

The great liquor boycott

In 1951 the licensing laws prohibiting opening of licensed premises throughout the country on St. Patrick's Day were still in vogue. These were archaic laws enforced from the time of the British to stave off drunken riots which before the law's enactment in the previous century were a common feature on this day.

At the annual general meeting of the Limerick Licensed Vintners' Association it was revealed that a deputation went to see the Minster to have the pubs opened. "We were received sympathetically, but that's as far as we got," said the chairman, Tom Mullane.

During the course of the meeting, Mr. Mullane proposed that a boycott of Dutch lager and gin be put in force as a protest against the presence of Dutch air naval personnel in the Six Counties. "The most effective protest we can make at the moment is to hit them in the pocket. We'll be doing that if we refuse to handle Dutch drink in our public-houses," said Mr. Mullane.

The Association unanimously decided to act on the chairman's suggestion and boycott the Dutch liquors.

Stephen Coughlan, B.C., thanked the publicans for their contribution to the O'Callaghan Tannery Worker's Fund. The tannery had been burned down some time previously.

April Fool's Day jokes

In a more leisurely age in the 1930's, April Fool's Day jokes were common and examples given in local newpapers included the one about the electrician who travelled all the way out to a country residence answering a call, only to find out he had been "had." Leaving the house he bumped into the delivery of a lorry load of eggs from a Nenagh supplier and soon after passed a builder's lorry containing a couple of tons of sand, all on their way to the same house as the result of a practical April 1st joker. A resident of Castle Street spent hours in the courthouse after being summonsed to defend his voting revision, and eventually on getting someone to decipher an Irish phrase at the bottom of the letter found it read: "Tis a grand day this April 1st."

Coonagh fishing comedy and Abbey outrage

A long standing dispute between the owners of the Lax Weir Fishery Co. in Corbally and local net fishermen had a farcical sequel in May 1925. The ongoing differences lay in the net fishermen's claims to fish certain fisheries down-river of the weir, which the Lax Weir Company claimed was their legal and exclusive property.

The weir company had the law on their side and in May, 1925, a launch containing a number of bailiffs, accompanied by Civic Guards and military, proceeded down river to protect the fishery near Coonagh.

A large company of fishermen, mainly from the area, were fishing the disputed waters when the upholders of the law arrived on the scene. The launch got in among the fishermen's boats but speedily got emeshed in the nets.

The fishermen decided at once to "improve the shining hour" and by means of the nets they drew the launch and its outraged occupants into the mud left by the outgoing tide and left them high and dry while they fished away to their hearts content for a considerable time longer. Jeers and laughter added to the discomfort of those who had become so innocently and unexpectedly marooned.

The occupants of the launch had to preserve their souls in peace until the tide arose sufficiently many hours later to enable them to leave their muddy perch, by which time the fishermen had departed to their homes, having concluded their labours for the day and highly delighted with the turn affairs had taken.

Seven years later the military, civic guards and bailiffs were again in action in what became known as the Battle of the Tail Race. This infamous incident took place in the waters below Ardnacrusha power station in July, 1932, when the Guild of Abbey Fishermen, in defiance of the law, cast their nets in waters in which they were forbidden to fish. With the main flow of the Shannon diverted to turn the turbines in the power house, thousands of salmon converged into the Tail Race with fatal results. Incensed at the slaughter of what was once their main source of livelihood, the fishermen defied the authorities, some of whom were armed. Shots were fired, and boats and nets were seized as hundreds watched the scene from the banks of the river, cheering and booing, and for some time, feelings ran high.

Great fire disasters

"It was something which at once excited pity, while at the same time there was in it elements depicting a spectacle of a nature never to be forgotten. As one could see across, there was nothing but flames, all devouring in their fury – leaping from one pile of resinous timber to another while everyone was caught in the vortex that lit up the night sky."

Thus was Limerick's first major fire of the century so dramatically and lyrically reported in the Limerick Chronicle in 1911. On the night of Thursday, June 1st, of that year, what was described as the greatest conflagration in living memory took place when the extensive timber yard and saw mills of James McMahon & Sons, Alphonsus Street, was burned to the ground.

Despite what was described as great work by the Corporation Fire Brigade, supplemented by those from the 1st Batt. Black Watch and Royal Engineers from the New Barracks, it was obvious after a short time that their task was hopeless. Michael O'Brien, St. Joseph Street, who worked as a cooper in McMahon's at the time of the fire, said in his later years that the flames were so high they could be seen as far away as Ennis. "The fire brigade might a well be throwing lolly-pops on it so great was the heat," he added.

So serious was the fire that it was feared that houses in nearby Clare View Terrace and Frederick Street would ignite and these were evacuated. The nearby gas works was also in danger, and if the combustible like gas came into contact with the flames "Limerick would have suffered a catastrophe from which it would not readily recover."

A horrific fire in the Griffin's Undertakers premises, Gerald Griffin Street, in 1912 claimed the lives of the owner, John Griffin, his wife, the housekeeper and a couple staying with them. A fire in the stables earlier in the night had been dealt with by the fire brigade, but it flared up again later on, spread to the residence and all five perished.

The following year three lives were lost when the drapery establishment of George Clancy, in William Street, was completely gutted. A nephew of the proprietor, George Clancy, died in the fire as did Peter McDonald, an assistant, and Mary Daly, a domestic servant.

Damage estimated at half a million pounds was the result of a disastrous fire which burned Roche's Stores to the ground in 1948. It was estimated that between eighty and ninety people would be out of work as a consequence. Two years later another disastrous fire occurred when O'Callaghan's Tannery, which was situated between Gerald Griffin Street and Mulgrave Street was completely gutted and many became unemployed as a result.

The city's greatest blaze of the century occurred on Tuesday morning, August 25th, 1959, when Limerick's biggest department store, Todds, caught fire. Within a short time the building was ablaze and the fire had spread to the whole block, engulfing Lipton's grocery store, Burton's men's shop and Nicholas' tobacconists. Eleven fire brigades fought the blaze before it was eventually brought under control. It was feared at one stage that the whole city centre would be destroyed, and such was the ferocity of the flames that it looked as if the Garda headquarters across the road in William Street, would also be engulfed.

1963 saw Goodwin's in William Street, described as one of the finest glassware, china and jewellery shops in the country, burned to the ground, and in the early hours of the morning of 7th December, 1974, Newsom's Hardware and McCarthy's Furniture, two major stores adjoining one another, were destroyed by fire and some neighbouring shops damaged.

The most tragic conflagration of all the was Dromcollogher Cinema fire in 1926, the story of which is on page 124.

Burnt-out shell of Todds after the disastrous fire in 1959.

John B. Keane: miscellaneous items

John B. Keane wrote his first story for the Leader on May 12, 1962, and in what was to prove a happy and lasting collusion, entertained readers of the newspaper with his acute observances in many hilarious stories over the next three decades and a bit.

His first effort was in praise of "Duckeggs" and he was observing that its great era was drawing to a close:

When our ancestors foregathered for the great trip to Clontarf they made the journey without tinned beef or sausage rolls in their haversacks. Their strength was the terrible strength of men who were reared on duckeggs and their anger was implacable against the herring-fed hosts of the foe.

If we are to be deprived of the duck egg, other more valuable commodities will follow in short order, and once the rot sets in, there is no telling where it will stop.

I am not saying that civilisation as we know it must come to an end, but it never does harm to be prepared, and a man with a couple of duckeggs under his belt has the equipment to cope with whatever a changing world has to offer him and the sustenance to endure the challenges of tomorrow.

The following week he waxed lyrical about "Grandfathers":

It is not the craze for small boys to boast about their elders anymore. Nowadays a grandfather is expected to behave like other human beings. He is an oddity if he sports whiskers, and a man with a doubtful background if he tells lies. It is fashionable to be ashamed if he dotes a bit and he is a character to be confined to his room if his mind wanders!

There was a time when elderly men were invested with the deeds of Robin Hood and the prowess of Alexander. There was an age when small boys could ask impossible questions with impunity and be assured that an answer was forthcoming, even if it meant much plucking of moustaches and thoughtful thumbing of waistcoat pockets.

They were men who could wink imperceptibly at small boys who turned to look at the choir during Mass and they could, without animosity, paralyse a stressful of disrespectful delinquents with a single paralysing glare.

They had, when called upon for a song, the grace to stand moist-eyed and stricken while they lamented the sad fate of an exiled maiden who expired upon a foreign shore. The veins would stand out on their faces like purple picture-cords and globules of moisture would glisten on their foreheads.

J.B. then followed up with "Crubeens", bemoaning the fact that the pleasures of this culinary delight was not broadcast abroad:

It is a well-known fact that you will not find a single crubeen for sale in

J. P. NEWSOM & CO.,

HOUSE FURNISHING AND BUILDERS' IRONMONGERS,

IRON AND HARDWARE MERCHANTS,

ARE NOW SHOWING IN THEIR NEW WAREROOMS

GRATES AND MANTELPIECES, BRASS FENDERS,

FIREIRONS AND COAL VASES.

OF NEWEST DESIGNS.

COOKING RANGES AND HOT-AIR STOVES,

FOR THE WINTER SEASON.

BUILDERS AND GENERAL IRONMONGERY WAREHOUSE,

20 AND 21, WILLIAM-ST., & DENMARK-ST.,

LIMERICK.

Newsoms is one of the few Limerick firms that has spanned three centuries. This dramatic picture was taken in 1974 when the premises was burned to the ground in a disastrous fire. The firm bounced back and built a new modern store that is now a familiar Limerick landmark.

Hyderabad, Timbuctoo or Calcutta, whereas they are as plentiful as piped water in Tubberneering and Newcastle West. We have imported our concepts of culture all over the eastern hemisphere, but we are guilty of neglect and lack of consideration for not having once invited a single black man to join us in a debate over a gallon of porter and a quarter stone of crubeens.

There is a clique, a sect, a saboteuring segment of our community who think it fashionable to look down their noses at crubeens, who shudder pretentiously at the thought of taking a pig's foot in their dainty hands and eating it with the relish that should be accorded to all delicacies of standing.

The same type of people are the ones who wouldn't dream of tapping their feet when a fife-and-drum band is passing, who would be ashamed of their lives to converse with an old woman who wore a shawl, who walk up the parish church as if they owned it, and who worry from morning 'till night about the impression they make on their betters. Their stomachs are out of tune, because they have sold a mighty heritage for frivolities like stuffed tomatoes and mandarin oranges. They have gone from us, for good and glory, to a world that has no room for potato cakes and Bendigo tobacco."

Visit of John F. Kennedy

The charasmatic John F. Kennedy, President of the USA, visited Limerick in 1963 where he is pictured above with members of Limerick Corporation at Greenpark Racecourse. To his left is the Mayor of Limerick, Mrs. Frances Condell, whose speech he described as being the best he had heard on his tour of Europe. Scenes of unprecedented enthusiasm were were witnessed as thouands turned out to give the president an ecstatic greeting. Five months later, on November 22nd, the President was assasinated in Dallas. In 1979 Greenpark was again the scene of unbridled enthusiasm, this time for the visit of Pople Poe John Paul II, and for many it was an all-night vigil to get prime viewing of the Pontiff's visit. It was described as the day "that the likes of it Limerick will never see again."

Dr. Tiede Herrema and family arrive back in Limerick where a civic reception was given in his honour.

Kidnap makes world headlines

Friday, October, 4th, 1975, started out as a normal day for Dr. Tiede Herrema, chief executive of the oft-troubled Ferenka Factory at Ballyvarrra, near Annacotty.

Setting out for work in his car, he left home in Castletroy shortly after 8 a.m. but a phone call to a Dublin newspaper three and a half hours later signalled the start of a drama that for three weeks made world headlines.

The phone call claimed that the Dutch executive had been kidnapped near his home and the abductors demanded the release of several Republican prisoners including Dr. Rose Dougdale, the Englishwoman who had become involved in I.R.A. activities. She was being held in Limerick Jail.

Road-blocks were immediately thrown up and the most extensive search ever carried out by the Gardai and Army got under way in the Limerick area, eventually spreading to different parts of the country. An unofficial strike at Ferenka was called off that evening.

The next day thousands marched through the city in condemnation of the kidnap and were addressed by the Mayor, Thady Coughlan. The Dutch Prime Minister cabled the Taoiseach expressing concern. The I.R.A. deny responsibility and Eddie Gallagher and Marion Coyle were named as being wanted in connection with the abduction.

Each day for the next few weeks the papers carried many stories of the search for the kidnappers and rumour and counter-rumour abound regarding the whereabouts of the kidnappers and their victim. The Mayor announced on the Wednesday that he was seeking an audience with the Pope to ask him to appeal personally to the kidnappers to spare Dr. Heremma's life.

The search went on relentlessly throughout the country, switching from one area to another as sightings of the kidnappers (all of them false alarms) were reported.

The first major news that Dr. Heremma was still alive came through the following Friday when Fr. Donal O'Mahony, a mediator, said he had made contact with the kidnappers and announced "the Doctor is tied to a chair, blind-folded with cotton-wool in his ears. He is mentally exhausted and does not know where he is," Fr. O'Mahony said.

The following Tuesday the search for Dr. Heremma was over, but he was still in the hands of his kidnappers. 1410 St. Kevin's Park, Monastaraven, became the focal point of the assembled world media as it was here the kidnappers and their victim were finally tracked down.

Reporting from the scene, Leaderman Billy Kelly said there was much rumour and counter rumour throughout the siege, such as outlandish claims being made that Dr. Herrema was wired to explosives. Dramatic shots were taken by staff photographer A. F. Foley of detectives pointing machine guns and pistols up at the bedroom window.

The siege lasted two weeks until eventually the release of Dr. Heremma was procured. The Dutchman was released, shaken but in one piece, with his captors, Eddie Gallagher and Marion Coyle, being taken into custody.

It was reported that Dr. Herrema's strong personality and level of physical fitness helped see him through the ordeal. He was back in Limerick after a few weeks recuperating in Holland and was accorded a civic reception in the Savoy where he got an emotional welcome. When driven through the streets of the city, many thousands turned out to greet him and several bands turned out to play. He was later made a Freeman of the City at a special ceremony.

Holocaust portents in tragic suicide

The issue of the Limerick Chronicle of November 1st, 1938, brought home the first indication of the Nazi persecution of the Jews that was sweeping Europe. An inquest heard that an Austrian Jewess named Mrs. Elsa Hoefler, aged about 56, had been found shot dead in the bedroom of the Hotel Crescent in 87 O'Connell Street. She had been staying with her husband Berish in the Tobin family home at 18 Newenham Street as paying guests. The jury returned a verdict of suicide while being of unsound mind, caused by a bullet wound.

Evidence was given by Mrs. Tobin, stat-

No. 87 O'Connell St., formerly Hotel Crescent, where Elsa Hoefler committed suicide.

ed to be also a Jewess, that the deceased had become depressed by the situation in Austria and the persecution of Jews. She constantly spoke of Hitler and all the money they had lost by fleeing before the persecution. A passport found with a number of letters showed that she had been allowed to stay just forty-eight hours in the United Kingdom. The passport, showing her maiden name, Elsa Reininger, was issued by the Czech Consul in Vienna. She was a native of Bohemia, a Czech province of the Austro-Hungrarian empire.

The deceased's husband, Herr Hoefler, when questioned at the inquest, said that he was a rich man before fleeing Vienna. "I had 300,000 Austrian shillings, and I have lost it all. My wife and daughter had property and securities. I could, through my own channels, bring only £440 to Ireland for my wife. My daughter lost all, every penny."

The deceased's daughter, Mrs. Gaskel Kaitcher, who had fled to Limerick before her parents, and who had been described in an earlier report as being very beautiful, said her mother was subject to depression and had been in a clinic for a year.

Both husband and daughter of the deceased were deeply affected during the inquest and the daughter had to be assisted from the courtroom on one occasion. Mr. Hoefler also broke down and there was an affecting scene between father and daughter.

The coroner said he would not read out any of the three letters left by the deceased, only to demonstrate the state of the deceased's mind by reading out a passage from one which stated: "I am compelled to go to my death."

Miss Maeve Moloney of the Hotel Crescent, gave evidence of finding the deceased laying across the bed and called the police. At the request of members of the Jewish community in Limerick, the Coroner had given permission to have the interment carried out on Friday as burials were not allowed on Saturday, the Jewish Sabbath.

A sensation was caused when, as the remains were being removed from the city morgue at Barrington's Hospital, the Civic Guards stopped the funeral and ordered the body to be returned to the morgue for further examination. After a post-mortem examination had been made on Saturday, and certain organs removed, permission for the burial was given.

On Sunday, October 30th, 1938, Elsa Hoefler was buried in the Jewish Cemetery in Castletroy. Chief mourners were Herr Berish Hoefler, husband; Mrs. Margaret Kaitcher, daughter; Herr Gatiskhal Kaitcher, son-in-law, and Simon Guwurtz, Chief Rabbi, Limerick.

Elsa was laid to rest in a grave that is unmarked.